\<designing web graphics.2\>

■ Words: Lynda Weinman
■ Design: Ali Karp

Designing Web Graphics.2

By Lynda Weinman

Published by: New Riders Publishing
201 West 103rd Street
Indianapolis, IN 46290 USA

Copyright © 1997 by Lynda Weinman
Printed in the United States of America 2 3 4 5 6 7 8 9 0
ISBN:1-56205-715-4
Library of Congress Cataloging-in-Publication
Data available upon request.

Warning and Disclaimer

Every effort has been made to make this book as complete and as accurate as possible, but no warranty or fitness is implied. The information is provided on an "as is" basis. The author(s) and New Riders Publishing shall have neither liability nor responsibility to any person or entity with respect to any loss or damages arising from the information contained in this book or from the use of the disks or programs that may accompany it.

Trademark Acknowledgements

All terms mentioned in this book that are known to be trademarks or service marks have been appropriately capitalized. New Riders Publishing cannot attest to the accuracy of this information. Use of a term in this book should not be regarded as affecting the validity of any trademark or service mark.

Publisher: Don Fowley
Publishing Manager: David Dwyer
Marketing Manager: Mary Foote
Managing Editor: Carla Hall

Designing Web Graphics.2 Credits

Product Development Specialist
John Kane

Software Specialist
Steve Flatt

Senior Editor
Sarah Kearns

Project Editor
Jennifer Eberhardt

Acquisitions Coordinator
Stacey Beheler

Administrative Coordinator
Karen Opal

**Cover Artwork, Spread
Illustrations, Photography**
Bruce Heavin

Cover Production
Aren Howell

Book Designer
Ali Karp
Alink Newmedia
■ alink@earthlink.net

Production Manager
Kelly Dobbs

Production Team Supervisors
Gina Rexrode, Joe Millay

Production Team
Dan Caparo, Megan Wade,
Daniela Raderstorf

Indexer
Sharon Hilgenberg

Lynda's early days exploring color theory issues, obviously in preparation for the web design series she authors today.

■ Lynda Weinman

Lynda Weinman writes full-time for a living now, but in the past has been a designer, animator, magazine contributor, computer consultant, instructor, moderator, and lecturer. She lives in California with her husband, seven-year-old daughter, 2 cats, and 5 computers. She has taught Web Design, Interactive Media Design, Motion Graphics, and Digital Imaging classes at Art Center College of Design in Pasadena, California (although she is currently taking a break from teaching). Lynda contributes regularly to *Web Techniques*, *MacUser*, *Step-by-Step Graphics*, *Web Studio*, and *How* magazines. She likes the web so much, she even has a domain for her name:

■ http://www.lynda.com

Lynda, get a life!

This book is dedicated to my dad, from whom I inherited my height, eyeglass prescription, and computer acumen.

A face is like a work of art.
It deserves a great frame.

Special thanks to Gai, Barbara, and Ruth from L.A. Eyeworks (fierce sister eyewear, yeah!) for featuring me in their ad campaign when the first edition of *Designing Web Graphics* was released. It's the only formal head shot I own of myself, and I actually felt glamorous for the first time in my life! Thanks to Greg Gorman and the L.A. Eyeworkers for letting me reprint it here and use it on the back cover. Photo Credit: Greg Gorman

Lynda's Acknowledgements

My daughter Jamie, who keeps me grounded in the real world, not just the World Wide Web. I love you my sweetheart, and can't wait to have more time with you now that this book is finished!

My brand spankin' new husband Bruce Heavin, without whom I could not have survived the last year of writing four books. Your support, love, and encouragment has made all the difference. And the beautiful covers you painted and incredible images you created didn't exactly suck either! There are no words to describe how much I appreciate and love you.

My book designer, Ali Karp, who cared more about the integrity of this second edition than anyone can measure. Who made sure everything was designed to work correctly with the information and pushed me and herself as hard as humanly possible. You are one awesome friend, collaborator and designer, girlfriend! ■ alink@earthlink.net

My very awesome New Riders team—**John Kane** and **Jennifer Eberhardt**. You were great to work with—let's do it again sometime <g>.

My dear friend **George Maestri** for helping me find the right publisher for the first *Designing Web Graphics*.

David Dwyer for listening to George.

■ In a not-so-glamorous, more true-to-life photo shoot, here I am striking more typical poses. Photo Credit: Bruce Heavin

My dear friend **Crystal Waters** who is always there for me, even when I talk about the web.

My dear friend **Joy Silverman** for her love and supportiveness. Plus when I grow up I want to look like her.

My other close women friends—**Ann Monn**, **Khyal Braun**, **Deborah Caplan**, and **Windy Litvak** who I rarely see, but always carry with me.

My moms—**Carolyn Graysen**, **Ann Weinman**, **Sharyl Heavin**, and **Françoise Kirkland**. Hey, I got lucky and have a lot of moms!

My bro **William Edward Weinman**, who heaped tons of great HTML advice on me and talked to me about my chapters even when he had no time to do so.

My sistah **Pamela** who just graduated from nursing school! Congrats, Pam. You rule!

Steve Weinman for the video, the palette help, and overall supportiveness.

Josh Weinman for the great party.

Mary Thorpe for her beautiful laugh, smile, heart, spirit, and support.

Christopher Schmitt for hanging in there with HTML and graphic help even though I barely had time to explain what I needed.

Web Design List Members **Hung Doan**, **Suzanne Stephens**, and **A. E. Fullerton** for your help. **All the listees** who provided tips, advice, suggestions, and URLs.

Ivan Hoffman for help, warmth, and advice.

Classic PIO Partners (800-370-2746) and **Digital Stock** (■ http://www.digitalstock.com) for use of their great stock photographs.

Erik Holsinger and **Mark Wheaton** for their help with video and sound information in the first edition of *Designing Web Graphics*. A lot of your work appears in the second edition, too. Thank you both again!

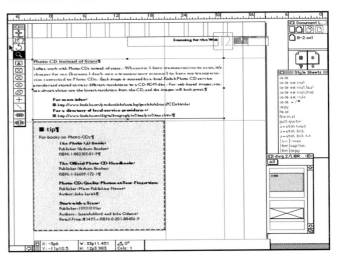

A designer's view of laying out the book—from desktop to finished document. We chose to mimic a web aesthetic with our design of *dwg.2*, using underlined text and colored pull quotes. Dashed line boxes were used for tips, notes, and warnings because it reminded us of Bruce's cover artwork. Our goal was to create a playful, inviting, accessible book that was specifically tailored to the information at hand.

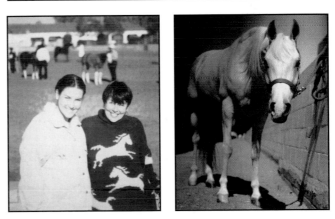

My favorite book designer, Ali, with her best friend/mom at a local horse show. To the right, Ali's horse Smoke—always ready to smile for her camera.

■ contents at a glance

1. Getting Started in Web Design   2

2. Understanding the Web Environment   24

3. Web File Formats   44

4. Low-Bandwidth Graphics   70

5. Hexidecimal Color   118

6. Browser-Safe Color   132

7. Transparent Artwork   164

8. Background Tiles   188

9. Rules, Bullets, and Buttons   204

10. Navigation-Based Graphics   222

11. Web-Based Typography   250

12. Scanning for the Web   276

13. Layout and Alignment Techniques   298

14. Animation   330

15. Sound   358

16. Interactivity   376

17. HTML for Visual Designers   406

    Glossary   416

    Design Resources   424

Introduction   xx

1   Getting Started in Web Design   2

Web Design as a Career Path   4
    Design Resources   4
How to Charge for Web Design   5
Learn to Use Search Engines   6
How to List Your Site with Search Engines   7
Choose Your Tools   8
Which Flavor: Mac or PC?   8
Macs Versus PCs   9
System Requirements   10
Software   12
Imaging Programs   12
Shareware and Freeware Programs   14
Learning HTML   15
What Does HTML Look Like?   16
HTML Software   18
Should You Learn HTML?   19
How to Learn HTML   20
Text-Based HTML Editors   21
WYSIWYG HTML Editors   22

2   Understanding the Web Environment   24

Welcome to the Weird World of Web Graphics   26
Designing for the Computer Screen, Not the Printed Page   28
Browser Differences   29
HTML for Different Browsers   30
    Browser Types Visiting BrowserWatch   31
Cross-Platform Hell!   32
Cross-Platform Color Calibration Issues   34
High Resolution Versus Low Resolution   38
    Measurements for the Web   38
Bit Depth   40

Monitor's Bit Depth   42
    How to Change Your Monitor's Bit Depth   43

3   Web File Formats   44

Compression File Formats   46
HTML for Embedding Images   47
    Naming Conventions for JPEGs and GIFs   47
GIF File Formats   48
GIFs for Illustration-Style Imagery   48
    GIF Pronunciation   48
GIFs for Photographic Imagery   49
Controlling Your Color Mapping   50
Interlaced GIFs   52
Transparent GIFs   53
    8-Bit Transparency   53
Animated GIFs   54
    Popular GIF animation authoring tools   54
    Some good animated GIF references   54
JPEG   56
Progressive JPEGs Versus Standard JPEGs   59
    Photoshop 4.0 Settings   59
PNG   60
Digital Watermarks   63
WebTV   64
    Designing for WebTV   64
WebTV Features   66
Unsupported WebTV HTML Tags   66
    The Price of WebTV   66
WebTV Design Tips   67
Comparing WebTV to the Net: www.lynda.com   68
Comparing WebTV to the Net: www.ikon.net   69

4   Low-Bandwidth Graphics   70

Low-Bandwidth Graphics   72
How to Know What Size Your File Really Is   74
    To Icon or Not to Icon   75

Making Small GIFs 76
Aliased Artwork 78
Dithering and Banding 80
To Dither or Not to Dither? 82
Photoshop Dither Settings 83
    GIF Choices 83
Photoshop's Indexed Color Dialog Box 84
Photoshop Palette Chart 86
How to Use the Image Compression Charts 88
Image Compression Charts: PNG Dithered 89
Image Compression Charts: PNG Nondithered 90
Image Compression Charts: GIF Dithered 91
Image Compression Charts: GIF Nondithered 92
Image Compression Charts: JPEG 93
Image Compression Charts: PNG Dithered 94
Image Compression Charts: PNG Nondithered 95
Image Compression Charts: GIF Dithered 96
Image Compression Charts: GIF Nondithered 97
Image Compression Charts: JPEG 98
Image Compression Charts: PNG Dithered 99
Image Compression Charts: PNG Nondithered 100
Image Compression Charts: GIF Dithered 101
Image Compression Charts: GIF Nondithered 102
Image Compression Charts: JPEG 103
Image Compression Charts: PNG Dithered 104
Image Compression Charts: PNG Nondithered 105
Image Compression Charts: GIF Dithered 106
Image Compression Charts: GIF Nondithered 107
Image Compression Charts: JPEG 108
24-Bit JPEGs Versus 24-Bit PNGs 109
Reducing Colors in GIF Files Using Photoshop 110
Reducing Colors in Photo-Paint 111
Reducing Colors in Paint Shop Pro 112
    The Windows 16 Palette 112
    Other Compression Tools and Resources 113
    Compression Rules in a Nutshell 113
Photoshop 4.0 Actions Palette 114
Step-by-Step Actions Palette Programming 114
Batch File Processing 117
Actions Palette Options 117

5   Hexadecimal Color   118

Hexadecimal Shmexadecimal	120
Hexadecimal Resources	123
Web Hex Converters	123
Hex Calculators	123
Color-Related HTML Tags	124
Adding Color Using HTML	124
Using Color Names Instead of Hex	126
Coloring Individual Lines of Text	128
Coloring Links	129
Inserting a Background Image	130
Adding Color to Tables	131

6   Browser-Safe Color   132

Computer Color	134
RGB Versus CMYK	135
Introduction to Browser-Safe Specs	136
Why Work Within a Limited Palette?	137
Hexadecimal-Based Artwork	137
Illustration-Based Artwork	138
Photograph-Based Artwork	140
What Does the Browser-Safe Palette Look Like?	141
Do Browser-Safe Colors Really Matter?	141
Browser-Safe Color Charts Organized by Hue	142
Browser-Safe Color Charts Organized by Value	144
What Is a CLUT and What Do You Do with One?	146
Changing Existing Colors	146
How to Load a Browser-Safe Swatch Palette into Photoshop	147
How to Use the Browser-Safe Swatch Sets	147
How to Load the Browser-Safe Palette into Paint Shop Pro	148
How to Load a Browser-Safe Palette into Photo-Paint	149
How to Load a Browser-Safe Palette into Painter	150
How to Ensure Your Artwork Stays Browser Safe	151
Mixing Photos and Illustrations with Browser-Safe Colors	152
Removing Unwanted Browser-Safe Colors	153
16-Bit Trouble?	153

Vector-Based Software: Illustrator, CorelDraw, and FreeHand   154
Working with CorelDraw   154
Working with Adobe Illustrator   155
    GIFs in Illustrator   155
Working with FreeHand   156
Working with Color Picker-Based Applications   157
    CMYK Is Not Browser Safe   157
What Are Hybrid-Safe Colors?   158
HTML for Hybrid Colors   159
Hybrid Color Background Tile Creation in Photoshop   160
    Importance of Value   160
Coloring Hybrid Tiles in Photoshop   161
    Photoshop Shortcuts   161
Custom Palettes for Shockwave Documents   162
Previsualizing Tiles in Photoshop   163

7 Transparent Artwork

164

Transparency   166
Creating Background Color the Hexadecimal Way   168
Creating Background Color Using Solid Patterns   169
    JPEG or GIF?   169
Transparent GIFs   170
    HTML for Transparent GIFs   170
When to Use Transparent Artwork   171
Making Clean Transparent Artwork   172
Photoshop Tips for Creating Aliased Images   173
Creating Illustration-Based Artwork for Transparent GIFs   173
Turning Prescanned Illustrations into Aliased Art   174
Photographic Source Art for Transparent GIFs   175
How to Deal with Glows, Soft Edges, and Drop Shadows with GIF Transparency   176
    Transparent GIF URLs   177
Transparent GIF Software   178
Cross-Platform   178
    Adobe Photoshop GIF89a Export Plug-In 178
    Fractal Design Painter 4.0   180
    Transparency Resources   181
    URLs for Online Transparency   181

Macintosh | 182
Transparency | 182
DeBabelizer | 182
Windows | 184
LView | 184
GIF Construction Set | 184
Paint Shop Pro | 185
8-Bit Transparency with PNG | 186
PNG File Size | 187

8 Background Tiles 188

Making Background Tiles | 190
Tiling Backgrounds | 191
Determining Tiled Pattern Sizes | 192
File Formats for Patterned Background Tiles | 194
The Code, Please! | 194
Seams or No Seams, That Is the Question | 196
Seams | 196
Aesthetics of Backgrounds | 197
No Seams, the Photoshop Way | 198
No Seams, the Painter 4.0 Way | 200
Recommended Reading | 201
Full-Screen Body Backgrounds? | 202
Other Tricks with Background Tiles | 203

9 Rules, Bullets, and Buttons 204

Rules, Bullets, and Buttons | 206
Horizontal Rules | 206
Horizontal Rules the HTML Way | 207
Fancier Horizontal Rule Tags | 208
Horizontal Rules the Do-It-Yourself Way | 210
Using Illustrator and Photoshop to Create Custom Horizontal Rule Art | 210
Vertical Rules | 213
Clip Art Rules, Too | 213
Clip Art | 213

Bullets 214
Creating HTML Bulleted Lists 215
Creating Ordered and Definition Lists 216
Creating Custom-Made Bullets 218
Creating Custom Bullet Art 219
Using Kai's Power Tools 219
Faking Interactive Buttons 220
Button Clip Art 221

10 Navigation-Based Graphics 222

Navigation Issues in Web Design 224
Storyboarding 225
    Storyboarding Your Site 225
Hot Images and Text 226
Identifying Hot Images 227
Creating Linked Images and Text 228
Turning Off Image Borders 228
Creating Navigation Bars 230
The Miraculous Server Include Tag 232
    Recommended Reading 232
What Are Imagemaps? 233
Client-Side Imagemaps Versus Server-Side Imagemaps 234
Creating Server-Side Imagemaps 235
Do You Really Need an Imagemap? 235
The Four Stages of a Server-Side Imagemap 236
Starting with the Graphic 237
Defining the Regions of an Imagemap 237
Using WebMap 238
Using MapEdit 239
Writing HTML to Support Server-Side Imagemaps 240
Creating Client-Side Imagemaps 241
Using Server-Side and Client-Side Imagemaps Together 242
Importance of the <ALT> Tag 243
Importance of <WIDTH> and <HEIGHT> Tags 243
    Imagemap Tutorial URLs 243
    Imagemap Software Tools 243
Frames for Navigation 244
HTML for Frames 245

Floating Frames   248
    Extra Frame-Related HTML Attributes   248
Aesthetic Cues for Navigation Graphics   249
    Rollovers Versus Buttons   249

Web-Based Typography   250

Web-Based Typography   252
Short Glossary of Key Typographic Terms   253
Glossary of Terms Not Possible with HTML   255
Interesting Typography-Based URLs   256
    HTML Type Versus Graphical Type   256
Aesthetic Considerations   257
    Printing Web Pages   257
HTML-Based Typography   258
    Headings   258
    Bold   258
    Italics   258
    Preformatted   258
    Blinking Text   258
    Changing Font Sizes   258
    Drop Cap   259
    Small Cap   259
    Centering Text   259
    Useful URLs   259
Fun with ASCII!   260
    Case Study: Hollywood Records   260
    HTML Font Choices   262
    Font Face Tag   262
    Font Size Differences Between Macs and PCs   263
Graphics-Based Typography   264
    Aliasing Versus Anti-Aliasing   264
Using Photoshop for Type Design   265
Working with Illustrator Type in Photoshop   268
Writing the HTML to Place Your Text Graphics into the Page   269
Mixing Graphic Type and HTML   270
    Case Study: Alice in Chains   270
HTML for Mixed Type Sizes   272
    Case Study: Art Center College of Design   274

Digital Font Foundries   275
    Font Legends   275

12 Scanning Techniques for the Web   276

Scanning for the Web   278
Scanner Equipment   279
For scanner comparisons, check out the following   280
Dictionary of Scanning Terms   280
Resolution   281
Resizing Images in Photoshop 4.0   282
    Do Not Resize Art in Indexed Color!   283
Scanning 3D Stuff   284
Photo CDs Instead of Scans   285
    For books on Photo CDs   285
Post Processing Scans with Photoshop 4.0   286
Correcting Color with Adjustment Layers in Photoshop 4.0   286
More Photoshop 4.0 Images Processing Tips   288
Levels   288
Color Balance   290
Dot Screen Patterns and Moirés   292
Selections   294
Photoshop Selection Tools   295
Photoshop Selection Modifiers   296
Painting Quickmask Selections in Photoshop 4.0   297
    More on Photoshop   297

13 Layout and Alignment Techniques   298

Alignment Hell   300
Defining the Size of a Web Page   302
JavaScript for Establishing Page Size   304
Using HTML for Alignment   306
Text Alignment Tags   307
Image and Type Alignment Tags   308
Image Alignment Tags   308

Horizontal and Vertical Space Tags	308
WIDTH and HEIGHT Attributes	309
Alternatives to HTML Using Artwork	310
Using Spacers for Alignment	310
Netscape Proprietary Alignment Tags	310
WIDTH and HEIGHT Attributes for Spaces	311
Aligning a Graphic to a Patterned Background	312
Tables for Alignment	313
WYSIWYG Tables	313
Data Tables	314
HTML Table Tags	315
Graphic Tables for Page Layout Design	318
Warning: Text in Tables Can Get Messed Up Easily	321
Alignment Without Tables	322
The Adobe Acrobat Solution	324
More Information on PDG Authoring	326
Cascading Style Sheets	327
Microsoft's CSS Gallery	328

14 Animation

330

Web Animation	332
The Aesthetics of Animation	333
Web Animation Technologies	334
Animated GIFs	334
Plug-Ins	335
Java	336
JavaScript	337
JavaScript Resources	337
QuickTime Movies	338
Embedding QuickTime Movie Tags	339
QuickTime VR	342
HTML Tags for QuickTime VR	343
AVI Movies	344
AVI Movie Tags for Embedding	344
Syntax Example	344
Server Push	345
Noteworthy Web Animation Tools	346
FutureSplash Animator (Mac/PC Compatible)	346

Shockwave/Director (Mac/PC Compatible)   347

webPainter (Mac Only)   348

3D Web Workshop (Mac Only)   348

PhotoDisc Animation Series (Mac/PC Compatible)   349

GIF Animation Tools   349

QuickTime: Web Motion (Mac Only)   349

Tech Notes: More on Animated GIFs   350

Tech Notes: More on Creating Movies   352

General Movie-Making Tips   352

Make Your Movies Small   353

Codecs   354

      Appropriate Codes for Web Movies   354

Cinepak—Available for QuickTime and AVI   355

Indeo—Available for QuickTime and AVI   355

MPEG   356

Glossary of Animation and Digital Video Terms   356

How to Create Animation Content   357

      Last Word Department   357

15 Sound   358

Sound on the Web   360

Sound Aesthetics   360

How to Get Sound Source Files into Your Computer   361

Digital Audio Terminology   363

To Stream or Not to Stream?   364

Making Small Audio Files   365

Rates and Bits   365

Audio File Formats   366

Tips for Making Web-Based Sound Files   367

HTML for Downloading Sound Files   368

Audio Helper Apps and Utilities   369

For Macs   369

For PCs   369

Automatic Music Without Downloading   370

MSIE Audio Tags   370

BGSOUND   370

Netscape Audio Tags   371

HTML Syntax   372

JavaScript Functions for LiveAudio   374
LiveAudio   374
LiveConnect   374
    Cross-Browser Compatibility   374
Other Sound Options   375

16 Interactivity   376

Interactivity   378
Interactivity Role Models   379
Interactivity Versus Difficulty   380
    What Kind of Server   380
Counters   382
Forms   383
    HTML for Buttons within Forms   383
Guestbooks   384
Ad Banners   388
Chat Environments and Avatars   390
Mouse Rollovers   392
JavaScript MouseOvers   392
Joe Maller's JavaScript Rollover   392
    Declaring Images in the Script   392
    Naming Image Objects   393
    What's "onMouseOver"?   393
    Functions   393
    Notes and Problems   394
Putting It All Together   394
Bill Weinman's JavaScript Rollover   395
Director/Shockwave/Lingo-Based Interactive Web Pages   396
Shockwave Versus JavaScript   397
Leroy's Click and Drag   398
Designing the Interface for the Anatomy Shockwave Project   400
Deconstructing the Lingo for Shockwave   402
    Director 5 Supports Shockwave   404
Shocking Director   405

17 HTML for Visual Designers — 406

HTML for Visual Designers 408
Naming Protocols 409
Common File Extensions 409
Relative Versus Absolute Path Names 410
    Checking Your Pages 410
Troubleshooting 411
Uploading Your Pages 411
The Basic Structure of an HTML Document 411
Common HTML Tags 412
    Head Tags 412
    Body Tags 412
    Text Tags 412
    Horizontal Rule Tags 413
    Text Alignment Tags and Attributes 413
    Image Alignment Tags and Attributes 413
    Image Tags 413
    List Tags and Attributes 414
    Table Tags 414
    Table Tags and Attributes 414
    Linking Tags and Attributes 415
    Frames Tags and Attributes 415
    Linking Tags and Attributes 415
    Comments Tag 415

Glossary — 416

Design Resources — 424

Index — 428

Introduction

Getting Started in Web Design

Understanding the Web Environment

Web File Formats

Low-Bandwidth Graphics

Hexadecimal Color

Browser-Safe Color

Transparent Artwork

Background Tiles

Rules, Bullets and Buttons

Navigation-Based Graphics

Web-Based Typography

Scanning Techniques for the Web

Layout and Alignment Techniques

Animation

Sound

Interactivity

HTML for Visual Designers

Glossary

Design Resources Appendix

Index

BROWSER SAFE COLORS

Web 3d typography

33FF

Photoshop

INDEX

Width="500"

<STRONG>

.Gif
.Jpg
Png

<img src="

Image compression
Limited palettes
IMAGE OPTIMIZATION
216 Colors

PARENCY

Height="600"

</A>

102 K

<cente>

Imaging techniques
Extending HTML
Web file formats
bgcolor="FFFFCC"

Animation, sound and

@link = "cyan"

LYNDA.COM

</center>

www.Design

Introduction

It's been a year since the first edition of *Designing Web Graphics*, and what a year it's been. My conviction that visual design would play a pivotal role in the advancement of the web has been validated by new and better HTML features, better browsers, better imaging tools, better techniques, and *better sites!* The need to concentrate on design for the web as a separate entity from programming has never been more timely.

If you are a professional visual designer, you are most likely being asked to design web sites or are currently already doing so. If you are a nondesigner making web sites, you are finding yourself in the role of visual designer, whether you feel qualified or not.

My goal is to speak to both the professional designer and the novice nondesigner in this book, and make sure to explain concepts and techniques as clearly as possible, avoiding hype, fluff, and intimidation. Who needs to be overwhelmed by technical writing when the subject at hand is technical enough?

At the same time the web has gotten more friendly toward designers, it's also gotten more complex. The early web a year ago was not only more primitive, it was also easier to learn. As more options and technologies emerge, the learning curve climbs upward as well. I write in a friendly, easy going style because I don't think the information needs to be presented in a complicated way. Whenever I can explain something in plain English and avoid jargon or assumptions, I do.

Web design is in its infancy. Anyone claiming to be an expert has been doing this work for maybe three or four years—at the most. My attitude is that we are all new at this stuff, even those so-called expert folks. I consider myself both a student and a teacher of web design. There's never been a reason to understand file compression, navigational techniques, color palettes, animation, and sound in one visual design discipline. And visual design should not be entirely separated apart from information design and/or programming design. Great sites work on all levels, not just visual design. The web makes it possible and necessary to combine many different disciplines at once, and it's one rare superhuman who can do it all well.

I am just as jazzed as the next person to see web technology advance and improve. All kinds of techniques are described here, from very advanced to very simple. **Keep in mind, however, that just because a site throws every new bell and whistle into its mix doesn't make it a great site. In fact, more often the reverse is true!**

The web is a publishing medium, and there's room for all types of publishers and all types of sites. I personally hope that the homespun nature of the web never gets edged out by the more advanced sites. At that point, we will have lost the true meaning behind this revolutionary new publishing model.

This web has leveled the playing field to spread across continents, economics, races, genders, and politics. It enables anyone to be a publisher or consumer of information. This is the first time in history that publishing has not been controlled by government, large institutions, the media, and/or big business. It's a mom-and-pop kind of world, where dog and cat home pages might get accessed as often as well-funded corporate sites. The web plays havoc with our sense of hierarchy. You can throw all the money in the world at a site, but basic publishing and design skills that are within reach of anyone are what will make a site stand apart from the crowd.

It's funny how we talk about web sites so differently from other types of visual design mediums. We don't look at a site as we would with printed artwork or text—we go to a site. We talk about web pages as if they are places. We use verbs such as surfing, navigating, browsing, and lurking to describe our actions as we view pages. What's going on? Why are these terms associated with viewing web sites?

The web is an environment. Even though we're looking at a flat screen, often sitting motionless except to move our mouse or type at a keyboard, we are moving. We are moving through information, through geography, through images, and through sounds and video. This is a dynamic medium and one of the most challenging design mediums ever created.

Good design, however, is not just about making beautiful images. There actually are design constraints and limits specific to this medium. It is my goal to bridge those limits and constraints, and to help designers, programmers, and hobbyists understand the medium to make the best use of it.

Good design aids communication; it doesn't exclude its intended audience. If you choose to ignore the limits of the web, you choose to exclude your public. This is not print, this is not TV, and this is not a CD-ROM. The web is its own, very different environment. It has its own quirks and rules and weaknesses, and this book is a place you can turn to learn about what they are.

How Is the Second Edition Different from the First?

The first edition of *Designing Web Graphics* shepherded a lot of other firsts. It was the first book written by a designer for designers on the subject of web design. It was the first book to address low-bandwidth graphics as a subject larger than a few page's mention. It was the first book to describe browser and cross-platform differences in detail. It was the first book to discuss cross-platform palette and color management. It was also the first book I ever wrote, and researching the subject spurred me to create my first web site.

That's not to suggest I'm a stranger to computer graphics. Far from it in fact. I got my first computer in 1982 and have been creating graphics and teaching almost ever since. The web is actually a throwback to more primitive days of computing. Before WYSIWYG editors existed, we used to have to add commands such as bold, italic, and underline in the form of tags. There was no such thing as a millions of color video card for a personal computer until the late 1980s. When I first looked around the web, even though I had never authored a page, I recognized many similarities to the olden days of computer graphics from the decade before.

That's not to say my first experiences were not frustrating. I downloaded an HTML editor, but didn't understand how to use it. I wanted to make images with transparent edges, but didn't understand how. I wanted to know why certain images had blue borders and some didn't. Why some appeared out of focus at first and then sharpened. It was such a strange new landscape, but I wanted so badly to understand it and be in control of it.

At that time, there were no web design books—only a few HTML books. I decided to write the first edition of *Designing Web Graphics* because I couldn't find the book I needed! Today, any respectable computer section in a bookstore has entire shelves devoted to the subject of web development. There are now dozens of books on web design, hundreds on HTML and Java, and probably hundreds more to come. Creating web sites has become the digital gold rush of the '90s.

There was a glaring need for my first book. Now that there all kinds of competing web design titles are out there, why is there a need to write *Designing Web Graphics* all over again? For one thing, readers write to me all the time. I didn't realize that people wrote to authors about their books! I thought people wrote only when they had complaints. I've been amazed by the volume of encouraging and grateful e-mails I've received about *Designing Web Graphics*, and I want to keep servicing the people who seem to appreciate my work. As a teacher, I used to have 18 to 100 students a semester who I might have the privilege of influencing or inspiring. What a rush to have tens of thousands of students all of a sudden! I like this book-writing thing, and as long as you readers spur me on, my guess is I'll keep going at it.

Besides all that, the web design landscape has evolved and changed over this past year. One of the major advancements has been the proliferation of new HTML editors that make web page authoring much more automatic and easy than in the past. The focus now is much less on the programming and much more on the content, speed, interactivity, and appearance of web sites. I'm very excited to produce a new, updated version of *Designing Web Graphics* that will address the many new design and graphics issues of web publishing.

When I proposed doing a second edition of this book, I thought it would be easier to produce than the first. Instead, I have practically rewritten the book from start to finish because there's that much more to write about now. Those of you who already own the first edition will find lots of new information in this second version.

What's New

Here's a brief list of what's new in *DWG.2*:

- Pricing Guidelines
- Copyright Information
- Equipment Suggestions
- HTML Editor Suggestions
- Hybrid-Safe Color Creation
- PNG
- WebTV Specifications
- Digital Watermarks
- PNG Transparency
- Client-Side Imagemaps
- Frames
- New Alignment Tags
- Scanning Tips
- GIF Animation
- Photoshop 4.0 Tips
- Programming Actions Palettes
- Embedded Sound
- Embedded QuickTime
- JavaScript Button Rollovers
- Expanded Typography Section

As you can see, there's a lot that has been added to this second edition of *Designing Web Graphics*. My publisher and I hope to come out with annual updates of this book, as long as the medium warrants it and we receive your encouragement to do so.

How This Book Works

Writing about web design is a tricky thing because there are so many overlapping concepts. For example, tables can be used for layout and alignment, or for cutting apart images to save on file size and downloading time. Teaching about linked graphics and navigation involves both image creation techniques and HTML or CGI. Sometimes, making the decision about which chapter to put with which subject is difficult! For this reason, I have intentionally structured this book so that readers can approach it in a nonlinear manner. Whenever a subject is mentioned in more than one chapter, it is clearly noted.

Those who use the web for information often wonder if they need to buy a book, when so much information is available for free right on the Net. Indeed, the Net is an invaluable resource, and this book is not meant to be a substitute for it but rather an enhancement. Few will dispute the advantages to having all the information you need in a compact, transportable, and easy-to-read form. Books have not lost their importance in the age of networked information, but must work in tandem with electronic resources to be as effective as possible. This book (of course!) has a sister web site at ■ http://www.lynda.com/dwg2/.

Although it might be possible to read or skim this book in a single day, the information inside is far too overwhelming to absorb in a single sitting. It took me many months to write the first *Designing Web Graphics* and many more months to write the second edition. Even with that many months, I could not have possibly understood the task at hand without many more years of experience under my belt as a computer graphics artist and teacher. The task of collecting all this information in one place is enormous and, frankly, never feels finished. The web changes and evolves constantly, but once the ink is dry on this book's pages, it will forever be there.

That's why there are many references to outside information sources in this book. Everything from other URLs, other books, magazines, conferences, newsgroups, mailing lists, and CD-ROMs are offered as support resources whenever a new subject is touched upon. I wrote this book with the full understanding that information will change and evolve, and gave you outside channels to get to that new information. Updates and errata will be posted at my web site as well. Just remember how to spell my name—with a "y"—and you'll be able to e-mail me or check in on my web site at any time. I can't promise to answer everyone, but I do whenever time permits.

lynda@lynda.com
■ http://www.lynda.com

■ what the chapters cover

1. **Getting Started in Web Design**   2
Pricing issues, equipment, and browser differences found on the web.

2. **Understanding the Web Environment**   24
Cross-platform computing issues, as well as the equipment and browser differences, that you'll find.

3. **Web File Formats**   44
In-depth coverage about GIF, JPEG, PNG, WebTV, and digital watermarks.

4. **Low-Bandwidth Graphics**   70
Concrete information and charts to help you learn to make the smallest possible images that will download quickly and look their best.

5. **Hexadecimal Color**   118
All the color tags you want, in one place, in one chapter.

6. **Browser-Safe Color**   132
Color on the web is a tricky thing because it is translated differently by many platforms and operating systems. This chapter shows how, when, and why to use browser-safe colors.

7. **Transparent Artwork**   164
GIF and PNG transparency, as well as nontransparency tricks that will fool them all.

8. **Background Tiles**   188
How to make seamless and seamed tiles with step-by-step tutorials for the images and HTML.

9. **Rules, Bullets, and Buttons**   204
How to create HTML code for horizontal rules, bullets, and buttons.

10. **Navigation-Based Graphics**   222
How to create linked images and imagemaps, and how to make artwork appear clickable.

11. **Web-Based Typography**   250
Type terminology explained along with practical HTML and Photoshop examples.

12. **Scanning for the Web**   276
Scanning at low resolution is very different from scanning for print mediums. This chapter explains it all and includes step-by-step Photoshop 4.0 lessons that teach how to use adjustment layers.

13. **Layout and Alignment Techniques**   298
Tables? Invisible GIFs? Alignment Tags? You've come to the right chapter.

14. **Animation**   330
Shockwave? Animated GIFs? JavaScript? Quick-Time? Again, you've come to the right chapter.

15. **Sound**   358
Embedding sound or downloading sound, that is the question. The answers are in this chapter.

16. **Interactivity**   376
Guestbooks, ad banners, counters, forms, and rollovers all equate to enhanced interactivity in your site design.

17. **HTML for Visual Designers**   406
Want that certain tag and want it NOW? This is the chapter for you.

Glossary   416
When you need to understand a web design term and you want it NOW, this is the chapter.

Design Resources   424
A list of great design resources: magazines, URLs, books, conferences, and schools.

Which <...ing web graphics> Book Is Right For You?

Now that there are three different books to choose from, I get a lot of e-mail from people saying they want to buy one of my books, but aren't sure which one is right for them.

Designing Web Graphics.2 is appropriate for designers and nondesigners who are planning or already creating web sites. This book is the cornerstone of my series, which is tailored for newcomers to web design. Surprisingly I get just as much e-mail from experienced web designers who've bought the first edition and have learned a lot of new information. *Designing Web Graphics.2* covers web design from A through Z. It is a comprehensive web design book that you'll use as a reference as you develop your own sites. Most people report that their copy of the first edition has become dog-eared, and that of every web book they own, it's the one book they keep by their computer at all times.

Deconstructing Web Graphics approaches learning web design through a different means. Because most of the HTML buffs I know taught themselves through viewing other's source code, I thought it would be great to select from inspirational sites and both view and explain their code for readers. Behind-the-scenes profiles are made of programmers, designers, photographers, and illustrators, and everything from Photoshop layers to Shockwave/Lingo files are analyzed and demystified. This book is great for experienced designers looking for inspiration and improvement, and non-hands-on people who want an overview of issues surrounding web design.

Coloring Web Graphics is half book, half software. The book is a definitive guide to color on the web. Everything from file compression to dithering to browser-safe colors is thoroughly explained. My co-author, Bruce Heavin, assembled hundreds of suggested browser-safe color combinations for web sites. The CD-ROM includes swatches that can be loaded into Photoshop, Paint Shop Pro, Painter, Photo-Paint, and FreeHand. The book offers lots of step-by-step tutorials, and the CD-ROM swatches provide endless ideas for successful and cross-platform compatible color schemes.

A Final Note from the Author

I view the web as a both a revolutionary place and a historical event unfolding before my eyes, in my lifetime. I am drawn to the web as a place of enormous possibility. It's a great honor to have something to contribute to this medium that might help make it a better place. Not just a better looking place, but a more usable and accessible place, too.

Although the web started as a grass-roots movement, it has quickly escalated to big business. Even if you don't own a computer, these days you can't escape noticing web addresses everywhere. URLs are in magazine ads, television commercials, billboards, and junk mail. The web has taken the world by storm, with an unstoppable momentum that has inspired new pressures on the public to participate.

This is both positive and negative. I view the historical time we're in now as a digital revolution. Anything that is digital is somehow supposed to be better than anything that isn't. It's causing a lot of people to lose job security, and there's a lot of anxiety about getting up to speed. I hear so many people complain that they'll never catch up, and they feel defeated. The stakes seem high, and unfortunately they are.

Personally, I enjoy the challenge of computers and the web, and am a participant by choice not pressure. I do, however, completely understand that digital is not for everyone, in the same way no religion or political belief is correct for everyone. It's my goal to write about this stuff in a comforting way, and help those through it who are lost, intimidated, or defeated. Those who catch the wave almost always have a good time once they know how to ride. Information is power. It's far better to understand than to fear.

The World Wide Web has brought people, platforms, and operating systems together that were never intended to necessarily mix. With that comes controversy, greed, very high stakes, and a sense of panic. If I can do anything to alleviate that fear and instead instill my own sense of excitement and fascination, my job will be done.

Thank you for sharing my work with me.

Lynda

■ New Riders Publishing

The staff of New Riders Publishing is committed to bringing you the very best in computer reference material. Each New Riders book is the result of months of work by authors and staff who research and refine the information contained within its covers.

As part of this commitment to you, the NRP reader, New Riders invites your input. Please let us know if you enjoy this book, if you have trouble with the information and examples presented, or if you have a suggestion for the next edition.

Please note, however: New Riders staff cannot serve as a technical resource for web graphics or for questions about software or hardware-related problems. Please refer to the documentation that accompanies your software or to the applications' Help systems.

If you have a question or comment about any New Riders book, there are several ways to contact New Riders Publishing. We will respond to as many readers as we can. Your name, address, or phone number will never become part of a mailing list or be used for any purpose other than to help us continue to bring you the best books possible.

You can write us at the following address:
New Riders Publishing
Attn: Publisher
201 W. 103rd Street
Indianapolis, IN 46290

If you prefer, you can fax New Riders Publishing at:
(317) 817-7448.

You can also send electronic mail to New Riders
at the following Internet address:
jkane@newriders.mcp.com

NRP is an imprint of Macmillan Computer Publishing.
To obtain a catalog or information, or to purchase any
Macmillan Computer Publishing book, call (800) 428-5331
or visit our Web site at ■ http://www.mcp.com.

Thank you for selecting *Designing Web Graphics.2*!

Getting Started in Web Design

Introduction

Understanding the Web Environment

Web File Formats

Low-Bandwidth Graphics

Hexadecimal Color

Browser-Safe Color

Transparent Artwork

Background Tiles

Rules, Bullets and Buttons

Navigation-Based Graphics

Web-Based Typography

Scanning Techniques for the Web

Layout and Alignment Techniques

Animation

Sound

Interactivity

HTML for Visual Designers

Glossary

Design Resources Appendix

Index

Becaus
design
that pa
pay ove
ing web
for $10
and a cl

If it help
by every
market
down at
but for t
design th
work or
below ma
much hig

I always r
business
Work for
Observe
any smart
a few jobs
besides un
being a de
being on ti
all factor in

When I ran
designer ma
and rarely, i
I truly unde
to finish. I
wanted, and
by committe
warning. I le
bill accordin
make in a giv
I would need
Even so, it to
bidding. Dor
make a financ

Introduction

Getting Started in Web Design

Understanding the Web Environment

Web File Formats

Low-Bandwidth Graphics

Hexadecimal Color

Browser-Safe Color

Transparent Artwork

Background Tiles

Rules, Bullets and Buttons

Navigation-Based Graphics

Web-Based Typography

Scanning Techniques for the Web

Layout and Alignment Techniques

Animation

Sound

Interactivity

HTML for Visual Designers

Glossary

Design Resources Appendix

Index

<H1>
BROWSER
typography
Web
<TAB
<img src="
<STRONG>
Width="500
.gif
.jpg
Png
Image compression
Limited palettes
IMAGE OPTIMIZATION
216 Colors
Height="600
</A>
<<center
Imaging techniques
Extending HTML
Web file formats
bgcolor="FFFFCC"
Sound and
alink="
LYNDA.COM
</center>
www Design
2

Welcome to the Weird World of Web Graphics

I don't know about you, but I feel enormous excitement to witness and participate in the emergence of the web as a new communication medium. I never imagined a scenario where everyone could be, depending on personal choice, an author or spectator, a publisher or subscriber, an information source or information retriever.

There's never been a distribution medium like the web. Where else could you reach a potential audience of millions of people without spending a fortune in time, money, and research to mail your work to them? It's platform-independent. The web doesn't care whether you're on a Mac, Windows, Sun, or SGI workstation. There are no geographical boundaries. Someone in Germany can look at my site as easily as someone who lives around the corner.

The web has no hierarchy. By looking at a site, you can't tell whether the author is male, female, black, white, Asian, Hispanic, handicapped, rich, poor, old, or young. If you have a cool site, there's no one stopping more viewers from visiting yours than any number of boring well-funded corporate sites. Is this really an example of where the best designer wins? So far, yes. It represents freedom of expression in its most idealistic, raw form.

Whatever valid criticisms exist of the web as a design medium, visuals play a huge role in the popularity of the World Wide Web. Artists have an opportunity to define the look and feel of the web, and I doubt there's ever been another case in history where individuals, not institutions, have had a chance to influence a medium of this importance and magnitude. This is the world unlike any of us ever dreamed—all connected across geographical and computer platform boundaries, all capable of being interactive spectators or active contributors.

Although the web may be considered by many the latest, most advanced technology in computing, it is a very disconcerting authoring environment for most artists. Graphics are indisputably one of the key components that have made the web so popular and exciting. Even so, the graphic tools and techniques available to create visuals are confusing and limited. Most visual designers and computer artists using today's advanced imaging programs are going to feel lost when first introduced to authoring for the web.

This is partially because the web, like all graphical user interfaces, is easy to view and use, but more difficult to create for. It's one of those ironies life is full of; if it's easy to use, it's generally hard to make. It used to be that you could define yourself as just a writer, an illustrator, a typographer, a layout artist, an animator, a sound designer, a programmer, or an interface designer and that was enough. The web merges all these separate disciplines into one integrated communication medium, and it's enough to make a single individual feel easily overwhelmed. A few superhumans do it all well, but they are the exception, not the rule.

There are many parallels to web design and the early days of desktop publishing. Remember what happened to typography with the invention of the laser printer? Designers were horrified to see page layouts generated with bad spacing, poor font choices, mismanaged type sizes, and an uneducated sense of placement. Things have settled down since then, and with a little maturity the same will be true of the web.

Designing for the Computer Screen, Not the Printed Page

Everything that is wonderful about the web—global accessibility, cross-platform compatibility, networked distribution, and ever-improving-technology—has a tradeoff somewhere down the graphics creation road. On a printed page, everyone sees the same thing (with the exception of those who are visually impaired). A printed page has fixed dimensions. A printed page is designed once and forever stays the same. A printed page cannot be changed once it is finished.

Creating artwork for the web is very different from other visual delivery mediums because you're publishing your work to people's computer screens instead of printed pages. Computer systems vary widely. Some have small screens, some large. Some have color, some do not. Different operating systems deal with color differently. Some people have fast Internet connections, some do not. Different browsers display artwork differently. Different computer platforms have different fonts. It's the biggest design nightmare you could ever dream up—and your one chance of harnessing control over it is to understand the nature of the beast.

You can't possibly design a page that will look the same under all conditions without pandering to the lowest common denominator. That is not the route I advocate in this book. I believe that knowledge gives you power—if you arm yourself with an awareness of what can work and what can go wrong, and take whatever measures within your control to avoid the common pitfalls of this medium, your design can triumph over the obstacles.

This chapter reviews browser differences, monitor settings, and cross-platform compatibility issues, and offers an overview of bit-depth settings and gamma. These issues represent some of the common pitfalls to which web designers can fall prey.

Browser Differences

What is a browser, and what does it do? It's software that reads web pages and displays them for you. Different browsers can interpret the visual content of a web page differently. If you are a designer, this means you have the maddening task of designing a presentation that is subject to change according to which browser it's viewed from.

In the first edition of *Designing Web Graphics*, the introduction chapter to browsers was called "Browser Hell!" Back then, there were dozens of browsers with huge gaps in feature sets. Browsers have improved to the point now where that chapter heading is no longer appropriate because we've emerged from the browser hell era of the past to the present era of the browser wars. Competition has served us web designers well. The major discrepancies between feature sets that existed a year ago have become much less problematic.

Why do browsers interpret the pages differently? Shouldn't there be fixed standards? The browser interprets HTML (**H**yper**T**ext **M**arkup **L**anguage) code, which is the type of programming required to author web pages. HTML uses tags for including links, graphics, and other media on a web page. **HTML was created as an attempt to be a universally accepted, cross-platform standard language for displaying information, text, and visuals on the web.** Standards usually involve a standards committee, and committees often take a long time to agree on what they will officially support.

Officially sanctioned HTML of the old days allowed for one-color text, text that was left-justified with paragraph breaks, left-justified images, and little else. This understandably created frustration among designers and web browser developers who wanted to see the web evolve faster than the time it took outside committees to make formal decisions.

Entrepreneurial developers (primarily Netscape) took matters into their own hands and made web browsers that supported more options, without the blessings or participation of the HTML standards committee. New HTML code was developed that was supported only on proprietary browser systems, starting with Netscape and followed by others. This created outrage among some, and an outpouring of support from others who created an avalanche of web pages that included these new, unofficial HTML features.

As designers, it is not surprising that we want as many design features for the web as we can get our hands on. HTML today enables us to do a lot more than it used to, and we are grateful for every small morsel of design flexibility newly thrown our way. The downside is that some of these new design options have created a more confusing web design environment.

HTML for Different Browsers

In the first edition of *Designing Web Graphics*, I showed a full-color chart of the same HTML page in 11 different browsers and how you couldn't predictably rely on colored backgrounds, invisible borders, transparent GIFs, or even tables between different browsers. The level of differences today don't warrant that kind of visual chart. Most of the tags this book discusses work in the major three browsers: Netscape, Microsoft Internet Explorer (MSIE), and Mosaic. AOL's browser is the only popular browser that seriously lags behind the rest, but now that AOL will let you use other browsers, this should not be of much concern to web designers.

An invaluable resource for checking on browser discrepancies was put together by Kevin Ready, co-author of the book *Hybrid HTML Design: A Multi-Browser HTML Reference*. You'll find a table that shows all known HTML tags and which browsers support which tags here:

■ http://www.browserbydesign.com/resources/appa/apa1.htm

The book, *Hybrid HTML Design,* details how to design pages that are not only intended for display in all browsers, but perform optimally in each as well.

Hybrid HTML Design: A Multi-Browser HTML Reference
Publisher: New Riders Publishing
Authors: Kevin Ready and Janine Warner
Retail Price: $35.00 ■ ISBN: 1-56205-617-4

You can get the latest updates about browser versions at this marvelous site created by Dave Garaffa:

■ http://www.browserwatch.iworld.com

Here's a chart that was prepared by the Browserwatch site, dated 11/01/96:

Browser Types Visiting BrowserWatch
(Must Have .25% Share Or Better) ▪ printed with permission

Netscape Navigator	64.8%
Microsoft Internet Explorer	20.3%
Cyberdog	3.21%
Ibrowse	2.87%
Lynx	1.19%
IBM WebExplorer	0.92%
QuarterDeck Mosaic	0.83%
SPRY_Mosaic	0.77%
Amiga-AWeb	0.49%
Opera-2.1	0.47%
AOL (For Windows)	0.46%
FFiNet32.DLL	0.27%
AmigaVoyager	0.24%

Cross-Platform Hell!

One of the coolest things about the World Wide Web is that it's cross-platform, and people on Macs, PCs, Suns, and SGIs all get to communicate together in the same location for the first time in history.

If you're curious to know the percentage of systems used to access the web, here's the breakdown according to ■ http://browserwatch.iworld.com/stats/stats.html:

Windows	61.5%
Macintosh	23.2%
Unix	6.92%
Amiga	3.63%
OS/2	2.53%
Unknown	1.98%
VM/CMS	0.05%
NeXT	0.04%
Sega Saturn	0.01%

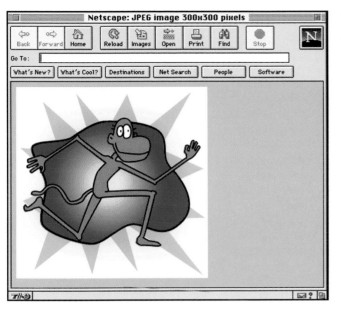

Here is an image viewed in a browser in 24-bit color.

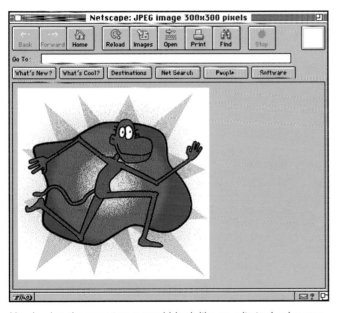

Here's what the same image would look like on a limited color monitor (4-bit or 16-color).

The unfortunate fact about cross-platform authoring is that viewers log on to the web by using different computers with different color spaces, color cards, monitor types, and monitor sizes. If you want to make yourself sad, spend hours creating a beautiful full-color graphic and then view it on someone's portable computer with a 4-bit color display. It's not a pretty sight. This is typical of some of the things that can happen unexpectedly to artwork that you post to your web site.

What can you do about such unplanned cross-platform discrepancies? In the case of viewers looking at your site from black-and-white portables or machines intended for video games, there's not much you can do except accept that the web will never offer full control over how your site is displayed. It's both the beauty of the medium and the curse of it. However, if you decide to make a site that relies on 24-bit color and a 21" monitor, you can see by the chart on the left how much you're probably limiting your potential audience.

Cross-Platform Color Calibration Issues

One of the problems with color on computer screens is that few monitors are calibrated accurately to one another. Shades of a color often vary wildly from computer to computer, and from platform to platform. (If you've ever owned two television sets, you know the color from set to set can vary wildly.) Anyone who works for a company with more than one computer knows that the colors shift between systems—even between identical operating systems and identical hardware.

Color calibration is a distressing problem for web designers who expect the colors they've picked to look the same on everyone's system. Macs, PCs, SGIs, and Suns all have different color cards and monitors, and none of them are calibrated to each other.

Mac

PC

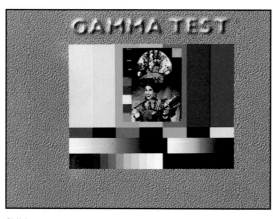

SUN

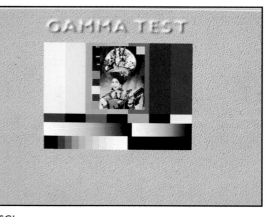

SGI

Because you now see for yourself that you have no control over the calibration of systems that your work will be viewed on, what can you do to make good-looking graphics that look good everywhere? What becomes more important than the colors you pick and what is stressed throughout this book is the contrast and value of a graphic. If you achieve contrast and value balance, the brightness and darkness, or color differences, on various platforms are going to be less objectionable.

Does your page pass the bit-depth test? Here's my home page viewed in **8-bit color**, **grayscale**, and **black and white**.

Across different computer platforms, the calibration problem is amplified by gamma differences. Gamma dictates the brightness and contrast of the computer's display. Macs, for example, are typically much brighter than PCs because of the differences in Macintosh's native gamma settings. Both calibration and gamma pose variables that are impossible to control in web design.

Although these numbers vary widely from different sources, it is generally reported that Mac and SGI monitors are close to the same, but PCs are much darker.

Average factory settings for Mac monitors	1.8 gamma
Average factory settings for SGI monitors	1.7 gamma
Average factory settings for PC monitors	2.5 gamma

Value is especially important in the context of web graphics. Differences in computer platforms, gamma settings, or a monitor's calibration can wreak havoc on the readability of images. A dark image created on one machine may come out black or appear tinted on another. Macintosh computers are generally lighter than Windows-based machines. Web pages can now also be viewed over television screens, which are calibrated differently from computer monitors altogether.

So how do you know if you are creating an image with values that will display properly on other machines? You can start by making sure your images have a good range from black to white. Don't place all the important information in the dark areas because they might go to black and fade out on someone's PC. And the same goes for light areas. There is no absolute control over how someone will see your images, so making them as readable as possible in terms of value should be your highest priority. Always view your images on other platforms to see whether your images achieve their intended values.

A great exercise is to temporarily throw your monitor in grayscale mode and then view your image to see whether its values are reading as you expected. This converts all the color data to blacks, whites, and grays. This change of settings yields much better feedback about brightness and contrast than a color display can.

Colors are notoriously deceptive when judging brightness and darkness because variables, such as a florescent color or subtle hand tinting, are overpowering when judging value.

Here's an example of the original image.

When viewing the image in grayscale, it almost disappears! This is because the values (lights and darks) are close together.

Here is the color-corrected version.   See how the grayscale version looks.

Personally, when working on my Mac, I try to make graphics a little lighter than I normally would, knowing that they'll display darker on PCs. When working on my PC, I do the opposite and make graphics slightly darker. There's no way to make it work perfectly everywhere, but knowing these general differences makes you an "informed" web designer so that you can make educated guesses about overall color brightness. I recommend that you always view your graphics on as many platforms as possible and make necessary changes when needed based on informed feedback.

Cross-platform authoring is possible on the web, but that doesn't necessarily mean it looks good. Take the following items into consideration, and you'll be able to make the best of a difficult design situation:

- ■ Your pages will look different on different computer monitors and platforms.
- ■ Check your pages on other platforms and make informed decisions for changes if necessary.
- ■ Pay attention to the brightness and contrast of a graphic, and it will look best even when viewed under poor monitor conditions.

High Resolution Versus Low Resolution

Because your delivery medium is a computer screen and not a printed page, high-resolution files are not part of web design life. High-resolution graphics are intended to be printed on high-resolution printers, not displayed on standard computer monitors. A typical screen resolution is 72 dpi and a high-resolution image is often 300+ dpi. You should always work at "screen resolution" when authoring images for the web (or any other screen-based medium, such as television or interactive multimedia). The accepted measurement of "screen resolution" is 72 dpi, or 72 dots per inch. This is because most standard computer monitors use 72 pixels for every inch of screen space.

For those of you who have worked with high-resolution files before, you may remember that in order to view them 1:1, you generally have to use the magnifying glass tool many times, resulting in a huge cropped image on your computer screen. The reason for this is that a computer screen can't physically display a high-resolution file. If you put a high-resolution file on the web, it can display only at 1:1 magnification, meaning that it will appear much bigger than you intended. Most likely, your goal for working in high resolution is to ensure the highest possible quality for your image, although in actuality, you would defeat that purpose.

> ■ **tip**
>
> Measurements for the Web
> Whenever working on images for the web, set your graphics to be measured in pixels, not inches. Inches are needed when creating artwork that will be printed on paper; pixels are the standard unit of measurement for screen-based bound images.

Here's a 72 dpi image in Netscape of my lovely daughter after eating melted chocolate. It appears exactly the way we want it to appear.

Go under the Image menu and select Image Size in Photoshop. This shows what the resolution is—in this case it's 72 dpi.

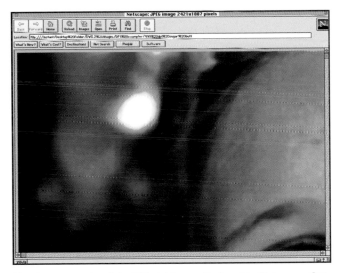

Here's an example of the 300 dpi image displayed in Netscape. Get the picture?

In this second example, the resolution is set to 300 dpi. In print graphics this would improve the appearance of this image significantly. In web graphics it results in an image that is way too big for the screen to display.

Bit Depth

Uh-oh, the dreaded bit-depth subject! For those math-phobic people, this topic will most likely sound intimidating. Bit depth is extremely important in understanding web graphics. Bit depth can refer to the number of colors in an image or the number of colors a computer system is capable of displaying. Bit-depth is "calculated" by figuring that 1-bit equals two colors and then multiplying 2 times 2 to arrive at each higher bit depth. Here's is a handy chart for convenient reference that identifies the different standard bit-depth levels.

32-bit	16.7+ million colors + 8-bit (256 level) grayscale mask
24-bit	16.7+ million colors
16-bit	65.5 thousand colors
15-bit	32.8 thousand colors
8-bit	256 colors
7-bit	128 colors
6-bit	64 colors
5-bit	32 colors
4-bit	16 colors
3-bit	8 colors
2-bit	4 colors
1-bit	2 colors

Here's a visual guide to refer to whenever you need it:

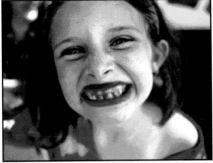 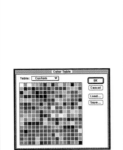

8-bit ▪ 45.3k ▪ 256 colors

 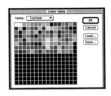

7-bit ▪ 38.2k ▪ 128 colors

 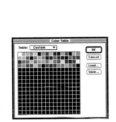

6-bit ▪ 32k ▪ 64 colors

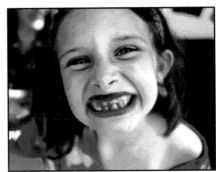 

5-bit ▪ 26.7k ▪ 32 colors

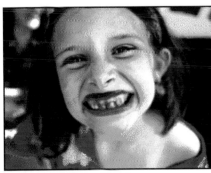 

4-bit ▪ 21.4k ▪ 16 colors

 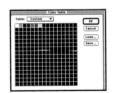

3-bit ▪ 15.9k ▪ 8 colors

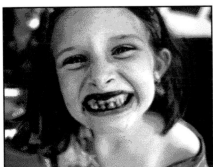 

2-bit ▪ 10.7k ▪ 4 colors

1-bit ▪ 7.2k ▪ 2 colors

Notice the lower the bit depth, the lower the quality and the lower the file size becomes? You will find much more information about how to choose which bit depth for your web graphics in Chapter 4, "Low-Bandwidth Graphics."

Monitor's Bit Depth

So far, bit depth has been defined as it relates to images. There are actually two instances where understanding bit depth is important. The first is to understand the bit depth of an image, and the second is to understand the bit depth of your end viewer's monitor. In this section, let's look at the monitor's bit depth, not the bit depth of images.

Most professional digital artists have 24-bit monitors (which can display up to 16.7 million colors). The average computer user—hence the average member of your web-viewing audience—has an 8-bit (256 color) monitor. This makes sense if you think about it because the majority of computer monitors are owned by average people who bought the least expensive version of their computer system, not professional graphic artists who might have greatly enhanced systems.

Herein lies a huge problem. The majority of people who create artwork for web sites are viewing the artwork under better conditions than the average end user. This makes for a communication gap—one this book hopes to bridge rather than skim over, or worse, ignore.

If a computer system has only an 8-bit color card, it cannot physically view more than 256 colors at once. When people with 256 color systems view your web screens, they cannot see images in 24-bit, even if they want to. They can't prevent it, and neither can you. Specific advice for working with 8-bit color and files is provided in Chapter 4, "Low-Bandwidth Graphics" and Chapter 6, "Browser-Safe Color."

■ step-by-step

How to Change Your Monitor's Bit Depth

I recommend that you always run a bit-depth preview test on your web pages before you send them out for the world to see. Change your monitor settings to 256 colors, and you'll see how your artwork translates under those conditions.

Instructions follow to change your computer's monitor to display in 256 colors so that you can preview the bad news before others do.

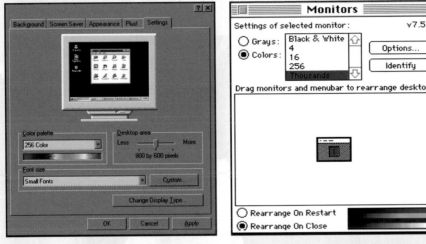

Windows 95: Access your display properties by using your right mouse button and selecting Display properties.

Macintosh: Open the control panel called "Monitors" or "Sights and Sound." (Control panel items are located in your System Folder.)

Windows 3.1: From Program Manager, display the Change System Settings dialog box by double-clicking on the Windows Setup icon (generally found in the Main program group) and choosing Change System Settings from the Options menu.

Introduction

Getting Started in Web Design

Understanding the Web Environment

Web File Formats

Low-Bandwidth Graphics

Hexadecimal Color

Browser-Safe Color

Transparent Artwork

Background Tiles

Rules, Bullets and Buttons

Navigation-Based Graphics

Web-Based Typography

Scanning Techniques for the Web

Layout and Alignment Techniques

Animation

Sound

Interactivity

HTML for Visual Designers

Glossary

Design Resources Appendix

Index

3
<H1>
<A>
<Img src="
<STRONG>
.Gif
.Jpg
Png
Width="500
Image compression
Limited palettes
IMAGE OPTIMIZATION
216 Colors
PARENCY
Height="600
</A>
10.2K
<center>
Sound and
Extending HTML
Web file formats
bgcolor="FFFFCC"
alink="cyan
LYNDA.COM
</center>
www.Design

Compression File Formats

What do all file formats for the web have in common? Compression. Compression is the key to making small graphics. Compression is not a necessary feature in other computer graphic file format specifications, which is why the file formats you'll find on the web might be new to you. Web-based image file formats have to implement impressive compression schemes in order to transform large images to small file sizes. Unfortunately, at times, with compression comes loss of quality.

Some web file formats use lossy compression techniques, meaning that there will be some loss of quality to the resulting images. Don't let that scare you, though; there is no way these file formats could impose the required amount of compression needed for web delivery and not sacrifice some quality. Remember once again, print quality is not expected on the web.

The two types of image file formats most commonly accepted by graphic web browsers are JPEGs and GIFs. One difference between them is that JPEGs can be 24-bit (include up to 16.7 million colors) and GIFs must be 8-bit or less (256 colors maximum).

JPEG stands for **J**oint **P**hotographic **E**xperts **G**roup, and GIF stands for **G**raphic **I**nterchange **F**ormat. These names tell you, in each respective acronym, which format is best for which kind of image. JPEGs were designed to compress photographs, and GIFs were designed to compress graphics.

There will be times when you will want to make a photograph into a GIF, such as with transparent GIFs and animated GIFs, and times when you want to make a graphic into a JPEG, such as when a logo or graphic is combined with a photograph. This chapter will help you answer which file format to use and why.

It's easy to convert to JPEGs and GIFs from other image file formats, such as PICT, BMP, TGA, TIFF, or EPS, if you have the proper software. Many other imaging programs support JPEGs and GIFs.

This section examines the pros and cons of web-based image file formats and gives you an understanding of how to choose which file format is appropriate for specific styles of artwork. The next chapter, "Low-Bandwidth Graphics," offers instruction and tips on how to make the smallest possible JPEGs and GIFs.

HTML for Embedding Images

Regardless of whether you're using a regular GIF, animated GIF, transparent GIF, interlaced GIF, JPEG, or Progressive JPEG format, the HTML is usually the same.

You must first learn to save the file with the proper extension. Here's a handy list:

To insert a graphic into an HTML page, use this tag:

`<IMG SRC="myimage.gif">`

To link an image to another image or HTML page,
use this tag:

`<A HREF="www.destination_url.com">`
`<IMG SRC="myimag.jpg"></A>`

To get rid of the border of an image that's been linked,
use this tag:

`<A HREF="www.destination_url.com">`
`<IMG SRC="myimage.jpg" BORDER=0></A>`

GIF	**.gif**
Interlaced GIF	**.gif**
Transparent GIF	**.gif**
Animated GIF	**.gif**
JPEG	**.jpg**
Progressive JPEG	**.jpg**

The HTML is the easy part—it's understanding how to optimize graphics, choosing which file format for which type of image, and making the images and content that will be much harder to master!

■ **note**

Naming Conventions for JPEGs and GIFs

When saving a JPEG or GIF file for a web page, always use the three letter extension of either .jpg or .gif at the end of your file name. Because many servers that store web graphics are Unix-based, it is important to pay close attention to whether your files are named with upper- or lowercase titles. The HTML document must exactly match the upper- or lowercase structure of the file name. For example, if you have something saved as "image.jpg" on your server, and your HTML reads "image.JPG", the file will not load! For more information on storing graphics on servers and file naming conventions, refer to Chapter 17, "HTML for Visual Designers."

GIF File Formats

Unlike most other computer graphic file formats, GIF (**G**raphic **I**nterchange **F**ormat) was designed specifically for online delivery because it was originally developed for CompuServe in the late 1980s. The file format compresses graphics beautifully, but can also be used for photographic images. Whenever you create graphics, such as logos, illustrations, or cartoons, we recommend the GIF file format.

GIF uses a compression scheme called LZW, which is based on work done by Lempel-Ziv & Welch. The patent for LZW compression is owned by a company called Unisys, which charges developers such as Netscape and Photoshop licensing and royalty fees for selling products that use the GIF file format. End users, such as ourselves (web designers) and our audience (web visitors), do not have to pay licensing fees or worry about any of this. There is some speculation that the GIF file format may be less prevalent at some point because of the fees, but we hope not. GIFs are accepted by all browsers, GIFs are small, and GIFs do things that many other file formats do not, such as animation, transparency, and interlacing.

The GIF file format, by definition, can contain only 256 colors or less. This is not the case with JPEGs, which by definition contain millions of colors (24-bit). Because GIFs are an indexed color file format (256 colors or less), it's extremely beneficial to have a thorough understanding of bit-depth settings and palette management when preparing GIF images.

There are two different flavors of GIF: GIF87a and GIF89a. GIF87a supports transparency and interlacing whereas GIF89a supports transparency, interlacing, and animation (more information on these features follow). As of this book's printing, the major browsers (Netscape, Internet Explorer, and Mosaic) all support both GIF format specifications. You don't really have to refer to the names GIF89a or GIF87a unless you want to sound techie. Most of us simply call these files by the features used, be it a transparent GIF, animated GIF, or plain vanilla GIF.

GIF compression is lossless, meaning that the GIF compression algorithm will not cause any unwanted image degradation. The process of converting a 24-bit image to 256 or fewer colors will cause image degradation on its own, however, so don't get too excited!

GIFs for Illustration-Style Imagery

GIFs work much better for graphics than photographs. By graphics, we mean illustrations, cartoons, or logos. Such graphics typically use areas of solid color, and GIFs handle compression of solid color better than the varied colors found in photographs. Because the GIF file format is lossless, illustrations with limited colors (less than 256) won't lose any quality. Because JPEG is a lossy method, it actually introduces image artifacts into solid color.

■ **note**

GIF Pronunciation

First of all, how is GIF pronounced? Some people say it with a soft g as in jiffy and some with a hard g as in gift. You have our blessing to say it either way. Because no one seems to agree, perhaps it could be said that there is no correct pronunciation?

GIFs for Photographic Imagery

GIFs are definitely designed to handle graphics better than photographs. But that doesn't mean there won't be times where you have to turn photographs into GIFs anyway. You may want to use transparency or animation, which are two features that JPEGs do not offer.

GIFs can be saved at any bit depth from 8 bits down to 1 bit. The bit depth refers to how many colors the image contains. Generally, the lower the bit depth, the smaller the GIF.

8-bit ▪ GIF 41.9k

7-bit ▪ GIF 33.9k

6-bit ▪ GIF 26.7k

5-bit ▪ GIF 21.5k

4-bit ▪ GIF 15.0k

3-bit ▪ GIF 11.8k

2-bit ▪ GIF 8.5k

1-bit ▪ GIF 7.1k

Your job when preparing a GIF is to take it down to its lowest bit-depth level and still maintain acceptable image quality. Depending on how important this image is, acceptable quality falls at 5-bit, which offers a 49% file size reduction over the 8-bit version.

Controlling Your Color Mapping

Color mapping refers to the colors that are assigned to a GIF image and can be taken from either the image or a predetermined palette of colors. Photoshop calls palettes that are derived from existing colors adaptive palettes. It enables you to apply external palettes (system or browser-safe are two examples) or makes a best-guess palette (adaptive) based on the content of your image. While the numbers of colors in an image (bit depth) affect the size of the graphic, the palette additionally affects the quality of your image. Some images can support fewer colors, while others cannot. If you understand how color affects size and quality, you will create better looking and faster loading web pages. For techniques required to assign color maps to images, check out Chapter 6, "Browser-Safe Color."

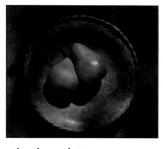 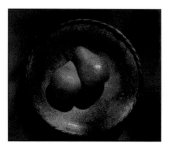 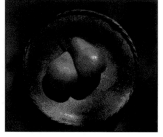

adaptive palette   **Mac System palette**   **216 browser-safe palette**

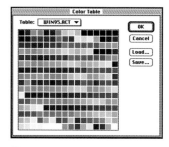 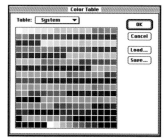 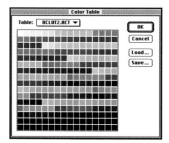

The adaptive palette looks the best because the colors are based on the content of the image. Paint Shop Pro calls this type of palette a Nearest Color palette. Photoshop calls it an adaptive palette.

The system palette image looks much worse. Although it has the same number of colors as the adaptive palette, the colors are unrelated to the image and detract from the quality.

The browser-safe palette looks worst of all. Not only does it use fewer colors, but just like the system palette, the colors are unrelated to the image.

It's clear that an adaptive or nearest color palette gives the best results to the image, but what about when it's seen in a browser? The following shows the results:

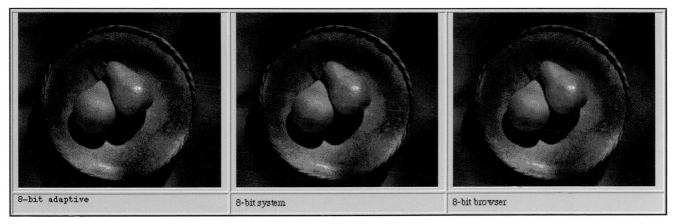

| 8-bit adaptive | 8-bit system | 8-bit browser |

This example demonstrates how the images display in an 8-bit web browser. See any differences? The differences are minor, if any, aren't they? This is what visitors to your site would see if they had only an 8-bit display.

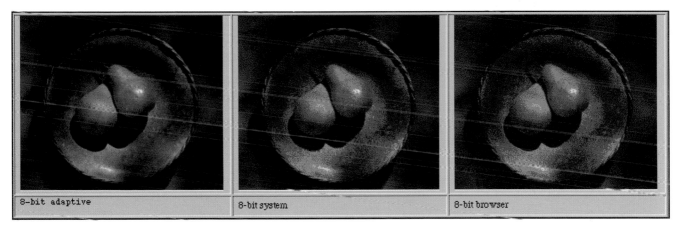

| 8-bit adaptive | 8-bit system | 8-bit browser |

This example demonstrates how the images display in a 24-bit web browser. The adaptive GIF looks the best, does it not? The moral of the story? Use adaptive palettes for photographs saved as GIFs, and let the 8-bit browsers out there remap your colors on-the-fly. This enables your 24-bit viewing audience to see these images at their best, and your 8-bit viewing audience is none the worse off.

Interlaced GIFs

If you've toured the web much, you've encountered interlaced GIFs. They're those images that start out blocky, and appear less and less blocky until they come into full focus.

Interlacing doesn't affect the overall size or speed of a GIF. In theory, interlacing is supposed to make it possible for your end viewer to get a rough idea of your visuals and to make a decision whether to wait or click onward before the image finishes rendering. Again—in theory—this is supposed to save time. Unfortunately for the end viewer, being forced to wait for the entire image to finish coming into focus to read essential information is often a frustrating experience. In other words, interlaced images save time if you don't have to wait for them to finish.

Our recommendation is that you do not use interlaced GIFs for important visual information that is critical to viewing your site. An imagemap or navigation icon, for example, must be seen in order to fulfill its function. Although interlaced GIFs serve their purpose on nonessential graphics, they only frustrate end users when used on essential graphics.

These examples simulate the effect of interlacing on a browser. The image starts chunky and comes into focus over time. This allows the end viewer to decide whether to wait for your graphic to finish or click onward.

Transparent GIFs

Transparent GIFs are used to create the illusion of irregularly shaped artwork. All computer-made images end up in rectangular-shaped files; it's the nature of the medium. Certain file formats, such as GIF, can store masked regions, which create the illusion of shapes other than rectangles. This "masked region" appears to be transparent.

Transparency comes in two forms: 8-bit transparency and 1-bit transparency. 8-bit transparency is the best, but it isn't supported by GIFs or by web browsers. 8-bit transparency is what is used by the file formats PSD (Photoshop), TGA, and PICT. 8-bit transparency is also called alpha channel-based transparency and can support up to 256 different levels of opacity (which is why it looks so great!). GIFs support 1-bit transparency, which makes it a much more limited type of masking. For more information on transparent GIFs, turn to Chapter 7, "Transparent Artwork."

Here's an example of artwork from Lynda's Homegurrrl site that has been defined to be transparent. The gray color was instructed to drop out within transparency software.

This shows the transparent artwork in context. Once the GIF transparency is recognized within browser software, the browser enables the rectangular artwork to appear irregularly shaped.

This image represents the type of compositing you can do in Photoshop and 8-bit transparency, where it can easily display differing levels of transparency, glows, and blurs. GIF transparency is unfortunately much more crude than this.

■ **note**

8-Bit Transparency

The only type of web file format that supports 8-bit transparency is PNG, which is discussed later in this chapter and in Chapter 7, "Transparent Artwork." GIF is much more common than PNG and supported by far more browsers, so it is still much more practical to get your GIF-making chops up to speed and make the best of what it offers.

Animated GIFs

Animated GIFs are part of the GIF89a specification. They are formally called multi-block GIFs because multiple images can be stored as separate blocks within one single GIF document. When the GIF document is viewed, the multiple images display, one at a time, and produce a streaming animation.

Streaming is a wonderful and appropriate method for displaying animation over the web. Streaming means that each frame of the animation displays one after the other, so that your end user doesn't have to wait for the whole file to download before seeing anything. Other animation formats in the past required that the entire movie download before a single frame could be viewed.

Animated GIFs function much like automated slide shows. They can include custom palette information and be set to play at different speeds. They can include interlacing and transparency, too! The beauty of animated GIFs is that they require no plug-ins, and the authoring tools to create them are often free and easy to learn. As well, major browsers (Netscape, Internet Explorer, and Mosaic) support them, so you can include them in web pages without worrying about compatibility or accessibility. Specific instruction on how to create animated GIFs and apply custom palettes is available in Chapter 14, "Animation."

Just like other GIF files, the number of colors and amount of noise in the frames affect the overall file size. If you have a 100-frame animation with each frame totaling 5k, your animated GIF will be 500k. It simply multiplies in size according to how many frames you create and the file size of the individual frame of artwork. On the other hand, your end viewer is really waiting for only 5k servings at a time, so it's nothing like the painful waiting that a standard 500k GIF would incur!

■ **note**

Popular GIF animation authoring tools:

GIF Construction Set/bookware (Windows/Win95)
■ http://www.mindworkshipcom/alchemy/alchemy.html

GIFBuilder/freeware (Mac)
■ http://iawww.epfl.ch/Staff/Yves.Piguet/clip2gif-
home/GifBuilder.html

Some good animated GIF references:

Royal Frazier's awesome site
■ http://member.aol.com/roalef/gifanim.htm

GIFBuilder's FAQ
■ http://iawww.epfl.ch/Staff/Yves.Piguet/clip2gif-
home/GifBuilder Doc/GifBuilder-FAQs.html

Here's a 30-frame animation, found on Lynda's Homegurrl site at ■ http://www.lynda.com/anim.html. It's hard to tell the subtle changes from frame to frame when viewed in sequence, but once the frames are played in motion over time the '50s man appears to be bobbing his head and waving his finger, and has little lines flowing from the side of his head. It totals 64k in size. Why? It's only two colors, with no anti-aliasing.

JPEG

The JPEG (pronounced jay-peg) file format offers a 24-bit alternative to the 8-bit GIF file format. This is especially great for photographic content because 24-bit photographs do not dither! One added advantage to dealing with JPEGs is that they don't need you to define the palette for them, unlike GIFs. Whenever an image format includes millions of colors (24-bit), palette and color mapping issues disappear. This is because enough colors are allowed to rely on the original image's color information, and substitute colors are no longer necessary.

JPEG ▪ **8.2k**   **GIF** ▪ **19.3k**   **JPEG** ▪ **7.1k**   **GIF** ▪ **17.6k**

JPEG ▪ **9.5k**   **GIF** ▪ **5.2k**   **JPEG** ▪ **2.5k**   **GIF** ▪ **17.3k**

JPEG handles images with subtle gradations beautifully. This is in part because the file format enables the image to remain in 24-bit. Compare the JPEG images to the left to the 8-bit GIF images to the right. The JPEGs compress photographic-style images better than graphic style images and look better too!

JPEG was developed specifically for photographic-style images. It looks to areas with subtle tonal and color changes and offers the best compression when it encounters that type of imagery. It actually does not compress solid color well at all!

Here's an image with a lot of solid color, saved as a low-quality JPEG. It totals 7.6k.

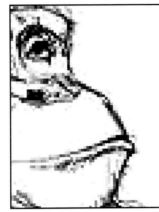

Here is a close-up of the artifacts present in the JPEG.

The GIF looks better (no artifacts!), but it is larger at 17.6k.

JPEG is a lossy compression algorithm, meaning that it removes information from your image and, therefore, causes a loss in quality. JPEG does a great job of doing this so the difference in information data is often not visible or objectionable. It does introduce artifacts in some instances, especially where it encounters solid colors. This is a by-product of its lossy compression methods.

Unlike the GIF file format, JPEGs require both compression and decompression. This means that JPEG files need to decompress when they're viewed. Although a GIF and a JPEG might be identical sizes, or sometimes even when the JPEG is smaller, the JPEG may take longer to download or view from a web browser because of the added time required to decompress.

Another difference between GIF and JPEG is the fact that you can save JPEGs in a variety of compression levels. This means that more or less compression can be applied to an image, depending on which looks best.

The following examples were taken from Photoshop. Photoshop employs the JPEG compression settings of max, high, medium, and low. In Photoshop, these terms relate to quality, not the amount of compression.

| 4.6k | 6.1k | 8.2k | 10.5k | 16.3k |

| 7.1k | 9.0k | 11.1k | 11.8k | 15.1k |

You can see by this test that there's not a whole lot of difference between low quality and high quality, except with graphics. As we've said, leave graphics for GIF and photographs for JPEGs. Although there are good reasons for saving photographs as GIF (animation, transparency, and interlacing), there are no good reasons for saving graphics as JPEGs, unless the graphics are combined with photographs. With photographic content in general, don't be afraid to try low-quality settings; the file size saving is usually substantial, and the quality penalties are not too steep.

Progressive JPEGs Versus Standard JPEGs

Progressive JPEGs are a new entrée into our web graphics file format vocabulary. This type of JPEG boasts much higher compression rates than regular JPEG and supports interlacing (where the graphic starts chunky and comes into focus). They were initially introduced by Netscape, and are now additionally supported by MSIE. Progressive-JPEG-making tools for Mac and PCs are listed at ■ http://www.in-touch.com/pjpeg2.html#software.

Pro-JPEGs boast superior compression to regular JPEGs. They also give you a wider range of quality settings. Instead of Photoshop's standard max, high, medium, and low settings, pro-JPEGs can be set in quality from 0–100. We simulated a comparison here by using the settings of 100, 75, 25, and 0.

max 28.9k

high 12.4k

med 10.5k

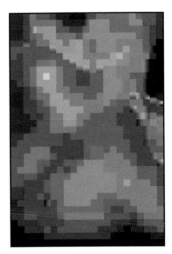

low 8.7k

The interface to Photoshop 4.0's JPEG Options.

■ note

Photoshop 4.0 Settings

There are lots of tools available to write progressive JPEGs, but here are the settings for Photoshop 4.0's version:

Baseline Standard: Enables you to save up to 10 quality levels.

Baseline Optimized: Enables you to save up to 10 quality levels—a little better file savings than Baseline Standard.

Progressive: Progressive JPEGs are often quite smaller, but are not supported by all browsers.

PNG

PNG (**P**ortable **N**etwork **G**raphics, or more fondly known as PNG Not GIF) holds great promise as a new web file format. The W3C (World Wide Web Consortium at ■ http://www.w3.org/pub/WWW/Press/PNG-PR.en.html) has made a formal endorsement of PNG, which strongly indicates that Netscape and MSIE will support it as an inline file format in the near future.

PNG is a lossless compression method, meaning that no quality loss is incurred when it's applied to images. Unlike GIF or JPEG, PNG can be stored at many different bit depths using different storage methods. GIF, for example, can be stored only in 8-bit or lower bit depths. JPEGs must be stored in 24-bit and no lower. PNG can be stored in either 8-bit or 24-bit or 32-bit. PNG also has a multitude of different filtering methods. This makes optimizing PNG images a daunting task, as you'll see by the PNG image charts in Chapter 4, "Low-Bandwidth Graphics."

PNG was developed by Thomas Boutell (visit his amazing site at ■ http://www. boutell.com, and the W3C spec pages for PNG at ■ http://www.boutell.com/ boutell/png/). Unlike JPEG and GIF, PNG was created to be a cross-platform file format and contains information about the characteristics of the authoring platform so that viewing software can automatically compensate and display the image correctly.

What this means is that Macs and PCs, which each utilize different gamma settings (see Chapter 2, "Understanding the Web Environment" for more information on gamma), can adjust properly for images created in the PNG file format. This is way cool!

For an excellent description of gamma, check out:
- http://www.cgsd.com/papers/gamma_intro.html

PNG also supports a far superior interlacing scheme than GIF. GIF interlacing gives a preview of the image after 1/8th of the image data has been recognized, whereas PNG gives a preview after only 1/64th of the image has loaded.

With alpha channel support (see Chapter 7, "Transparent Artwork," for a step-by-step example of creating PNG transparency), all the transparency problems of halos, matte lines, and fringing will be history. Alpha channels offer superior masking results, meaning that designers will be able to prepare images with glows, blurs, soft edges, and fades that will display beautifully on web browsers that support PNG.

Unfortunately, when this chapter was written, the major browsers (Netscape, MSIE, and Mosaic) still did not support PNG. There were a couple of plug-ins that enabled you to see PNG files, but neither supported transparency properly. They are:
- http://iagu.on.net/jsam/png-plugin/
- http://codelab.siegelgale.com/solutions

Photoshop 4.0 supports creating images in the PNG file format. The Photoshop documentation does not explain what any of the PNG settings do, unfortunately! When in doubt about image formats, I turn to my trusty book:

Graphic File Formats
Publisher: O'Reilly & Associates
Authors: James D. Murray and William VanRyper
Retail: $79.95 ▪ ISBN: 0932102085

Photoshop doesn't include any documentation about the PNG settings, but here's what I've pieced together from my research:

Interlace
■ **None:** No interlacing
■ **Adam7**: The sequel to the popular television show Adam 12, featuring pre-pubescent cops... No, wait! This function has a funny name, but all it does is interlace the image.

Filter
■ **None:** Like the name says, this filter offers no compression whatsoever!
■ **Sub:** Compares and averages pixel values next to each other on a horizontal axis.
■ **Up:** Compares and averages pixel values next to each other on a vertical axis.
■ **Average:** Averages all the pixel values in the document.
■ **Paeth:** Uses linear calculations to average and compare the different pixel values.
■ **Adaptive:** Best guess.

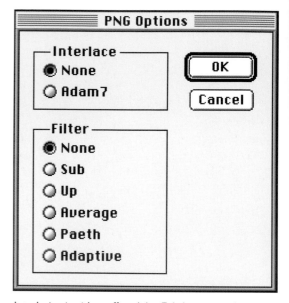

Interlacing is either off or Adam7 (who names these things?). Filtering is applied to the data before it's compressed, and the filtering process is reversed after the image is decompressed, restoring the data to its original values. This is how PNG compression can generate file savings and also be lossless at the same time.

Digital Watermarks

The term watermark is traditionally used to describe special printed paper that guarantees proof of authenticity and ownership. Dollar bills are a good example of watermarked currency that has special information embedded in the paper stock to prevent counterfitting.

Digital watermarks are a new technology that follows a similar principle, only the embedded copyright information is not visible until loaded into a computer that can read it. Watermarking technology can embed copyright notification, ownership, audience (adult or general interest material), and usage information (restricted, or royalty free). The watermark signature can be read by Digimarc's PictureMarc plug-in.

Digimarc (■ http://digimarc.com/) offers a digital watermarking service that offers watermarking software and a database/retrieval service for professionals. Digimarc's fee structure is listed on its site.

The PictureMarc plug-in for Photoshop is digital watermarking software that enables you to embed watermarks into digital documents for print or web-based submission. When PictureMarc is invoked, you are given the opportunity to obtain your own creator ID, which links your images to up-to-date contact information that is stored on the Digimarc site.

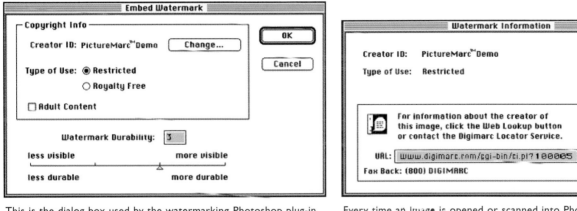

This is the dialog box used by the watermarking Photoshop plug-in PictureMarc, distributed by ■ http://digimarc.com/.

Every time an image is opened or scanned into Photoshop, PictureMarc performs a quick detection and adds a © to the image window's title bar.

By clicking on the © on the title bar, PictureMarc launches your web browser, displays detailed information about the image, and lists whatever contact details you have provided.

This service supports CMYK, RGB, LAB, Grayscale, and Index Color colorspaces and works with any file format type that Photoshop supports on NT, Win95, Win3.1, and Mac (68000 and PPC) platforms. A minimum image size of 256x256 pixels is required, which makes its usefulness for the web limited to larger images, thereby unfortunately excluding navigational graphics, buttons, bullets, and rules.

WebTV

Just when you thought you might have this web graphics thingy licked, along comes another display medium to add to the stack of cross-platform, cross-browser, and cross-operating systems considerations.

WebTV Networks, Inc. has released the first (expect more of these types of systems from other companies, too) set-top box to offer Internet/web connection through standard television sets.

The advent of web delivery via television screens introduces a new audience to our pages, as well as opens a new can of worms for our authoring concerns. WebTV is the subject of controversy among web designers. People have differing opinions about whether WebTV is a good or bad thing, whether you should or should not design for it, and whether it makes pages look ugly or acceptable.

As you can see by the set-up screen on the next page, WebTV allows end viewers to set up their preferences for text size and size adjustments. Here's one more area where you have to relinquish that precious design control most of us crave.

Television is a very different medium than the computer. It has lower resolution: a standard computer monitor displays 640x480 pixels, whereas a standard television monitor displays 544x378. Television uses NTSC color space, which is very sensitive to highly saturated colors, such as pure reds, greens, blues, yellows, cyans, and magentas. Television is interlaced, meaning that it displays two alternating images to create a single image. This can cause single pixel lines to jitter. The WebTV system uses a convolution filtering system to reduce flicker, and it works quite well.

The majority of people who have actually viewed WebTV (go to your local electronics store to check it out) are impressed at how well their pages translate. Expect that the font tags you use (for more information on HTML font tags, check out Chapter 11, "Web-Based Typography") will be altered to a largeish, sans serif typeface as shown on the next page.

■ **note**

Designing for WebTV

If you're curious to know how to design for WebTV, check out their developer docs at:

■ http://webtv.net/devdocs/styleguide/sguide-2.html#MARKER-9-1

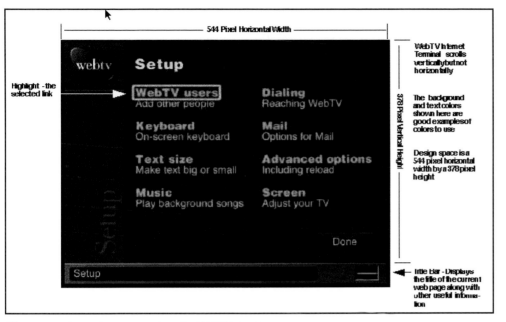

This screen shows the setup options for WebTV viewing.

The WebTV home page shows how large the type displays and how the cursor creates a yellow bounding box on top of linked graphics.

WebTV Features

WebTV supports:
Animated GIFs
Tables
Background Color
Colored Text
Background Tiles
Sound (RealAudio v2, AU, WAV, VMF,
AIFF, Shockwave audio, GSM, MPEG II
audio, and layer 3 MPEG I)
Inline JPGs, GIF89a

WebTV does not support
VRML plug-ins
JavaScript
QuickTime
Proprietary plug-ins
Java
Frames

WebTV plans to support:
JavaScript
Java
Frames

Unsupported WebTV HTML Tags

HTML Committee
<APPLET>
<a TITLE REL REV URN>
<DFN>
<dl COMPACT>
<form ENCTYPE>
<FRAME>
<FRAMESET>
<img ALT LOWSRC>
<meta NAME>
<NEXTID>
<ol COMPACT>
<PARAM>
<pre WIDTH>
<SCRIPT>
<STYLE>
<table HEIGHT>
<td NOWRAP>
<ul COMPACT>
<textarea WRAP>

Netscape
<BLINK>
<body ALINK>
<EMBED>
<isindex PROMPT>
<li VALUE>
<SERVER PUSH>
<WBR>

Internet Explorer
<font FACE>
<img DYNSRC LOOP>
<PLAINTEXT>

> ■ **note**
>
> The Price of WebTV
>
> Many of the plug-in-based and streaming movie technologies are too RAM intensive. Remember, WebTV is not a computer, and has a price-point that doesn't support high-end dedicated hardware.

WebTV Design Tips

A list follows that offers design tips if you would like your sites to be WebTV friendly. This was culled from the Design Tips list found on the WebTV site at ■ http://www.webtv.net and includes my comments, annotations, and tips as well.

■ Some designers say not to use full red or full white; both cause screen distortion. Many sites use pure-white backgrounds for their web pages, however, and so far those that I've personally viewed over WebTV have looked acceptable.

■ Use client-side imagemaps instead of server-side imagemaps; it works better with a remote control. See Chapter 10, "Navigation-Based Graphics," for details on programming client-side imagemaps.

■ Avoid small text sizes in HTML and graphics. If you do use small text sizes, WebTV will convert them to a larger font on-the-fly. You don't really have to redesign your pages; it's just that WebTV will go in and change your small typefaces for you.

■ Avoid narrow columns; images are scaled and text will wrap frequently.

■ Try to reduce the number of items on your page because television audiences are used to looking at one focal point.

■ Use light-colored text against dark-colored backgrounds; television audiences find it easier to read.

■ Don't use horizontal single pixel lines because they flicker on television sets.

■ Use images with size hints (the <IMG> WIDTH and HEIGHT attributes) to speed up load time.

■ The best way to ensure your page looks good on WebTV is to view it on a WebTV Internet terminal.

Comparing WebTV to the Net: www.lynda.com

Net: ■ http://www.lynda.com viewed through Netscape.

WebTV: Click on the arrows to scroll up or down an entire screen. The type will be enlarged by the WebTV browser to enhance readiblity on a television monitor.

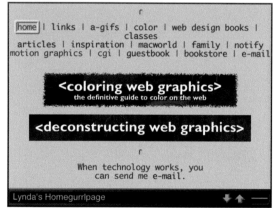

WebTV: The navigation bar at the bottom of my site shows the way WebTV links are highlighted in yellow bounding boxes.

Comparing WebTV to the Net: www.540.com

WebTV: Here's a screen from ■ http://www.540.com. It has image-based type, instead of HTML-based type.

WebTV: Image-based type is not altered by the Preferences that are set in WebTV.

WebTV: Ikon's home page includes both imagemaps and HTML-based text.

WebTV: The imagemaps work just fine, and the HTML-based text is enlarged just like on my site. These sites really hold up pretty well, considering!

Introduction

Getting Started in Web Design

Understanding the Web Environment

Web File Formats

Low-Bandwidth Graphics

Hexadecimal Color

Browser-Safe Color

Transparent Artwork

Background Tiles

Rules, Bullets and Buttons

Navigation-Based Graphics

Web-Based Typography

Scanning Techniques for the Web

Layout and Alignment Techniques

Animation

Sound

Interactivity

HTML for Visual Designers

Glossary

Design Resources Appendix

Index

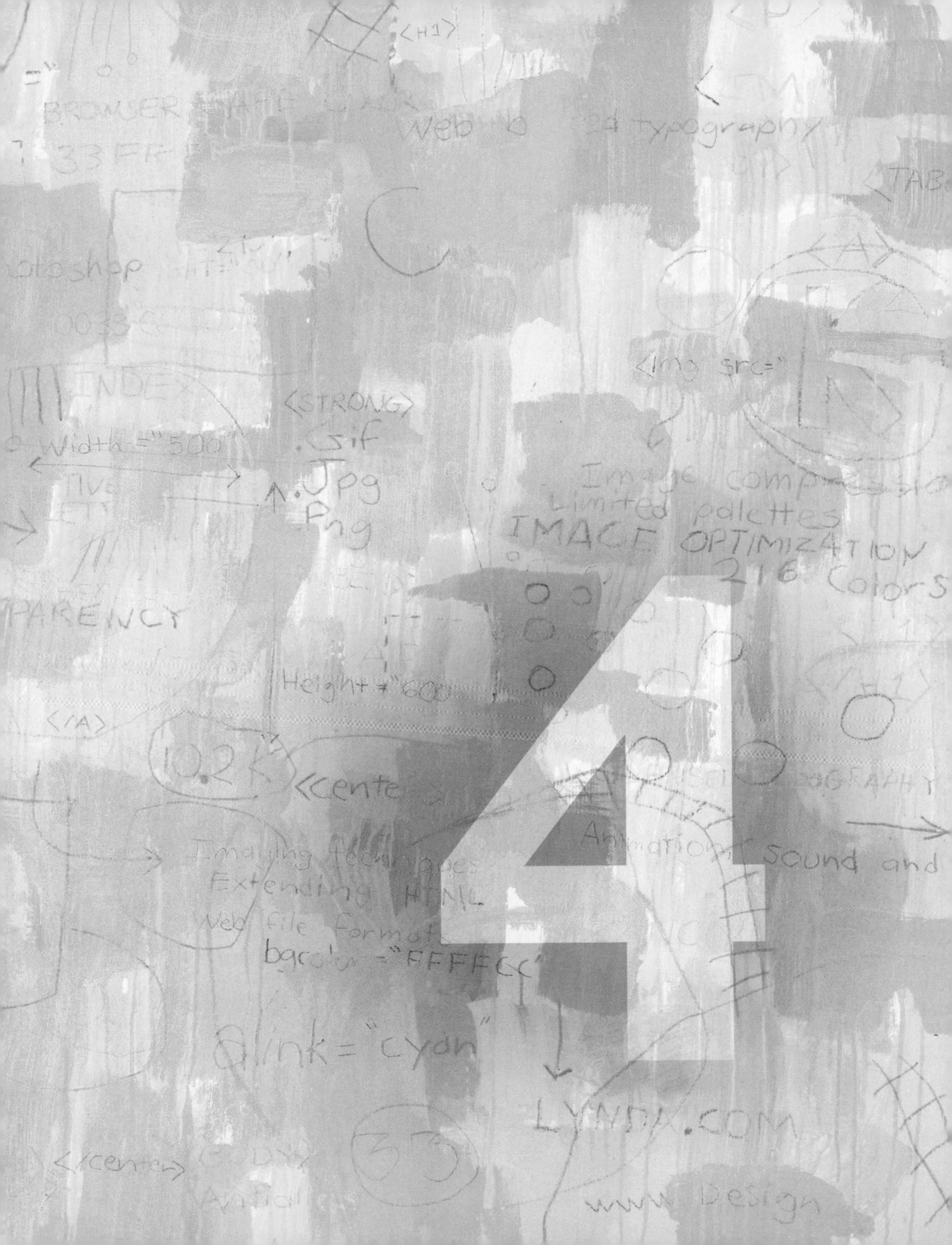

Low-Bandwidth Graphics

There's never been a design medium before where speed was an important judgment factor. No one looks through a magazine and says, "Oh, this image was only 90mb, and look, this one was just 5mb!" On the web, unlike other design mediums, file size makes it impossible to see the artwork if it's too big. **The truth with web graphics is that an image can be stunning and communicate critical information, but if it's too big, your audience will never wait around long enough to see it. Making images speedy means learning how to make small file sizes, and that's precisely what this chapter advocates.**

So you know images on the web have to be small, but how small is small? If you are a digital print designer, you probably don't blink at large file sizes, and working on images ranging from tens to hundreds of megabytes is a common, everyday fact of life. Even if you aren't working in graphics or print, you've been hearing that web graphics have to be small—but again, how small is small? A handy rule of thumb is to consider that the average person viewing the web is using a 14.4 modem, and you can expect it to take one second per kilobyte for an image to transfer. This means that a 60k file would take one minute to download, and one of your 10mb files could take almost 3 hours!

How do you translate your many-megabyte-sized file down to something small enough to fit on an average floppy disk? The two file formats of the web, GIF and JPEG, both offer impressive compression schemes. Saving in these formats, as long as your images are less than 640x480 pixels, at 72 dpi in RGB, will make fitting them on a floppy disk easy regardless of how complex your graphic is. Even though fitting a large graphic on a floppy may seem like a giant accomplishment if you're used to large files, this file size still won't cut it for the web.

This chapter walks you through the stages of making smaller images, not in dimensions but in file size. You'll learn how to "read" the file size of a graphic, understand what the file format is doing to an image, and know which file formats to use on which types of images. In the end, you should have a much better sense of to how to create the smallest possible images for web delivery.

One thing to keep in mind while designing your graphics is that print quality is not expected on the web, and a big difference exists between what looks good on paper and what looks good on screen. You will always need to work in RGB at 72 dpi for the web. This is because 72 dpi is the resolution of computer screens. You are delivering your end result to computer screens, not high-resolution printers. CMYK and high resolution are reserved for print graphics only. You'll love this change once you get over the shock of it. In print, you never know what you'll get until it's printed; for online graphics, what you see IS what you get. It'll probably be hard to go back to those huge, unwieldy print resolution files once you've experienced the luxury of working small.

How to Know What Size Your File Really Is

Your new web vocabulary will include measuring web images by kilobytes, or k, from now on. For those who are mathematically mindful, a kilobyte is composed of 1024 bytes; a megabyte is composed of 1,048,576 bytes; and a gigabyte has 1,073,741,824 bytes. Files measuring in the megabytes and gigabytes will not be allowed on well-designed web pages—they take too long to view! Because of this, you'll often get the directive from a client to keep page sizes within a certain file size limit. Or you might have an internal goal of not exceeding 30k per page. It's necessary to understand how to read the file size of a document if you're trying to make it fall within a certain target range of acceptability.

How can you tell how many kilobytes an image is? Most Photoshop users think the readout in the lower left corner of a document informs them about the file size. Not true! These numbers relate to the amount of RAM Photoshop is allocating to your image and its scratch disk virtual memory scheme.

The size reading at the bottom left corner of a Photoshop window is deceptive. It refers to how much RAM and disk space the Photoshop 3.0 file takes up, and has no relation to what the file size will be once saved in a web image file format, like GIF or JPEG.

You also might look to your hard drive for the file size. Notice that the file size numbers are all nicely rounded figures: 11k, 33k, and 132k. Your computer rounds up the size of a file to the next largest number depending on how large your hard drive partition is. Have you ever had a file read two different file sizes on a hard drive and a floppy? That's because the computer rounds off the size of the file depending on what size storage media it's on.

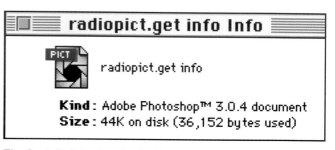

A Mac file menu, showing rounded file sizes. The rounding relates to how the hard drive is partitioned and not the true file size.

On a Mac, the only way to get information about the true byte size of a file is to do a Get Info command. First, highlight the file you want to check in the Finder, go to the File menu, and then choose Get Info.

The Get Info dialog box for the Mac, showing the disk size of 44k and the true file size of 36k.

Using Win95 on the PC, the file size shown in the menu is very close to the actual file size, with rounding to the next lowest number occurring. Under DOS you can get a more accurate reading of the file size, but it is not much different from what you see in Windows.

Making graphics and images that work on the web requires that images have as small a file size as possible. Understanding how compression affects image size and what types of file formats are appropriate for images is key to responsible web design.

■ note

To Icon or Not to Icon

Photoshop typically saves images with an icon. The icon is a small, visual representation of what the image looks like, which the file references. Photoshop icons take up a little extra room on your hard drive. This ultimately won't matter because when you send the files to your server, you'll transmit them as raw data, which will strip off the icon anyway. But if your goal is to get a more accurate reading of the true file size, you should set your preferences in Photoshop to not save an icon.

To set your preferences to not save the icon, choose File, Preferences, General. In the General dialog box, set the Image Previews to Ask When Saving.

The General Preferences dialog, where icons can be turned off.

In Photoshop 4.0, go under File, Preferences, choose File Saving, and this dialog box will enable you to set icons on or off.

Making Small GIFs

The GIF file-compression algorithm offers impressive file size reduction, but the degree of file size savings has a lot to do with how you create your GIF images. Understanding how GIFs compress is the first step in this process.

GIFs use a compression scheme known as LZW compression, which looks to patterns of data. Whenever it encounters areas in an image that do not have changes, it can implement much higher compression. This is similar to another type of compression called run-length compression (used in BMP, TIFF, and PCX formats), but LZW writes, stores, and retrieves its code a little differently. Similar to many types of run-length compression, however, GIF compression searches for changes along a horizontal axis, and whenever it finds a new color, adds to the file size.

  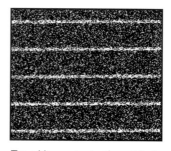

Here's an original image saved as a GIF image that contains horizontal lines. It is 6.7k.

Here's the identical image, only flipped on its side so that the lines are vertical. It's 72% bigger at 11.5k!

Try adding noise to the original. You'll be expanding the file size by more than eight times to 56k!

So what does the line test really teach? That artwork that has horizontal changes compresses better than artwork that doesn't. That anything with noise will more than quadruple your image's file size. That large areas of flat color compress well, and complicated line work or dithering does not.

Aside from the visual complexity of the image, there are two additional factors that affect file size: bit depth and dithering methods. With all GIFs, the fewer colors (lower bit depth), the smaller the resulting file. You should remember this fact when considering whether to improve image quality through anti-aliasing.

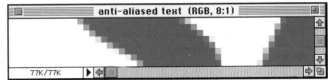

Here's an example of aliased text. It resulted in a file that totaled 3.8k when saved as a GIF.

Here's an example of anti-aliased text. It resulted in a file that's 5k when saved as a GIF. The anti-aliasing caused the file to be 32% larger!

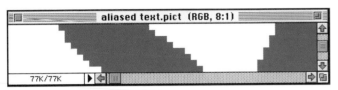

aliased text.pict (RGB, 8:1)

77K/77K

Close-up view: Aliasing doesn't disguise the jaggy nature of pixel-based artwork.

anti-aliased text (RGB, 8:1)

77K/77K

Close-up view: Anti-aliasing creates a blended edge. This blending disguises the square-pixel-based nature of computer-based artwork.

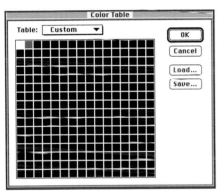

Color Table

Table: Custom

OK
Cancel
Load...
Save...

The aliased artwork used only 4 colors.

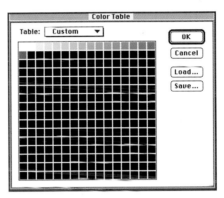

Color Table

Table: Custom

OK
Cancel
Load...
Save...

The anti-aliased artwork used 18 colors.

Aliased Artwork

Most computer artists have never considered working with aliased artwork. It's assumed that artwork will always look better if it has anti-aliased edges. This is simply not true! Artists have never had to factor size of files into their design considerations before. Having something load 32% faster is nothing to balk at. In many cases, aliased artwork looks just as good as anti-aliased artwork, and choosing between the two approaches is something that web designers should consider whenever possible.

As well as considering whether to use aliased or anti-aliased graphics, you should also always work with browser-safe colors when creating illustration-based artwork for the web. Examples of how browser-safe colors improve the quality of illustrations are demonstrated in Chapter 6, "Browser-Safe Color."

Here's an example of a 700x1134 pixel GIF file created by Bruce Heavin that totals only 7.1k! Why? Lots of solid color and no anti-aliasing. This image has only 4 colors.

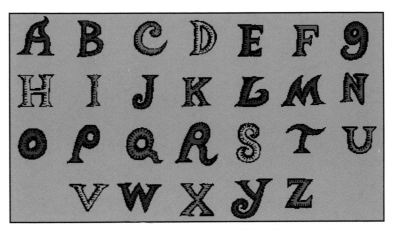

Artwork by Yuryeong Park for the Hot Hot Hot site ■ http://www.hothothot.com. The entire site is done in aliased graphics, and no page exceeds 30k, even though there are several images per page.

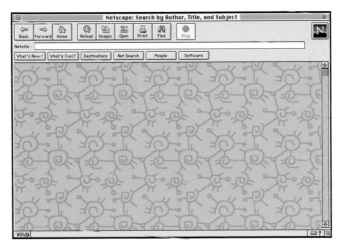

A background tile repeated in Netscape, by Bruce Heavin. The source tile is only 2.23k. The savings from aliased graphics can really add up!

Dithering and Banding

When an image with millions of colors is converted to an image with 256 colors or less, image quality is lost. Basically, when colors are removed from the image, some sacrifices have to be made. This can take place in two forms: dithering or banding. Here are some definitions to remember:

- **Dithering** is the positioning of different colored pixels within an image that uses a 256-color palette to simulate a color that does not exist in the palette. A dithered image often looks noisy, or composed of scattered pixels.

- **Adaptive palettes** are used to convert the image to 256 colors based on existing colors within the image. Generally, adaptive-based dithering looks the best of all dithering methods.

- **Screen dithering** is what happens when a 24-bit or 16-bit image is viewed on a computer with a 256-color card. The image's color is reduced to 256 colors, and the "dither" looks uniform, as if a pattern was used.

- **Banding** is a process of reducing colors to 256 or less without dithering. It produces areas of solid color and generates a posterized effect.

Understanding the terminology of dithering and banding is important in web design because these are often effects that are undesirable. Bringing down the quality of images is necessary at times for speed considerations, but riding the line between low file size and good enough quality means that you will often encounter unwanted results. These new terms help define the problems you'll encounter when creating web graphics and will be used throughout the rest of the book.

Screen dithering takes the form of a repeated pattern, and creates a moiré appearance.

The dots within a "screen dithered" image look uniform, based on a generalized screen pattern.

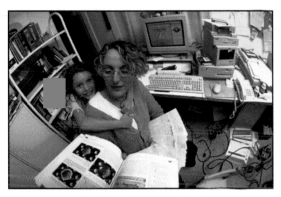

This is an example of **image dithering** using an adaptive palette. It will typically look a lot better than "screen dithering" because the dither pattern is based on the content of the image, not a preset screen.

Even though the image is composed of pixellated dots, they are less obvious and objectionable because there's no obvious pattern or screen.

The **banding** in this image is obvious. It looks like a posterization effect.

Here's a close-up of the banding. Instead of the dots you'll find in dithering methods, the computer takes the image and breaks it into regions of solid color.

To Dither or Not to Dither?

Dithering methods play a huge role in creating smaller GIFs. Any type of "noise" introduces added file size. Unfortunately, whenever you're working with photograph-based GIFs, dithering of one type or another must be employed to reduce the 24-bit color.

Saved with dithering: 30.1k　　　　Saved without dithering: 23.7k

In this example, the GIF that did not use dithering is an impressive 21% smaller. The only problem is, it looks awful! Sometimes file savings does not warrant loss of quality. Whenever a photograph contains glows, feathered edges, or subtle gradations, you will have to use dithering when converting from 24-bit to 8-bit in order to maintain quality.

Saved with dithering: 40.2k　　　　Saved without dithering: 38.2k

There's almost no perceivable difference between these two images, regardless of whether a dithering method is used to convert to 8-bit color or Photoshop's dither none method was chosen. Why? This image has a lot of solid areas of color to begin with. The file savings between 40.2k and 38.2k is not huge either, but the non-dither method still yields a smaller file size.

Instructions for how to set up dither and no-dither methods for Photoshop, Paint Shop Pro, and Photo-Paint are described later in this chapter. All programs offer the capability to set the "dithering" or "no dithering" method.

To summarize, in order to make smaller GIFs, you should:

- Try to save the file at the lowest possible bit depth, while monitoring quality.

- Try to avoid dithering, if the image can withstand it.

Photoshop Dither Settings

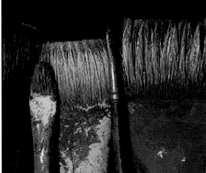

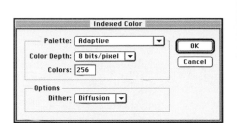

Dither Diffusion establishes a dither in the image.

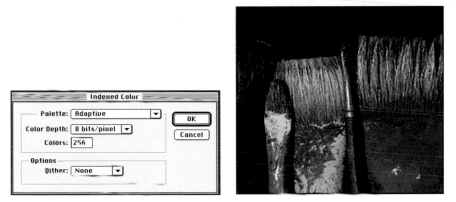

Dither None avoids dithering altogether but sometimes creates unwanted banding.

■ **note**

GIF Choices

There is never one pat answer for making the smallest possible GIFs. Choices between bit depth and dithering methods should always be based on the image's content. In general, images with subtle gradations will need to be dithered. Images with areas of solid color will look fine without dithering.

Photoshop's Indexed Color Dialog Box

The Indexed Color dialog box has three important functions: setting the resolution, the palette, and the dither. The resolution affects the bit depth of the image. The palette sets which colors are used, and the dither tells the program which color reduction method to use—dithering, screen, or no dithering.

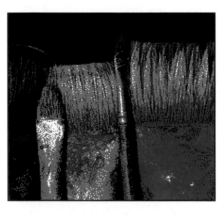

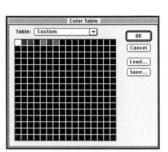

3-bit ▪ 19.8k

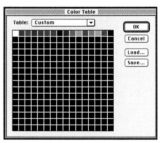

4-bit ▪ 26k

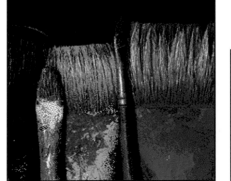

5-bit ▪ 31.2k

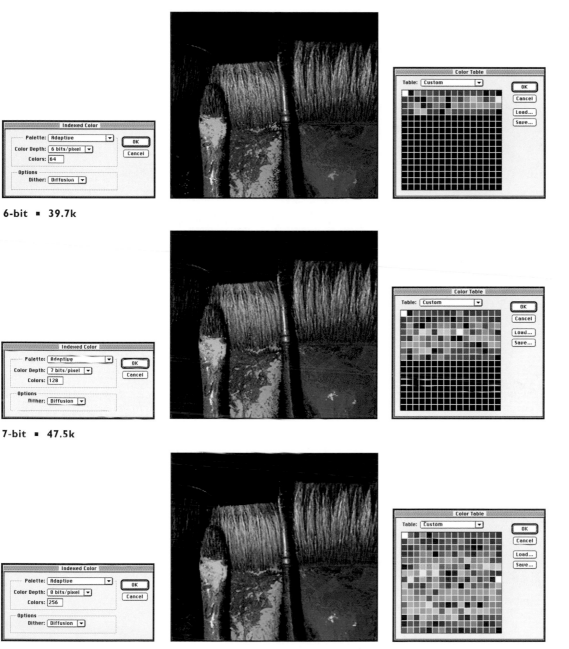

6-bit ▪ 39.7k

7-bit ▪ 47.5k

8-bit ▪ 55.4k

When you convert from RGB to Indexed Color mode, you are presented with the dialog box on the left. The middle row of images shows the results of the respective color-depth changes. The Color Table images on the right show the resulting colors contained within each image.

Photoshop Palette Chart

Adaptive: An adaptive palette is created from 256 colors found within the image ▪ 55.4k

Custom: Custom enables you to load a palette of your choosing ▪ 48.3k

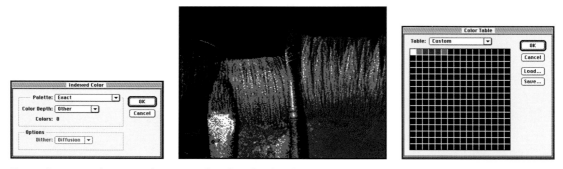

Exact: An exact palette uses the exact colors found within the image

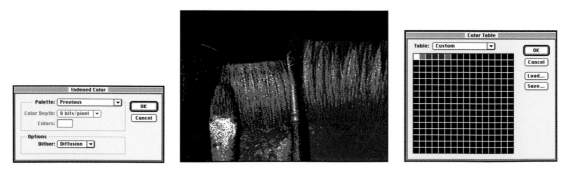

Previous: Uses the palette from the last conversion

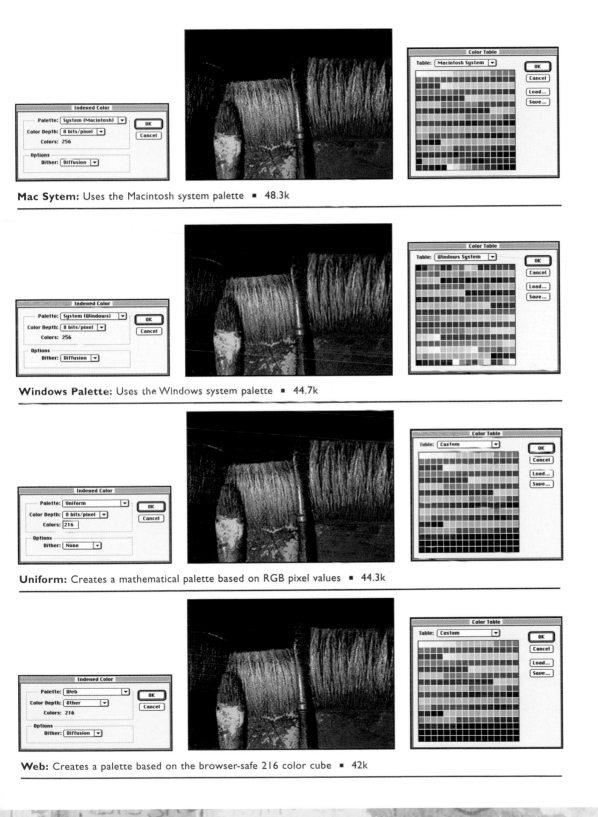

Mac Sytem: Uses the Macintosh system palette ■ 48.3k

Windows Palette: Uses the Windows system palette ■ 44.7k

Uniform: Creates a mathematical palette based on RGB pixel values ■ 44.3k

Web: Creates a palette based on the browser-safe 216 color cube ■ 42k

How to Use the Image Compression Charts

The next time someone asks you, "Which is better, PNG, GIF or JPEG?" you can answer confidently that there is no one compression that is better than another. Different types of compression are meant to work with different specific kinds of images. Creating the absolute smallest image you can requires that you understand the differences between images and the differences between compression methods.

You can use the following pages as guides to compressing your own images. If you have a specific image in mind, compare it to this page to see which type of image catagory it falls under. Turn to those pages and compare the file savings of PNG, GIF, and JPEG compression methods. This should help you find a ballpark compression setting and save you the time of putting each of your images through all these settings!

The four images on the right are put through the following types of compression methods:

PNG	Dithered ▪ 8-bit/below
	Not Dithered ▪ 8-bit/below
GIF	Dithered ▪ 8-bit/below
	Not Dithered ▪ 8-bit/below
JPEG	Low, Med, High, Max

The Image Compression Charts work with these four specific types of images:

Lynda Illustration is a good representative image of a flat-style illustration graphic.

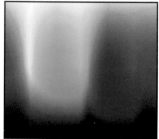

Spectrum represents a good example of a soft focus, gradation, and very colorful image.

Kitty Cats Photoshop is a good example of a gradated background combined with a cartoony illustration.

Sourpuss is a good example of a standard photograph with skin tones.

Image Compression Charts ▪ PNG Dithered

1-bit

2-bit

3-bit

4-bit

5-bit

6-bit

7-bit

8-bit

The 4-bit version of this graphic looks as good as the 8-bit version. Using the sub filter, the PNG file is only 15.4k.

	sub	up	average	paeth	adaptive
1-bit	12.8k	15.1k	14k	14.7k	13.7k
2-bit	13.3k	14.8k	14.3k	14.5k	14.4k
3-bit	11.9k	13.1k	13.2k	13k	12.8k
4-bit	**15.4k**	17.5k	18.9k	17.2k	17.4k
5-bit	17.4k	20.1k	22.2k	19.8k	20.2k
6-bit	18.1k	20.6k	23k	20.3k	20.8k
7-bit	18.6k	21.2k	23.6k	20.9k	21.1k
8-bit	18.6k	21.2k	23.6k	20.9k	21.3k

Image Compression Charts ▪ PNG Nondithered

1-bit

2-bit

3-bit

4-bit

5-bit

6-bit

7-bit

8-bit

The 4-bit version is still the best choice, but without dithering it's shrunk to 12.4k using the sub filter PNG method. Not bad!

	sub	up	average	paeth	adaptive
1-bit	8k	8.6k	8.3k	8.4k	8.1k
2-bit	10.1k	11k	10.9k	10.7k	10.6k
3-bit	12.9k	12.7k	13k	12.8k	12.7k
4-bit	**12.4k**	14k	14.7k	13.9k	13.8k
5-bit	13.3k	15.2k	16.2k	15.2k	14.9k
6-bit	13.8k	15.6k	16.9k	15.5k	15.2k
7-bit	13.9k	15.8k	17k	15.8k	15.4k
8-bit	14k	15.8k	17k	15.8k	15.5k

Image Compression Charts ▪ GIF Dithered

1-bit

2-bit

3-bit

4-bit

5-bit

6-bit

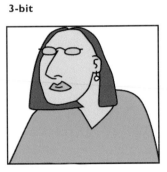

7-bit

8-bit

The 4-bit dithered GIF offers the best quality at the lowest file size price. At 6.3k, it's significantly smaller than its PNG counterpart.

	GIF Dithered
1-bit	5.4k
2-bit	5.2k
3-bit	4.3k
4-bit	**6.3k**
5-bit	9.1k
6-bit	9.8k
7-bit	10.2k
8-bit	10.2k

Image Compression Charts • GIF Nondithered

1-bit

2-bit

3-bit

4-bit

5-bit

6-bit

7-bit

8-bit

The 4-bit nondithered GIF is the best possible choice for this image. It yields the best quality at the lowest file savings. At 4.7k, it beats out dithered GIFs and all the PNG and JPEG examples.

	GIF Nondithered
1-bit	2.1k
2-bit	3.3k
3-bit	4.2k
4-bit	**4.7k**
5-bit	5.4k
6-bit	6.1k
7-bit	6.5k
8-bit	6.5k

Image Compression Charts ▪ JPEG

low	med	high	max

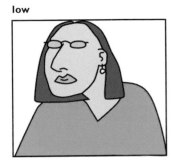   

baseline standard

baseline optimized

progressive

The low JPEG picked up some unwanted compression artifacts, but the medium version looks great. Still at 9.3k, it's much larger than the nondithered GIF.

	standard	optimized	progressive
low	7.7k	8.7k	7.5k
med	9.5k	10.6k	**9.3k**
high	13.3k	14.6k	12.9k
max	30.4k	20.6k	17.9k

Image Compression Charts ▪ PNG Dithered

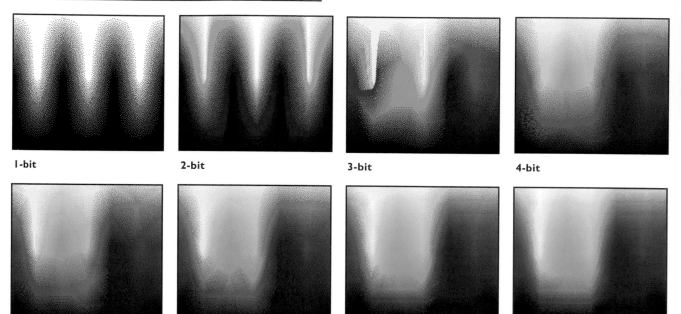

1-bit 2-bit 3-bit 4-bit

5-bit 6-bit 7-bit 8-bit

The spectrum gradient doesn't hold up well in low bit depths. I would pick 8-bit as the only acceptable example here. Once again, the sub filter yields the highest compression results at 30.9k.

	sub	up	average	paeth	adaptive
1-bit	11.2k	14.9k	13.5k	14.2k	13.4k
2-bit	15.7k	29k	18.5k	19.4k	19.4k
3-bit	17.7k	23.9k	24.1k	22.8k	23.7k
4-bit	21.7k	29.6k	30.8k	28.1k	29k
5-bit	23.8k	32.6k	34k	30.8k	32k
6-bit	26.1k	35.2k	38k	33.5k	34.4k
7-bit	28.1k	38.1k	41.8k	36.3k	37.4k
8-bit	**30.9k**	41k	45.4k	38.9k	37.5k

Image Compression Charts · PNG Nondithered

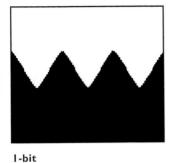
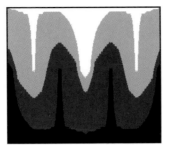

1-bit 2-bit 3-bit 4-bit

5-bit 6-bit 7-bit 8-bit

As you can see, none of these examples are acceptable. The subtle gradient is totally lost without dithering. The files sizes are significantly smaller, but the quality is so poor that it's of no use.

	sub	up	average	paeth	adaptive
1-bit	3.9k	3.9k	4k	3.9k	3.9k
2-bit	5.1k	4.6k	5.2k	4.7k	4.6k
3-bit	5k	4.9k	5.7k	4.9k	4.9k
4-bit	5.5k	5.4k	6.6k	5.4k	5.4k
5-bit	6.4k	6.1k	7.8k	6k	6.2k
6-bit	7.21k	7k	9.5k	7k	7k
7-bit	8.6k	8.4k	11.6k	8.2k	8.3k
8-bit	10k	10.2k	14.4k	10k	9.9k

Image Compression Charts ▪ GIF Dithered

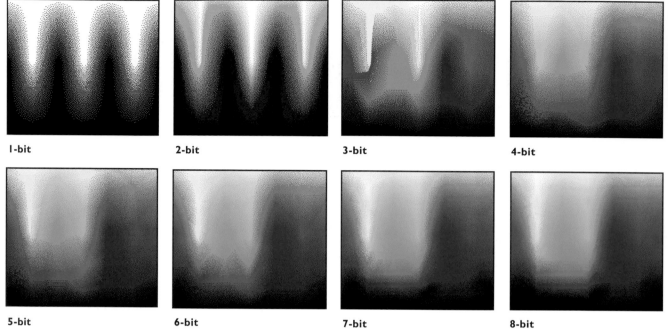

1-bit   2-bit   3-bit   4-bit

5-bit   6-bit   7-bit   8-bit

The 8-bit dithered GIF has the least amount of obvious dithering. At 33k it's large for a web graphic, but within an acceptable range. This graphic fared a little better as a PNG using the sub filter, at 30k.

	GIF Dithered
1-bit	6.7k
2-bit	10.5k
3-bit	13.8k
4-bit	17.9k
5-bit	20.7k
6-bit	24.3k
7-bit	28.2k
8-bit	33k

Image Compression Charts · GIF Nondithered

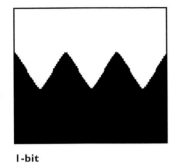

1-bit

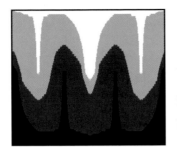

2-bit

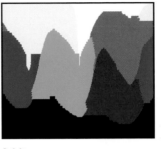

3-bit

4-bit

5-bit

6-bit

7-bit

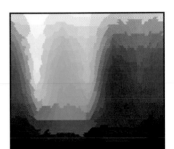

8-bit

The nondithered GIF has unusable quality, regardless how much these small file sizes tempt you.

	GIF Nondithered
1-bit	.9k
2-bit	3k
3-bit	2.6k
4-bit	3.4k
5-bit	5k
6-bit	7k
7-bit	10k
8-bit	14.1k

Image Compression Charts • JPEG

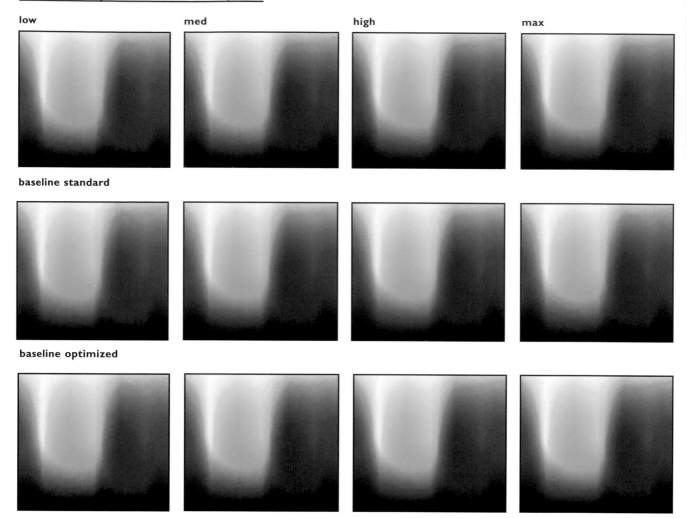

low   med   high   max

baseline standard

baseline optimized

progressive

Once again, the low-quality JPEG setting is perfectly acceptable. It's only 3.8k—less than 1/10th the size of PNG or GIF with better quality to boot. JPEGs will always yield the smallest and best-looking graphics if the image includes gradients or soft focus.

	standard	optimized	progressive
low	4.3k	3.7k	3.8k
med	4.9k	4.4k	4.4k
high	9.5k	8.2k	8.3k
max	13.3k	11.7k	11.4k

Image Compression Charts ▪ PNG Dithered

1-bit

2-bit

3-bit

4-bit

5-bit

6-bit

7-bit

8-bit

This image doesn't look great as a PNG, but of all the settings the 4-bit version yields acceptable quality and small enough size. The sub filter yields the smallest file size for this graphic. A 4-bit dithered GIF, however, looks identical and is significantly smaller than the dithered PNG.

	sub	up	average	paeth	adaptive
1-bit	11.4k	14.1k	13k	13.6k	12.2k
2-bit	13.3k	16.1k	16k	15.7k	16k
3-bit	14.2k	16.8k	16.6k	16.3k	16.8k
4-bit	**16.4k**	19.8k	19.5k	19.2k	19.6k
5-bit	19.7k	23.5k	24.6k	22.8k	23.1k
6-bit	22.1k	26k	27.6k	25.4k	25.6k
7-bit	24.7k	28.8k	30.6k	28.2k	28.8k
8-bit	27.2k	31.7k	33.5k	31.1k	30.6k

Image Compression Charts ▪ PNG Nondithered

1-bit

2-bit

3-bit

4-bit

5-bit

6-bit

7-bit

8-bit

The gradient background in this image looks terrible as a nondithered graphic. Use dithering, even though the file sizes will be larger.

	sub	up	average	paeth	adaptive
1-bit	4.9k	5k	5k	5k	5k
2-bit	6.5k	6.6k	7.2k	6.7k	6.7k
3-bit	7.8k	7.9k	8.6k	7.9k	7.9k
4-bit	8.6k	8.7k	9.4k	8.7k	8.8k
5-bit	12.3k	13k	14.9k	13k	13.2k
6-bit	14.6k	15.1k	17k	15.2k	15.6k
7-bit	16.6k	17k	19k	17.3k	17.6k
8-bit	18.2k	18.6k	20.5k	19k	18.9k

Image Compression Charts ▪ GIF Dithered

1-bit   **2-bit**   **3-bit**   **4-bit**

5-bit   **6-bit**   **7-bit**   **8-bit**

This image doesn't look great as a GIF, but of all the settings the 4-bit version yields acceptable quality and small enough size. This 4-bit dithered GIF, however, looks identical to the 4-bit dithered PNG, but is significantly smaller.

	GIF Dithered
1-blt	4.3k
2-bit	7.1k
3-bit	7.9k
4-bit	**10.3k**
5-bit	13.1k
6-bit	15.6k
7-bit	19.5k
8-bit	23.5k

Image Compression Charts ▪ GIF Nondithered

1-bit   **2-bit**   **3-bit**   **4-bit**

5-bit   **6-bit**   **7-bit**   **8-bit**

The gradient background in this image looks terrible as a nondithered graphic. Use dithering, even though the file sizes will be larger.

	GIF Nondithered
1-bit	1.5k
2-bit	2.9k
3-bit	4k
4-bit	5.2k
5-bit	8k
6-bit	10.4k
7-bit	13.2k
8-bit	15.9k

Image Compression Charts ▪ JPEG

low  med  high  max

baseline standard

baseline optimized

progressive

This image looks great as a low baseline standard JPEG. It is smaller than the GIF or PNG, too! This is because gradients and soft edges always look best as JPEGs.

	standard	optimized	progressive
low	8.4k	8.1k	8.1k
med	12.2k	10.2k	10.2k
high	16.1k	15.6k	15.5k
max	24.7k	23.9k	23.5k

Image Compression Charts · PNG Dithered

1-bit   2-bit   3-bit   4-bit

5-bit   6-bit   7-bit   8-bit

This image doesn't hold up well in 8-bit and lower bit depths. Even in 8-bit, little dots appear on Jamie's nose. The sub filter created the lowest file size of all the 8-bit PNG examples, but at 73.5k it's well above an acceptable range for the web.

	sub	up	average	paeth	adaptive
1-bit	17.7k	23.7k	21.8k	22.7k	21.5k
2-bit	22.1k	27.1k	24.7k	26.2k	27.1k
3-bit	30.7k	37.4k	37.5k	35.9k	36.6k
4-bit	37.9k	45.6k	45.6k	44k	42.9k
5-bit	46.2k	54.3k	54.3k	52.8k	54.9k
6-bit	57.1k	66.1k	66.1k	64.65k	66.7k
7-bit	65.6k	75k	75k	73.4k	75k
8-bit	**73.5k**	82.5k	90.5k	80.8k	78.6k

Image Compression Charts ▪ PNG Nondithered

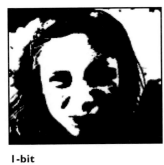
1-bit

2-bit

3-bit

4-bit

5-bit

6-bit

7-bit

8-bit

Unless you're looking for a posterized style, none of these examples are acceptable. The skin tones and subtle tones in Jamie's face make this image a difficult subject for 8-bit and lower nondithered compression types.

	sub	up	average	paeth	adaptive
1-bit	7.2k	7.2k	7.4k	7.2k	7.3k
2-bit	12.9k	12.5k	12.8k	12.5k	12.3k
3-bit	19.9k	19.6k	22.7k	19.6k	19.7k
4-bit	25.6k	26.1k	31.2k	26.1k	26.2k
5-bit	33.4k	34k	40k	34k	34.1k
6-bit	43.2k	45k	53.1k	44.8k	44.4k
7-bit	50.9k	53.1k	63.5k	52.7k	53.3k
8-bit	60k	63.3k	74.8k	62.5k	61.8k

Image Compression Charts ▪ GIF Dithered

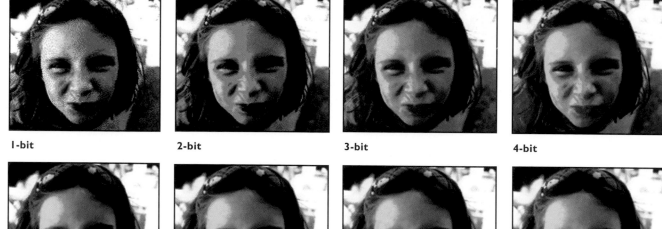

| | 1-bit | 2-bit | 3-bit | 4-bit |

1-bit　　**2-bit**　　**3-bit**　　**4-bit**

5-bit　　**6-bit**　　**7-bit**　　**8-bit**

This image doesn't hold up well in 8-bit and lower bit depths. Even in 8-bit, little dots appear on Jamie's nose. Even though the 8-bit GIF at 65k is smaller than its 8-bit PNG counterpart, it's still well above an acceptable size range for the web.

	GIF Dithered
1-bit	10.8k
2-bit	15k
3-bit	22.8k
4-bit	28.2k
5-bit	36.7k
6-bit	46.2k
7-bit	54.9k
8-bit	65k

Image Compression Charts · GIF Nondithered

1-bit **2-bit** **3-bit** **4-bit**

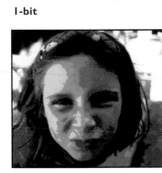

5-bit **6-bit** **7-bit** **8-bit**

Unless you're looking to create a posterized style image, none of these settings yield acceptable quality.

	GIF Nondithered
1-bit	4.1k
2-bit	8.6k
3-bit	14.1k
4-bit	19.4k
5-bit	26.4k
6-bit	35.3k
7-bit	43.5k
8-bit	54.2k

Image Compression Charts ▪ JPEG

low   med   high   max

baseline standard

baseline optimized

progressive

The low quality JPEG looks great—all the subtleties in Jamie's skin tone are preserved. And at 12.6k the size is right, too!

	standard	optimized	progressive
low	12.9k	12.5k	**12.6k**
med	17.6k	17.3k	17.2k
high	29.8k	29.2k	29.3k
max	50.5k	49.3k	48.7k

24-Bit JPEGs Versus 24-Bit PNGs

On the preceding Image Compression Charts, you may have noticed that PNG was compared using only 8-bit and lower bit-depth settings. That is because 24-bit PNG files are quite huge!

This is a 24-bit max quality JPEG. It is 49.3k.

This is a 24-bit PNG using the sub filter. It is 224k!

Applying PNG compression in 24-bit has the advantage over JPEG of being lossless. JPEG uses lossy compression, which means it permanently throws away information in an image. PNG is compressed using any number of filters and is then decompressed when viewed. This enables PNG to retain every original detail and pixel, with no loss of quality or difference between its original noncompressed source.

On low-resolution images for the web, the quality difference between JPEG and PNG is imperceptible. My recommendation is that you always choose JPEG over PNG for photographic style 24-bit images. The only time PNG compression compares favorably is when it is used in 8-bit and lower bit depths. PNG has two advantages over JPEG and GIF: it can store gamma information and will adjust automatically for the gamma of its target platform (gamma is explained in Chapter 2, "Understanding the Web Environment"), and PNG supports 8-bit transparency (otherwise known as alpha channels). You can find examples of PNG transparency in Chapter 7, "Transparent Artwork."

Reducing Colors in GIF Files Using Photoshop

Chapter 3, "Web File Formats," described the file-saving advantages of working with limited color palettes whenever using the GIF file format. Here's how to implement procedures that create the smallest possible GIF files.

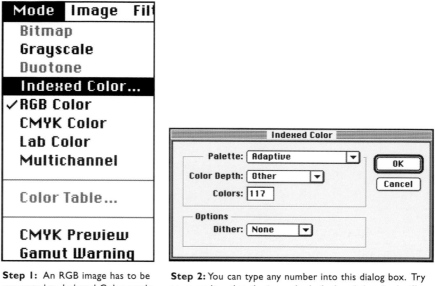

Step 1: An RGB image has to be converted to Indexed Color mode before it can be saved as a GIF. Under the Mode menu, choose Indexed Color.

Step 2: You can type any number into this dialog box. Try to go so low that the image looks bad, and then back off a step. This ensures that you've pushed the limits to how few colors are needed in order to make a small file that still maintains acceptable quality.

Reducing Colors in Photo-Paint

Photo-Paint has an interface similar to Photoshop's Indexed Color dialog box.

Convert to 256 Colors

Palette type:
- ○ Uniform
- ● Adaptive
- ○ Optimized
- ○ Custom...

Dither type:
- ● None
- ○ Ordered
- ○ Error diffusion

Colors: 200

OK   Cancel   Help

- A **Uniform palette** type produces the same palette over and over again. This is the appropriate type when you are using Photo-Paint's batch processing feature and want to convert a series of images to the same palette.

- An **Adaptive palette** type produces a color palette based on the colors found within the image. It is similar to the Exact setting in Photoshop.

- An **Optimized palette** type produces the best 256 colors for re-creating the image. This feature is the same as Photoshop's Adaptive palette setting.

- A **Custom palette** type allows you to assign a specific palette (such as the browser-safe 216) to an image.

- A **None Dither** type produces a banding effect. An **Ordered Dither** type produces a **screen dither** effect.

- An **Error Diffusion Dither** type produces a random dither based on the image itself.

- **Colors** determines at what bit depth the image is saved.

Reducing Colors in Paint Shop Pro

Here is Paint Shop Pro's version of decreasing color-depth options.

```
Decrease Color Depth - X Colors                          [×]

 ┌─Palette──────┐  ┌─Reduction Method─┐  ┌─Options──────────────┐
 │              │  │                  │  │ ☐ Boost Marked Colors by │
 │ Number of Colors │ ○ Nearest Color │  │   [0]    (1 to 10)    │
 │ [17]  [17-256]│  │ ● Error Diffusion│  │ ☐ Include Windows' Colors │
 │              │  │                  │  │ ☐ Reduce Color Bleeding │
 └──────────────┘  └──────────────────┘  └──────────────────────┘

         [  OK  ]   [ Cancel ]   [  Help  ]
```

- **Number of Colors** dictates the color depth of the image.

- The **Nearest Color** reduction method is the same as Dither None in Photoshop and Photo-Paint. It creates a banded appearance.

- **Error Diffusion** will create dithering based on the image itself.

- **Boost Masked Colors** allows you to select colors within the document and have the palette weigh toward favoring those colors.

- **Include Windows' Colors** ensures that the 16 colors within Windows are reserved in the image's color table.

- **Reduce Color Bleeding** reduces the left-to-right color bleeding that sometimes occurs with the Error Diffusion Settings.

■ **note**

The Windows 16 Palette

Sixteen colors are reserved for a native palette assigned to Windows machines. Unfortunately, only the last six colors are browser safe. There are some cases where you might want to use these colors in a Windows-based Intranet, where cross-platform compatibility is not an issue. The win16.clut is located at my web site: ■ ftp://luna.bearnet/com/pub/lynda/.

The 16 reserved native colors for Windows systems. Only the last 6 colors are browser safe.

■ **note**

Other Compression Tools and Resources

GIF/JPEG Smart Saver
Windows 95 and NT file optimization tool that includes previews so you can judge side to side how much compression a GIF or JPEG can withstand. A demo is availabe for downloading at
■ http://www.ulead.com/products/noslip.htm

HVS Color
A Windows or Mac Photoshop and DeBabelizer plug-in that optimizes GIF images with a proprietary algorithm.
■ http://www.digfrontiers.com/

GIF Wizard
An online file reduction service—runs any image through its automatic filter and reduces the file size on-the-fly. Way, way, way cool!
■ http://www.raspberryhill.com/gifwizard.html

PhotoGIF
Mac-only Photoshop plug-in that includes transparency tools and image and palette optimization features, and works with animated GIFs, too!
■ http://www.boxtopsoft.com/PhotoGIF/

ProJPEG
Mac-only Photoshop plug-in that offers baseline or progressive JPEG support and previews the results before you commit.
■ http://enlil.boxtopsoft.com/ProJPEG

The Bandwidth Conservation Society
Cool tutorials and great information about image optimization.
■ http://www.infohiway.com/faster/index.html

■ **note**

Compression Rules in a Nutshell

- ■ Avoid noise in GIF images.

- ■ Whenever possible, don't dither GIFs.

- ■ Use the least amount of colors in a GIF while maintaining acceptable quality.

- ■ Always try the lowest amount of JPEG compression while maintaining acceptable quality.

- ■ PNG compresses better on 8-bit.

Photoshop 4.0 Actions Palette

Photoshop 4.0 has a wonderful new addition called the Actions palette that makes life easier for those of us who regularly perform repetitive Photoshop tasks. The Actions palette enables us to create macros, which automate multiple Photoshop commands with the click of a button.

Macros are created by having Photoshop observe your actions during a recording session, which enables the program to memorize your steps. In addition to repeating multiple commands to a single image, actions can be applied to hundreds of images at a time. This is called batch processing.

Imagine you had 100 images that you wanted to index to a specific palette, shrink down to thumbnails, and save in the GIF file format. It might take you anywhere from 3–5 minutes for each image in order to finish this operation manually. An Action palette could do this task to 100 images in a matter of a few minutes. No one likes doing a repetitive task for hours on end when a computer can do it in minutes!

Step-by-Step Actions Palette Programming

Here's a step-by-step exercise to teach yourself Action palettes for web graphics authoring. This tutorial will teach you to create an action that makes a small thumbnail of a larger image by resizing it to a specific size, indexing the image to an adaptive palette, and then saving the image as a GIF.

Step 1: This demonstration will use this large streaking monkey image, illustrated by Bruce Heavin.

Step 2: Under Window, select Show Actions. Make sure you are not in the Button mode. To turn this off, go to the arrow in the upper right corner of the Actions palette and pull down the menu to toggle the "Button Mode" off. When you are out of Button mode, your Actions palette should look like this.

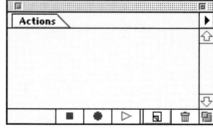

Step 3: It's always best to work on a copy of the image when programming a macro. This is so you don't damage the original image in the process of creating the action process. That's not to say that you will damage a file; it's simply a recommended precautionary measure. Copies can be made easily in Photoshop by selecting the Duplicate function from the Image menu.

Step 4: Click on the upper arrow of the Actions palette to access the setting New Action or the page icon at the bottom of the screen to initiate the recording session. A dialog box will prompt you to name your action, define a function key, and select a color for the button. Insert the name, "Thumbnail maker", or any other name that is appropriate for what you plan to record. When you're finished, press Record to begin.

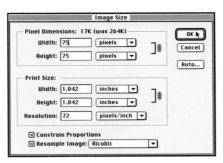

Step 5: The first step in this recording session will be to establish the amount of image size reduction. Under the menu item Image, select Image Size. This example shows changing the settings to 75 pixels high with constrained proportions checked. Once OK is pressed, the monkey image will shrink down to icon size.

Step 6: The results of the image size scaling should match what you requested.

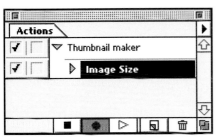

Step 7: The Actions Palette will now show the Thumbnail maker macro. Click on the twirly triangle to see the Image Size command. The Image Size layer can be twirled down as well.

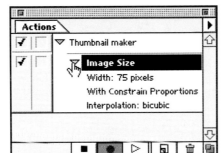

Step 8: If you want to change the settings, you can press Stop (the square at the bottom of the palette). Highlight Image Size and drag it into the little trash can and repeat the process again till you get it right. Press Record to continue the macro so you can add more functions to the actions set.

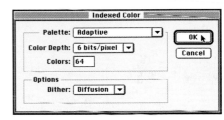

Step 9: Select Image, Mode, Indexed Color. Click OK once you have entered the setting you want.

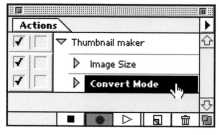

Step 10: Now the Actions palette should include the last operation.

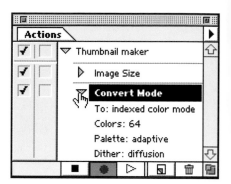

Step 11: The details of the action will be visible by pressing on the little twirly arrow.

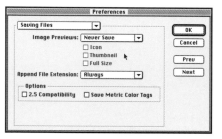

Step 12: The last action remaining to program is the save command. Before doing so, make sure your preferences are set up the way you want. Under File, Preferences, Saving Files, choose Append File Extension to "Always." This is so Photoshop will know to put the .gif extension at the end of the new thumbnail image. Choose Never Save in the Image Preview pull-down menu so that the file will be as small as possible. Icon's and previews make larger files.

Step 13: Choose File, Save As, and type the name of the file. The GIF extension will be filled in automatically.

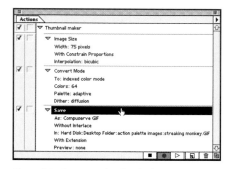

Step 14: Once you're finished programming the macro, press Stop on the recorder so that further actions won't be recorded. The Actions palette should now contain the actions that were recorded and should look something like this.

Batch File Processing

Now that the Actions macro is complete, you can create a batch process to apply the macro to a folder of images. Again, if this is your first time or if you simply want to be cautious, work on a backup of the folder, not the only copy!

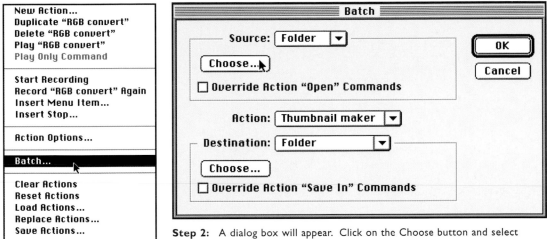

Step 1: To begin, hold down the upper right arrow to select Batch from the Actions palette options.

Step 2: A dialog box will appear. Click on the Choose button and select the folder that contains the images you wish to process. Next, select from the Actions pull-down to see the list of actions. In this example, the choice Thumbnail maker is selected. In the Destination pull-down, choose Folder. Click the Choose button to tell the computer where your folder is located. When everything is selected to your specifications, press OK and you can go get a cup of coffee for a moment while the computer does its business. If you have nothing else to do, you can watch the computer do its action to each of the images as they go by. Tada! You're a god! Well at least a Photoshop actions god.

Introduction

Getting Started in Web Design

Understanding the Web Environment

Web File Formats

Low-Bandwidth Graphics

Hexadecimal Color

Browser-Safe Color

Transparent Artwork

Background Tiles

Rules, Bullets and Buttons

Navigation-Based Graphics

Web-Based Typography

Scanning Techniques for the Web

Layout and Alignment Techniques

Animation

Sound

Interactivity

HTML for Visual Designers

Glossary

Design Resources Appendix

Index

BROWSER

33 FF

Web typography

otoshop

INDEX

<STRONG>

.Gif
.Jpg
.Png

Width="500"

<Img src="

Image compression
Limited palettes
IMAGE OPTIMIZATION
216 Colors

PARENCY

Height="600"

</A>

10.2 K

Imaging
Extending HTML
Web file formats
bgcolor="FFFFCC"

Animation, sound and

alink="cyan"

LYNX.COM

www.Design

Using Color Names Instead of Hex

You don't have to use hexadecimal numbers inside the color attribute tags; you can use words, too. Here's a list of color names that will work in Netscape.

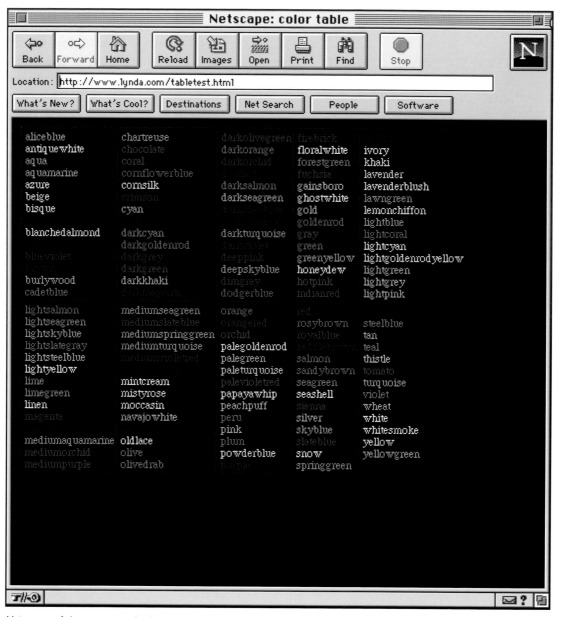

Using any of the names inside the color attribute tags will generate colored text in Netscape.

```
<HTML>
<HEAD>
<TITLE>Adding Color to
My Page</TITLE>
</HEAD>
<BODY BGCOLOR="lightgreen"
TEXT="darkgreen">
<H1>This page is where I will
play with color using all the
nifty color tags I can learn.
</H1>
</BODY>
</HTML>
```

1

1 You don't have to use hexadecimal numbers to define color—certain color names work as well. Here's an example of using "lightgreen" and "darkgreen" as color names within the **<BODY>** tag.

Netscape: Adding Color to My Page

Back Forward Home Reload Images Open Print Find Stop

Location: file:///Thing%20%231/Desktop%20Folder/color.html

What's New? What's Cool? Destinations Net Search People Software

This page is where I will play with color using all the nifty color tags I can learn.

Here's an example of using color names instead of hexadecimal values to define color.

Coloring Individual Lines of Text

You can also assign specific colors to individual lines of text by using the <FONT> tag. Here's some sample code.

```
<HTML>
<HEAD>
<TITLE>Adding Color to
My Page</TITLE>
</HEAD>
<BODY BGCOLOR="660099"
TEXT="CCCCFF">
<H1>This page is where I
<FONT COLOR="99FFFF">will </FONT>
<FONT COLOR="CCFF99">play </FONT>
<FONT COLOR="CC99CC">with </FONT>
<FONT COLOR="CC0000">color </FONT>
using all the nifty color
tags I can learn.
</H1>
</BODY>
</HTML>
```

1 The **<FONT>** tag can contain a color attribute, which can be specified by using color names or hex numbers. It must be closed with a **</FONT>** tag each time you want the specific colored text attribute to end.

Here's an example of using the **<FONT>** tag to insert color attributes so that individual words or letters can be colored.

Coloring Links

Link color can affect the border color around linked images or the color of linked text. Here's an example of how to set this up in an HTML document.

```
<HTML>
<HEAD>
<TITLE>Adding Color to
My Page</TITLE>
</HEAD>
<BODY BGCOLOR="660099"
TEXT="CCCCFF" LINK="CCFF00">
<H1>Here's an example of a
<A HREF="http://www.stinkabod.com">text-
based hyperlink</A>.
<P>Here's an example of a
linked graphic with a fat,
colored border: </H1>
<P>
<A HREF="http://www.stinkabod.com"> <IMG
SRC="fourlynda.gif" BORDER=10></A>
</BODY>
</HTML>
```

1

2

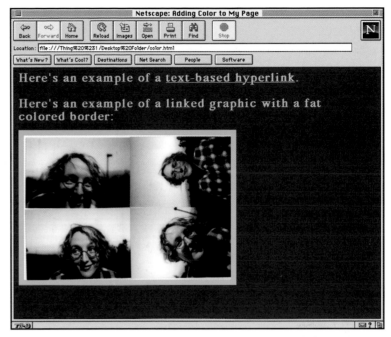

Here's an example of creating colored links. The border around the graphic was made wider with the **BORDER** attribute.

1 The **LINK** attribute within the **<BODY>** tag establishes the color for the linked text or graphic. The **<A HREF></A>** tag produces linked text.

2 The **<IMG SRC>** tag inserts an image, and the **BORDER** attribute enables you to set a width for the border, measured in pixels. Note: If you don't want a border, you can set this to **BORDER=0**.

Inserting a Background Image

If you want to use an image in the background of your web page, instead of a hex color, this is how you would structure the HTML.

```
<HTML>
<HEAD>
<TITLE>Adding Color
to My Page</TITLE>
</HEAD>
<BODY
BACKGROUND="tile.gif"
TEXT="CCCCFF" LINK="CCFF00">
<CENTER>
<A HREF="http://www.stinkabod.com"><IMG
SRC="fourlynda.gif"
BORDER=10></A>
<CENTER>
</BODY>
</HTML>
```

1 The **BACKGROUND** attribute within the **<BODY>** tag enables you to insert an image into the background of the web page. This image can be any kind of image (.jpg or .gif), and can be a solid color, a hybrid color, a seamless tile image, or a repeating tile image.

Here's an example of inserting a background image. You can insert a solid color image, a hybrid color image, a seamless tile image, or a repeating tile image. It's the same code, just a different graphic file!

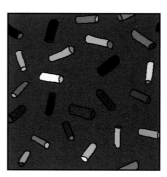

tile.gif

Adding Color to Tables

The BGCOLOR attribute works in table cells as well as the body of the HTML document. Here's some sample code that demonstrates this technique:

```
<HTML>
<HEAD>
<TITLE>Adding Color
to My Page</TITLE>
</HEAD>
<BODY BGCOLOR="660099"
TEXT="CCCCFF">
<CENTER>
<TABLE BORDER>
<TR><TH BGCOLOR="003366" HEIGHT=200
WIDTH=200>Hello</TH>
<TH BGCOLOR="990033" HEIGHT=200
WIDTH=200>Hola!</TH>
<TR><TD BGCOLOR="666600" HEIGHT=200
WIDTH=200
ALIGN=MIDDLE>You</TD><TD BGCOLOR="996666"
HEIGHT=200 WIDTH=200 ALIGN=MIDDLE>Me</TD>
</TABLE>
</CENTER>
</BODY>
</HTML>
```

1 The **<CENTER>** tag instructs the table to be centered in the page.

2 The **<TABLE>** tag establishes the beginning of the table command. The **BORDER** attribute assigns an embossed border to the table.

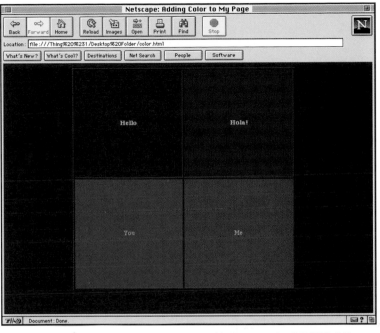

Here's an example of coloring cells within a table by using the **BGCOLOR** attribute within the **<TABLE>** tag.

3 **TR** initiates a table row. **TH** stands for table header. Everything within the **<TH>** tag will automatically be bold and centered. The **BGCOLOR** attribute allows a color to be established within the table cell and can be specified by using hexadecimal color or color names. The **<HEIGHT>** and **<WIDTH>** tags assign dimensions to the table cells by using pixel-based measurements. The **ALIGN= MIDDLE** attribute centers the text within the table cells.

Introduction

Getting Started in Web Design

Understanding the Web Environment

Web File Formats

Low-Bandwidth Graphics

Hexadecimal Color

Browser-Safe Color

Transparent Artwork

Background Tiles

Rules, Bullets and Buttons

Navigation-Based Graphics

Web-Based Typography

Scanning Techniques for the Web

Layout and Alignment Techniques

Animation

Sound

Interactivity

HTML for Visual Designers

Glossary

Design Resources Appendix

Index

6

Computer Color

Creating color artwork for the web is very different from other color delivery mediums because you're publishing your work to people's screens instead of printed pages. Computer screen-based color is composed of projected light and pixels instead of ink pigments, dot patterns, and screen percentages.

In many ways, working with screen-based color can be more fun than working with printed inks. No waiting for color proofs or working with CMYK values that are much less vibrant than RGB. No high-resolution files. No dot screens to deal with. Yes, working on the computer for computer delivery is a lot easier in some ways, but don't be fooled into thinking that what you see on your screen is what other people will see on theirs. Just like its print-based counterpart, computer screen-based color has its own set of nasties and gremlins.

The web differs from the printed page in more ways than you might imagine. It is not enough to approach web authoring with good ideas and great artwork. Understanding the medium is necessary in order to ensure that others view your designs and colors as you intended.

Here's a short list of the things that are different about the web as a publishing medium as it pertains to color:

- People view your artwork with monitors that have a wide variety of bit-depth settings.
- Various computer monitors have differing color calibration and gamma default settings.
- Different operating systems affect the way colors are displayed.
- Different web browsers affect the way colors are displayed.
- People judge your site not only by its artistic content, but by its speed. Color can affect speed, believe it or not!

Creating color images and screens for the web can be done without understanding the medium's limitations, but the results may not be what you are hoping for. The focus of this chapter is to describe the web and computer color environment, and to clue you in on known pitfalls and solutions that will offer maximum control over how your artwork is ultimately seen.

RGB Versus CMYK

The color of a pixel is made up of three projected colors of light that mix together optically. The projected lights form the colors red, green, and blue. Once mixed together, these three colors create a color space called RGB. Sometimes you'll also hear about CMYK color space, which is formed from cyan, magenta, yellow, and black. CMYK color space on a computer is used to simulate printing inks and is used commonly by print designers. Web designers are "screen" based, hence we use RGB color space only.

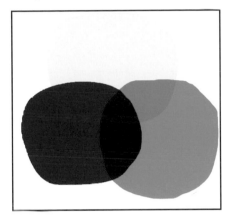

CMYK colors are subtractive, meaning that mixing multiple colors creates black. This color space was created for computer graphics that will be printed on paper.

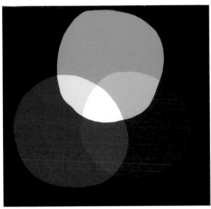

RGB color is additive, meaning that mixing multiple colors creates white. This color space was created for computer graphics that will be viewed on computer screens.

Introduction to Browser-Safe Specs

Browser software is your window into the web. You can't see web pages without the browser, so the browser plays a huge role in how your images are displayed, especially when viewed on 256-color systems.

Fortunately, the most popular browsers (Netscape, Mosaic, and Internet Explorer) all share the same palette management process. They work with the system palettes of each respective platform: Mac, Windows, and Win95. This means that any artwork you create will be forced into a variety of different palettes, depending on which operating system it is viewed from.

Although these three palettes look entirely different, they share 216 common colors. If you use the shared colors, referred to in this book as "browser-safe" colors, you will eliminate a lot of cross-platform inconsistencies with color artwork published over the web.

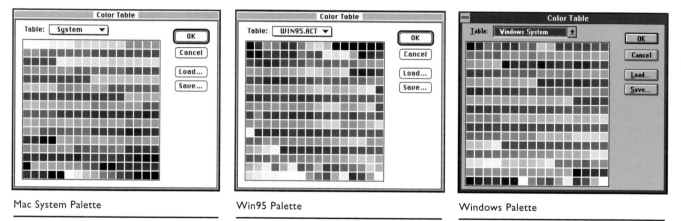

Mac System Palette   Win95 Palette   Windows Palette

Thankfully, there are common colors found within the 256 system palettes—216 common colors, in fact. Each operating system reserves 40 colors out of the possible 256 for its own use. This means that if you stick to the 216 common colors, they will be universally honored between browsers, operating systems, and computer platforms.

Why Work Within a Limited Palette?

Although it is wonderful and nice to design using a large monitor and 16 million+ color range, most people who view your work will have computers capable of seeing images in only 256 colors on a monitor that can't go beyond 640x480 in size. When we work with colors other than that of the 216 browser-safe colors, the browsers will convert the colors anyway. This will have an adverse effect on your artwork, as the following examples demonstrate.

Hexadecimal-Based Artwork

Web page color schemes are generally chosen by using hexadecimal values instead of embedded artwork (see more details in Chapter 5, "Hexadecimal Color"). If you choose a one-color background on your millions-of-color monitor and the end user views the image on a 256-color monitor, the browser will convert it to one of the 216 colors anyway. It will shift the colors you've chosen to its own palette.

Hexadecimal code is used instead of RGB values within HTML. If you don't understand what I mean, be sure to read Chapter 5, "Hexadecimal Color."

Here's a site that used the following hexadecimal code:

```
<BODY BGCOLOR="#090301" TEXT="#436E58" LINK="#CF7B42" VLINK="#323172" ALINK="#ffffff"
```

You should be able to tell, just by looking, that these colors are not browser safe! Remember, browser-safe hex combinations are always formed from variations of 00, 33, 66, 99, CC, and FF.

Mac 8-bit display

PC 8-bit display

This comparison demonstrates the kind of color shifting that occurs with hexadecimal-based artwork, on 8-bit systems, if the colors used are not browser safe.

Illustration-Based Artwork

With illustration-based artwork, if you create logos, cartoons, or drawings in colors outside of the 216—you guessed it—the browser converts it anyway! Instead of shifting the color, which is what happens with hexadecimal-based color, it dithers the artwork. Ugh!

On a millions-of-color display, you might not notice any differences between these two different colored versions of Bruce's cat image.

On an 8-bit display, look at what happens to the top version. It is filled with unwanted dots, caused by ditherings. Why? The colors in the bottom image are browser safe, and the colors in the top are not.

Here's a close-up of the dithering present in the nonbrowser-safe version of this illustration, on 8-bit (256-color) systems.

The close-up of the version created with browser-safe colors will not dither, regardless of the bit depth the end viewer's system supports.

Photograph-Based Artwork

Photographs are the one type of artwork that really do not benefit from using browser-safe colors. The reason is that the browsers convert photographs, but do a great job of it, unlike the terrible job they do with hexadecimal-based artwork and illustration-based artwork.

Viewed in 24-bit

Viewed in 8-bit

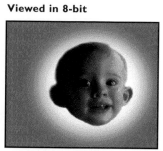

adaptive ■ 8-bit file ■ 35k

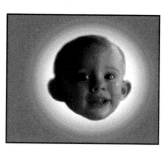

browser-safe palette ■ 50k

jpeg (low quality) ■ 11k

The images on the left of this study were all viewed from a browser in 24-bit. Which ones on the left have the highest quality? The JPEG, which is a 24-bit file, and the adaptive file, which is an 8-bit file based on the colors within the image, not the browser-safe palette. The right-side images show how these photographs looked within a browser viewed from a millions+ color system (24-bit). The right-side images all look worse than when viewed in the 24-bit browser, but are there any significant quality benefits from having saved them with different methods? I think not. The results of this study? It is not necessary to convert photographic-based images to the browser-safe palette or even an 8-bit palette. The browser does its dithering dirty work, regardless of how you prepare the image. It's best to leave the image in an adaptive palette or 24-bit file format so that the photographs will have the added advantage of looking better in 24-bit browser environments. JPEGs will always produce the smallest file size for photographs and have the added advantage of being a 24-bit file format, unlike GIF which cannot save images at bit depths higher than 8-bit (256 colors).

What Does the Browser-Safe Palette Look Like?

The 216-color palette for the web has only 6 red values, 6 green values, and 6 blue values which range in contrast. Sometimes this palette is referred to as the 6x6x6 palette, or the 6x6x6 cube. This palette is a predetermined palette which, as of yet, can't be changed.

The RGB values found within the 216-color palette have some remarkable similarities: the numbers are all formed from variations of 00, 51, 102, 153, 204, and 255.

The hexadecimal values found within the 216-color palette have some remarkable similarities, too: they are all formed form variations of 00, 33, 66, 99, CC, and FF.

It should be no surprise that these colors were picked by math, not beauty. Knowing the pattern of the numeric values is useful because you can check your code or image documents to see whether they contain these values.

Here's a version of the browser-safe palette, straight out of the computer.

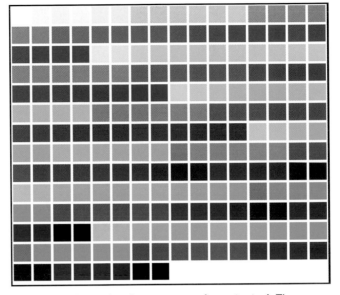

Notice how these colors have no sense of organization? They are organized by math, not beauty.

■ note

Do Browser-Safe Colors Really Matter?

You may think that all this hubbub over browser-safe colors need not apply to you. If you think your site will be viewed only from millions of color monitors (24-bit), you might be right. It's always important to decide who your audience is before you design a site and create artwork that is appropriate for your viewers.

My recommendation is, if you are going to pick colors for backgrounds, type, text, links, and illustrations, why not choose cross-platform compatible colors? There may come a day years from now when everyone has video cards that support more than 256 colors, but the majority of systems today do not.

Browser-Safe Color Charts Organized by Hue

330000 R=051 G=000 B=000	**660000** R=102 G=000 B=000	**990000** R=153 G=000 B=000	**CC0000** R=204 G=000 B=000	**FF0000** R=255 G=000 B=000	**663333** R=102 G=051 B=051	**993333** R=153 G=051 B=051	**CC3333** R=204 G=051 B=051	
CC0033 R=204 G=000 B=051	**FF3366** R=255 G=051 B=102	**990033** R=153 G=000 B=051	**CC3366** R=204 G=051 B=102	**FF6699** R=255 G=102 B=153	**FF0066** R=255 G=000 B=102	**660033** R=102 G=000 B=051	**CC0066** R=204 G=000 B=102	
CC0099 R=204 G=000 B=153	**FF33CC** R=255 G=51 B=204	**FF00CC** R=255 G=000 B=204	**330033** R=051 G=000 B=051	**660066** R=102 G=000 B=102	**990099** R=153 G=000 B=153	**CC00CC** R=204 G=000 B=204	**FF00FF** R=255 G=000 B=255	
FF99FF R=255 G=153 B=255	**FFCCFF** R=255 G=204 B=255	**CC00FF** R=204 G=000 B=255	**9900CC** R=153 G=000 B=204	**CC33FF** R=204 G=051 B=255	**660099** R=102 G=000 B=153	**9933CC** R=153 G=051 B=204	**CC66FF** R=204 G=102 B=255	
330099 R=051 G=000 B=153	**6633CC** R=102 G=051 B=204	**9966FF** R=153 G=102 B=255	**3300CC** R=051 G=000 B=204	**6633FF** R=102 G=051 B=255	**3300FF** R=051 G=000 B=255	**000000** R=000 G=000 B=000	**000033** R=000 G=000 B=051	
666699 R=102 G=102 B=153	**6666CC** R=102 G=102 B=204	**6666FF** R=102 G=102 B=255	**9999CC** R=153 G=153 B=204	**9999FF** R=153 G=153 B=255	**CCCCFF** R=204 G=204 B=255	**0033FF** R=000 G=051 B=255	**0033CC** R=000 G=051 B=204	
3399FF R=051 G=153 B=255	**6699CC** R=102 G=153 B=204	**99CCFF** R=153 G=204 B=255	**0099FF** R=000 G=153 B=255	**006699** R=000 G=102 B=153	**3399CC** R=051 G=153 B=204	**66CCFF** R=102 G=204 B=255	**0099CC** R=000 G=153 B=204	
00CCCC R=000 G=204 B=204	**33CCCC** R=051 G=204 B=204	**66CCCC** R=102 G=204 B=204	**99CCCC** R=153 G=204 B=204	**00FFFF** R=000 G=255 B=255	**33FFFF** R=051 G=255 B=255	**66FFFF** R=102 G=255 B=255	**99FFFF** R=153 G=255 B=255	
006633 R=000 G=102 B=051	**339966** R=051 G=153 B=102	**00CC66** R=000 G=204 B=102	**66CC99** R=102 G=204 B=153	**33FF99** R=051 G=255 B=153	**99FFCC** R=153 G=255 B=204	**00FF66** R=000 G=255 B=102	**009933** R=000 G=153 B=051	
009900 R=000 G=153 B=000	**339933** R=051 G=153 B=051	**669966** R=102 G=153 B=102	**00CC00** R=000 G=204 B=000	**33CC33** R=051 G=204 B=051	**66CC66** R=102 G=204 B=102	**99CC99** R=153 G=204 B=153	**00FF00** R=000 G=255 B=000	
66CC33 R=102 G=204 B=051	**99FF66** R=153 G=255 B=102	**66FF00** R=102 G=255 B=000	**336600** R=051 G=102 B=000	**669933** R=102 G=153 B=051	**66CC00** R=102 G=204 B=000	**99CC66** R=153 G=204 B=102	**99FF33** R=153 G=255 B=051	
333300 R=051 G=051 B=000	**666600** R=102 G=102 B=000	**666633** R=102 G=102 B=051	**999900** R=153 G=153 B=000	**999933** R=153 G=153 B=051	**999966** R=153 G=153 B=102	**CCCC00** R=204 G=204 B=000	**CCCC33** R=204 G=204 B=051	
CC9900 R=204 G=153 B=000	**FFCC33** R=255 G=204 B=051	**996600** R=153 G=102 B=000	**CC9933** R=204 G=153 B=051	**FFCC66** R=255 G=204 B=102	**FF9900** R=255 G=153 B=000	**663300** R=102 G=051 B=000	**996633** R=153 G=102 B=051	
CC3300 R=204 G=051 B=000	**FF6633** R=255 G=102 B=051	**FF3300** R=255 G=051 B=000	**333333** R=051 G=051 B=051	**666666** R=102 G=102 B=102	**999999** R=153 G=153 B=153	**CCCCCC** R=204 G=204 B=204	**FFFFFF** R=255 G=255 B=255	

FF3333 R=255 G=051 B=051	**996666** R=153 G=102 B=102	**CC6666** R=204 G=102 B=102	**FF6666** R=255 G=102 B=102	**CC9999** R=204 G=153 B=153	**FF9999** R=255 G=153 B=153	**FFCCCC** R=255 G=204 B=204	**FF0033** R=255 G=000 B=051
993366 R=153 G=051 B=102	**FF3399** R=255 G=051 B=153	**CC6699** R=204 G=102 B=153	**FF99CC** R=255 G=153 B=204	**FF0099** R=255 G=000 B=153	**990066** R=153 G=000 B=102	**CC3399** R=204 G=051 B=153	**FF66CC** R=255 G=102 B=204
663366 R=102 G=051 B=102	**993399** R=153 G=051 B=153	**CC33CC** R=204 G=051 B=204	**FF33FF** R=255 G=051 B=255	**996699** R=153 G=102 B=153	**CC66CC** R=204 G=102 B=204	**FF66FF** R=255 G=102 B=255	**CC99CC** R=204 G=153 B=204
9900FF R=153 G=000 B=255	**330066** R=051 G=000 B=102	**6600CC** R=102 G=000 B=204	**663399** R=102 G=051 B=153	**9933FF** R=153 G=051 B=255	**9966CC** R=153 G=102 B=204	**CC99FF** R=204 G=153 B=255	**6600FF** R=102 G=000 B=255
000066 R=000 G=000 B=102	**000099** R=000 G=000 B=153	**0000CC** R=000 G=000 B=204	**0000FF** R=000 G=000 B=255	**333366** R=051 G=051 B=102	**333399** R=051 G=051 B=153	**3333CC** R=051 G=051 B=204	**3333FF** R=051 G=051 B=255
3366FF R=051 G=102 B=255	**003399** R=000 G=051 B=153	**3366CC** R=051 G=102 B=204	**6699FF** R=102 G=153 B=255	**0066FF** R=000 G=102 B=255	**003366** R=000 G=051 B=102	**0066CC** R=000 G=102 B=204	**336699** R=051 G=102 B=153
33CCFF R=051 G=204 B=255	**00CCFF** R=000 G=204 B=255	**003333** R=000 G=051 B=051	**006666** R=000 G=102 B=102	**336666** R=051 G=102 B=102	**009999** R=000 G=153 B=153	**339999** R=051 G=153 B=153	**669999** R=102 G=153 B=153
CCFFFF R=204 G=255 B=255	**00FFCC** R=000 G=255 B=204	**00CC99** R=000 G=204 B=153	**33FFCC** R=051 G=255 B=204	**009966** R=000 G=153 B=102	**33CC99** R=051 G=204 B=153	**66FFCC** R=102 G=255 B=204	**00FF99** R=000 G=255 B=153
33CC66 R=051 G=204 B=102	**66FF99** R=102 G=255 B=153	**00CC33** R=000 G=204 B=051	**33FF66** R=051 G=255 B=102	**00FF33** R=000 G=255 B=051	**003300** R=000 G=051 B=000	**006600** R=000 G=102 B=000	**336633** R=051 G=102 B=051
33FF33 R=051 G=255 B=051	**66FF66** R=102 G=255 B=102	**99FF99** R=153 G=255 B=153	**CCFFCC** R=204 G=255 B=204	**33FF00** R=051 G=255 B=000	**33CC00** R=051 G=204 B=000	**66FF33** R=102 G=255 B=051	**339900** R=051 G=153 B=000
CCFF99 R=204 G=255 B=153	**99FF00** R=153 G=255 B=000	**669900** R=102 G=153 B=000	**99CC33** R=153 G=204 B=051	**CCFF66** R=204 G=255 B=102	**99CC00** R=153 G=204 B=000	**CCFF33** R=204 G=255 B=051	**CCFF00** R=204 G=255 B=000
CCCC66 R=204 G=204 B=102	**CCCC99** R=204 G=204 B=153	**FFFF00** R=255 G=255 B=000	**FFFF33** R=255 G=255 B=051	**FFFF66** R=255 G=255 B=102	**FFFF99** R=255 G=255 B=153	**FFFFCC** R=255 G=255 B=204	**FFCC00** R=255 G=204 B=000
CC6600 R=204 G=102 B=000	**CC9966** R=204 G=153 B=102	**FF9933** R=255 G=153 B=051	**FFCC99** R=255 G=204 B=153	**FF6600** R=255 G=102 B=000	**993300** R=153 G=051 B=000	**CC6633** R=204 G=102 B=051	**FF9966** R=255 G=153 B=102

Browser-Safe Color Charts Organized by Value

FFFFFF R=255 G=255 B=255	**FFFFCC** R=255 G=255 B=204	**FFFF99** R=255 G=255 B=153	**CCFFFF** R=204 G=255 B=255	**FFFF66** R=255 G=255 B=102	**CCFFCC** R=204 G=255 B=204	**FFFF33** R=255 G=255 B=051	**CCFF99** R=204 G=255 B=153
99FF99 R=153 G=255 B=153	**CCFF00** R=204 G=255 B=000	**CCCCFF** R=204 G=204 B=255	**66FFFF** R=102 G=255 B=255	**FFCC66** R=255 G=204 B=102	**99FF66** R=153 G=255 B=102	**CCCCCC** R=204 G=204 B=204	**66FFCC** R=102 G=255 B=204
33FFFF R=051 G=255 B=255	**CCCC66** R=204 G=204 B=102	**66FF66** R=102 G=255 B=102	**FF99CC** R=255 G=153 B=204	**99CCCC** R=153 G=204 B=204	**33FFCC** R=051 G=255 B=204	**CCCC33** R=204 G=204 B=051	**66FF33** R=102 G=255 B=051
FF9966 R=255 G=153 B=102	**99CC66** R=153 G=204 B=102	**33FF66** R=051 G=255 B=102	**CC99CC** R=204 G=153 B=204	**66CCCC** R=102 G=204 B=204	**00FFCC** R=000 G=255 B=204	**FF9933** R=255 G=153 B=051	**99CC33** R=153 G=204 B=051
9999FF R=153 G=153 B=255	**33CCFF** R=051 G=204 B=255	**CC9966** R=204 G=153 B=102	**66CC66** R=102 G=204 B=102	**00FF66** R=000 G=255 B=102	**FF66CC** R=255 G=102 B=204	**9999CC** R=153 G=153 B=204	**33CCCC** R=051 G=204 B=204
00FF00 R=000 G=255 B=000	**CC66FF** R=204 G=102 B=255	**6699FF** R=102 G=153 B=255	**00CCFF** R=000 G=204 B=255	**FF6666** R=255 G=102 B=102	**999966** R=153 G=153 B=102	**33CC66** R=051 G=204 B=102	**CC66CC** R=204 G=102 B=204
FF6600 R=255 G=102 B=000	**999900** R=153 G=153 B=000	**33CC00** R=051 G=204 B=000	**FF33FF** R=255 G=051 B=255	**9966FF** R=153 G=102 B=255	**3399FF** R=051 G=153 B=255	**CC6666** R=204 G=102 B=102	**669966** R=102 G=153 B=102
996699 R=153 G=102 B=153	**339999** R=051 G=153 B=153	**CC6600** R=204 G=102 B=000	**669900** R=102 G=153 B=000	**00CC00** R=000 G=204 B=000	**CC33FF** R=204 G=051 B=255	**6666FF** R=102 G=102 B=255	**0099FF** R=000 G=153 B=255
339933 R=051 G=153 B=051	**CC3399** R=204 G=051 B=153	**666699** R=102 G=102 B=153	**009999** R=000 G=153 B=153	**FF3300** R=255 G=051 B=000	**996600** R=153 G=102 B=000	**339900** R=051 G=153 B=000	**FF00FF** R=255 G=000 B=255
CC3333 R=204 G=051 B=051	**666633** R=102 G=102 B=051	**009933** R=000 G=153 B=051	**FF0099** R=255 G=000 B=153	**993399** R=153 G=051 B=153	**336699** R=051 G=102 B=153	**CC3300** R=204 G=051 B=000	**666600** R=102 G=102 B=000
6633CC R=102 G=051 B=204	**0066CC** R=000 G=102 B=204	**FF0033** R=255 G=000 B=051	**993333** R=153 G=051 B=051	**336633** R=051 G=102 B=051	**CC0099** R=204 G=000 B=153	**663399** R=102 G=051 B=153	**006699** R=000 G=102 B=153
9900CC R=153 G=000 B=204	**3333CC** R=051 G=051 B=204	**CC0033** R=204 G=000 B=051	**663333** R=102 G=051 B=051	**006633** R=000 G=102 B=051	**990099** R=153 G=000 B=153	**333399** R=051 G=051 B=153	**CC0000** R=204 G=000 B=000
990033 R=153 G=000 B=051	**333333** R=051 G=051 B=051	**660099** R=102 G=000 B=153	**003399** R=000 G=051 B=153	**990000** R=153 G=000 B=000	**333300** R=051 G=051 B=000	**3300FF** R=051 G=000 B=255	**660066** R=102 G=000 B=102
330066 R=051 G=000 B=102	**0000CC** R=000 G=000 B=204	**330033** R=051 G=000 B=051	**000099** R=000 G=000 B=153	**330000** R=051 G=000 B=000	**000066** R=000 G=000 B=102	**000033** R=000 G=000 B=051	**000000** R=000 G=000 B=000

FFFF00 R=255 G=255 B=000	**FFCCFF** R=255 G=204 B=255	**99FFFF** R=153 G=255 B=255	**CCFF00** R=204 G=255 B=102	**FFCCCC** R=255 G=204 B=204	**99FFCC** R=153 G=255 B=204	**CCFF33** R=204 G=255 B=051	**FFCC99** R=255 G=204 B=153
FFCC33 R=255 G=204 B=051	**99FF33** R=153 G=255 B=051	**CCCC99** R=204 G=204 B=153	**66FF99** R=102 G=255 B=153	**FFCC00** R=255 G=204 B=000	**99FF00** R=153 G=255 B=000	**FF99FF** R=255 G=153 B=255	**99CCFF** R=153 G=204 B=255
FF9999 R=255 G=153 B=153	**99CC99** R=153 G=204 B=153	**33FF99** R=051 G=255 B=153	**CCCC00** R=204 G=204 B=000	**66FF00** R=102 G=255 B=000	**CC99FF** R=204 G=153 B=255	**66CCFF** R=102 G=204 B=255	**00FFFF** R=000 G=255 R=255
33FF33 R=051 G=255 B=051	**CC9999** R=204 G=153 B=153	**66CC99** R=102 G=204 B=153	**00FF99** R=000 G=255 B=153	**FF9900** R=255 G=153 B=000	**99CC00** R=153 G=204 B=000	**33FF00** R=051 G=255 B=000	**FF66FF** R=255 G=102 B=255
CC9933 R=204 G=153 B=051	**66CC33** R=102 G=204 B=051	**00FF33** R=000 G=255 B=051	**FF6699** R=255 G=102 B=153	**999999** R=153 G=153 B=153	**33CC99** R=051 G=204 B=153	**CC9900** R=204 G=153 B=000	**66CC00** R=102 G=204 B=000
6699CC R=102 G=153 B=204	**00CCCC** R=000 G=204 B=204	**FF6633** R=255 G=102 B=051	**999933** R=153 G=153 B=051	**33CC33** R=051 G=204 B=051	**CC6699** R=204 G=102 B=153	**669999** R=102 G=153 B=153	**00CC99** R=000 G=204 B=153
00CC66 R=000 G=204 B=102	**FF33CC** R=255 G=051 B=204	**9966CC** R=153 G=102 B=204	**3399CC** R=051 G=153 B=204	**CC6633** R=204 G=102 B=051	**669933** R=102 G=153 B=051	**00CC33** R=000 G=204 B=051	**FF3399** R=255 G=051 B=153
FF3366 R=255 G=051 B=102	**996666** R=153 G=102 B=102	**339966** R=051 G=153 B=102	**CC33CC** R=204 G=051 B=204	**6666CC** R=102 G=102 B=204	**0099CC** R=000 G=153 B=204	**FF3333** R=255 G=051 B=051	**996633** R=153 G=102 B=051
9933FF R=153 G=051 B=255	**3366FF** R=051 G=102 B=255	**CC3366** R=204 G=051 B=102	**666666** R=102 G=102 B=102	**009966** R=000 G=153 B=102	**FF00CC** R=255 G=000 B=204	**9933CC** R=153 G=051 B=204	**3366CC** R=051 G=102 B=204
009900 R=000 G=153 B=000	**CC00FF** R=204 G=000 B=255	**6633FF** R=102 G=051 B=255	**0066FF** R=000 G=102 B=255	**FF0066** R=255 G=000 B=102	**993366** R=153 G=051 B=102	**336666** R=051 G=102 B=102	**CC00CC** R=204 G=000 B=204
FF0000 R=255 G=000 B=000	**993300** R=153 G=051 D=000	**336600** R=051 G=102 B=000	**9900FF** R=153 G=000 B=255	**3333FF** R=051 G=051 B=255	**CC0066** R=204 G=000 B=102	**663366** R=102 G=051 B=102	**006666** R=000 G=102 B=102
663300 R=102 G=051 B=000	**006600** R=000 G=102 B=000	**6600FF** R=102 G=000 B=255	**0033FF** R=000 G=051 B=255	**990066** R=153 G=000 B=102	**333366** R=051 G=051 B=102	**6600CC** R=102 G=000 B=204	**0033CC** R=000 G=051 B=204
003366 R=000 G=051 B=102	**3300CC** R=051 G=000 B=204	**660033** R=102 G=000 B=051	**003333** R=000 G=051 B=051	**330099** R=051 G=000 B=153	**660000** R=102 G=000 B=000	**003300** R=000 G=051 B=000	**0000FF** R=000 G=000 B=255

What Is a CLUT and What Do You Do with One?

CLUT is an acronym for **C**olor **L**ook**U**p **T**able. A color lookup table is the file that assigns the specific colors to any 8-bit or lower bit-depth computer image. CLUTs can be applied to images two different ways in Photoshop.

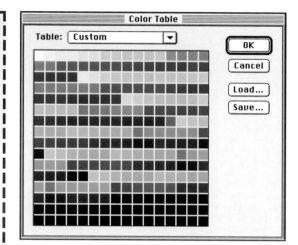

If your image is already in Index mode, go to the Mode menu and choose Color Table, which opens the Color Table dialog box. By clicking the Load or Save button, you can create and apply custom CLUTs to images. If you want to test it on the browser-safe CLUT, download the Photoshop file bclut2.aco from my ftp site ■ ftp://luna.bearnet.com/pub/lynda/.

If your image is not in 256 colors yet, choose Index Color under the Image, Mode menu to display the Indexed Color dialog box.

How to Load a Browser-Safe Swatch Palette into Photoshop

The same file, bclut2.aco (available from my ftp site ■ ftp://luna.bearnet.com /pub/lynda/), can be loaded into the Swatch Palette by following these steps:

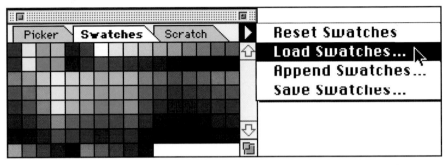

Step 1: Choose Windows, Palettes, Show Swatches. Using the upper right arrow, choose Load Swatches from the pull-down menu.

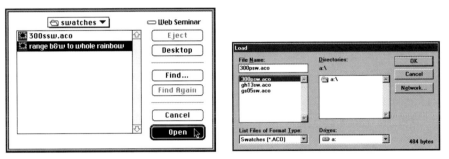

Step 2: Select any file with an .aco extension. The custom set appears as a new set in Photoshop's Swatch Palette.

How to Use the Browser-Safe Swatch Sets

Use browser-safe colors when you are creating custom artwork, illustrations, cartoons, and/or logos for web delivery.

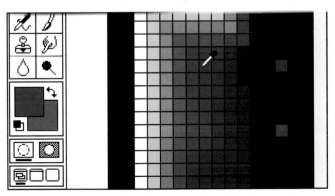

Use the Eyedropper Tool to click on a color within the swatch set. This causes the color to appear in the Foreground Color area of the Photoshop Toolbox. Choose any paint tool, and it will use the color you selected from the swatch set.

How to Load the Browser-Safe Palette into Paint Shop Pro

You can also download a CLUT for Paint Shop Pro from my ftp site. Go to
■ ftp://luna.bearnet.com/pub/lynda/ and select netscape.pal.

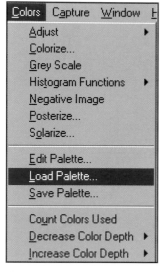

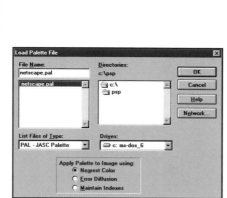

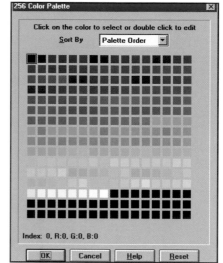

Step 1: Under the Color menu, select Load Palette.

Step 2: Select the file netscape.pal.

Step 3: The palette will appear. It can be sorted by Palette Order, Hue, and Luminance by changing the Sort By setting.

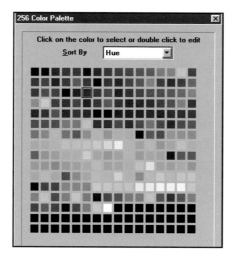

Step 4: Double-click on the foreground color in the Toolbar. In this example, it's turquoise.

Step 5: The color palette that you just loaded becomes active. Double-click on a browser-safe color you would like to paint with. Click OK, or press the Return key.

Step 6: The browser-safe color appears in the foreground color picker. Select any painting tool, and it will use this color.

How to Load a Browser-Safe Palette into Photo-Paint

Photo-Paint 6.0 supports the ability to load a custom palette into its color table. Download the file 216clut.cpl from my ftp site

■ ftp://luna.bearnet.com/pub/lynda/.

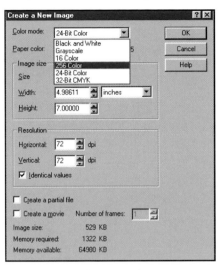

Step 1: Open a 256-color document or create a new 256-color document.

Step 2: Under the Image menu, select Color Table.

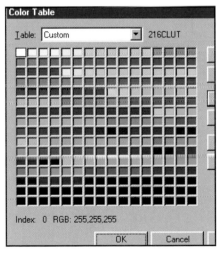

Step 3: The Color Table window will open, where you can load and save custom palettes. To load the browser-safe palette, choose the file named 216clut.cpl.

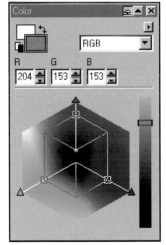

This places the colors in the palette bar at the bottom of the screen and inside the Color window. Photo-Paint has a really neat interface when you pick a color, showing you the color cube and where your selection is being pulled from.

How to Load a Browser-Safe Palette into Painter

Painter enables you to save its own version of swatch sets, called Color Sets. You'll find a browser-safe CLUT for Painter named clut, located inside the Painter folder on my ftp site ■ ftp://luna.bearnet.com/pub/lynda/. Drag this file into Painter's Color, Weaves, and Grad Folder on your hard drive before you begin.

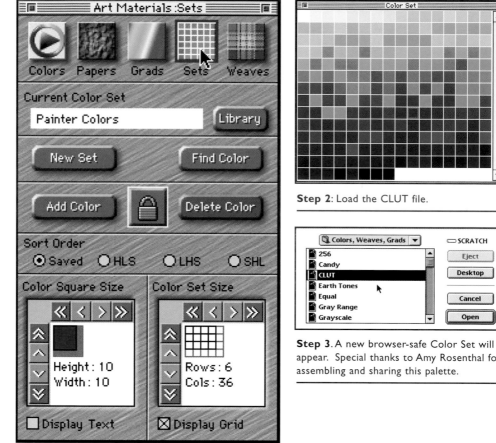

Step 2: Load the CLUT file.

Step 3. A new browser-safe Color Set will appear. Special thanks to Amy Rosenthal for assembling and sharing this palette.

Step 1: Open the Art Materials Palette, highlight Sets, and then click on the Library button.

How to Ensure Your Artwork Stays Browser Safe

If you work with browser-safe colors when you create artwork, you still have the important task of ensuring that those colors remain browser safe during the file format conversion process.

Unfortunately, files that are converted to JPEGs do not retain precise color information. The lossy compression method used throws away information, and unfortunately some of that information has to do with color control. Because of this, there is no way to accurately control color using the JPEG file format.

Chapter 3, "Web File Formats," emphasized that JPEGs are not good for graphics. Not only do they compress graphics poorly, but they introduce artifacts into images, which alters color.

What this means is that you cannot accurately match foreground GIFs to background JPEGs, or foreground JPEGs to background GIFs. Even if you prepare images in browser-safe colors, they will not remain browser safe when converted to JPEG, no matter what you do. Chapter 3 already established that JPEGs are not good for solid colors. This is one more reason not to use JPEGs when dealing with flat-style illustration, logos, cartoons, or any other graphical image that would not lend itself to having unwanted dithering.

Here's an example of a solid browser-safe color, with the hex readout of 51, 153, 153.

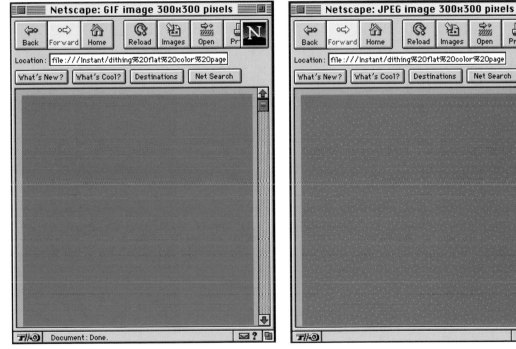

When saved as a GIF file, this color stayed browser safe.

When saved as a JPEG, the color shifted from 51, 153, 153 to 154, 154, 156. It is no longer browser safe, as evidenced by the dither when displayed in Netscape under 8-bit monitor conditions. Note: If you use the highest quality JPEGs, color inconsistency can be avoided, but you will suffer larger files sizes. Seems like if one thing doesn't get you, something else does!

Mixing Photos and Illustrations with Browser-Safe Colors

Next follows an example in which an image was created that used a photographic background, and browser-safe colors for the type.

Here's a 24-bit image that uses a photographic-style background with flat-style lettering. The letters were created using browser-safe colors.

This is an example of the image saved with an adaptive palette as a GIF.

This is an example of the image saved with the browser-safe palette as a GIF.

When viewed from Netscape in 256 colors, the adaptive palette version caused the lettering to dither.

When viewed from Netscape in 256 colors, the browser-safe palette version caused the lettering to look fine.

GIFs, on the other hand, do offer precise color control. If you create an image that is less than 256 colors by using browser-safe colors, Photoshop will let you save it with an Exact Palette. The only problem is when you create images that exceed 256 colors. In order to save these types of images as GIFs, some of the colors must be discarded.

This is when it's useful to use a Custom Palette setting in Photoshop and load the bclut2.aco file from my ftp site ■ ftp://luna.bearnet.com/pub/lynda/. You can't trust an adaptive palette to preserve browser-safe colors.

Removing Unwanted Browser-Safe Colors

At times you will apply the browser-safe palette to a file in order to ensure that the colors within honor the 216 color limit. The problem is that you might want to later reduce the file size even further than 216 by reducing the number of colors.

The following example shows you how to apply a browser-safe palette and then reduce the depth.

Bruce created an illustration in colors other than browser safe.

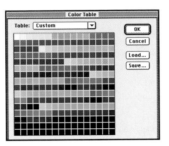

He converted them to browser-safe colors by choosing Image, Mode, Index Color and loading the 216 browser-safe CLUT file (called bclut2.aco) from my ftp site. Note: In Photoshop 4.0 there is a built-in 216 color table called Web that you can select from the Table menu.

The image is now browser safe, but it is also 216 colors! That's a few too many colors than are necessary for this image. By leaving the image this way, it would be 6.8k.

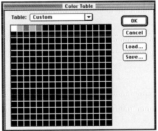

There's no reason for the image to include all 216 colors. By changing the image back to RGB mode and then back to Indexed Color mode, Bruce chose Exact Palette the second time. This image needs to be assigned only 7 colors! When saved as a GIF with only 7 colors, the image is 5.8k, a 14% file size savings that doesn't affect visual image quality in the least.

Vector-Based Software: Illustrator, CorelDraw, and FreeHand

The two most popular image file formats for the web, GIF and JPEG, are bitmap-based formats. Bitmap artwork is composed of pixel-based artwork, meaning that every pixel takes up memory and is accounted for in the file format. Vector file formats are based on code that instructs the computer to draw the artwork and furnishes information such as the radius of a circle or the length of a line.

Most vector-based drawing programs enable you to move objects around on the screen, align artwork with grids using precise control, and offer much more elaborate type layout treatments than their bitmap counterparts. For this reason, many artists work with vector-based software programs to begin with, and later export their artwork into bitmap programs where the images can be saved as GIFs and JPEGs. This section evaluates processes for creating browser-safe vector-based artwork in three popular vector-based imaging programs: Adobe Illustrator, Macromedia's FreeHand, and CorelDraw.

For more in-depth information about these three programs, check out these URLs:

- http://www.adobe.com/prodindex/illustrator/main.html
- http://www.macromedia.com/software/freehand/index.html
- http://www.corel.com/products/graphics&publishing/draw7/index.htm

Working with CorelDraw

At the time of this chapter, the current shipping version of CorelDraw supported the capability to output files in RGB. The only problem was that it didn't allow you to specify the palette. The next version, 7.0, promises to allow custom palette assignments. It's best to create artwork in CorelDraw that is close to the colors you want to use and then bring the artwork into Photo-Paint to convert the colors to the browser-safe CLUT. The Photo-Paint 216 palette is called 216clut.cpl. and is available from my ftp site ■ ftp://luna.bearnet.com/pub/lynda/.

Working with Adobe Illustrator

Adobe Illustrator is an extremely useful program that does many things better than Photoshop. Some of the reasons to use Illustrator are its better handling of text, and its ability to position artwork accurately and create object-oriented artwork that is resolution independent.

The only problem using Illustrator for web graphics is that it works only in CMYK. It's impossible to load the browser-safe color chart or swatch sets into a CMYK environment. Most artists who use Illustrator for browser-safe color artwork create the artwork in black-and-white in Illustrator and then import the artwork into Photoshop, where they use the browser-safe swatches.

Illustrator is a popular software program because of its superior type handling, accurate positioning features, and resolution-independent drawing tools. Unfortunately it works only in CMYK color, so it's impossible to author web color images directly. Create artwork in black-and-white first, and save it as a native Illustrator file.

When you open the file in Illustrator, you'll be prompted to rasterize the artwork. This converts the artwork from the Illustrator vector format to the Photoshop bitmap format.

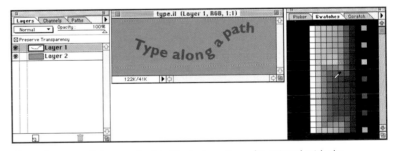

Once the artwork is rasterized in Photoshop, it can be painted with the browser-safe color swatches, just like artwork that originated in Photoshop.

■ note

GIFs in Illustrator

Version 6.0 of Adobe Illustrator will let you save GIF files and convert them to a specified palette, including one that contains the 216 browser-safe colors.

Working with FreeHand

Artists who use FreeHand for its excellent type-handling tools and vector-drawing tools are in luck! FreeHand allows users to work directly in RGB and will support the 216 palette.

FreeHand works with RGB percentages rather than specific RGB values. It's possible to mix browser-safe colors right in RGB within FreeHand. Just use these conversions:

%	RGB	HEX
100%	255	FF
80%	204	CC
60%	153	99
40%	102	66
20%	51	33
0%	0	0

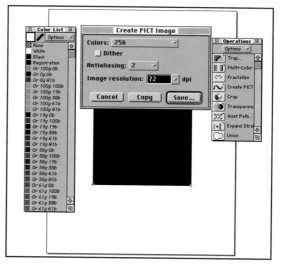

Thanks to the generosity and work of Amy Rosenthal, you can download a FreeHand CLUT, called clut.bcs, from my ftp site ■ ftp://luna.bearnet.com/pub/lynda/.

The following steps will enable you to access this palette in FreeHand:

Step 1: Open the Color List Palette. Under Options, choose Import. Locate the clut.bcs file.

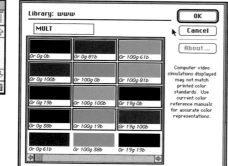

Step 2: Double-click on the file name clut.bcs and this window will appear. Hold the Shift key down to select all the color chips within the set, and click OK. A new Color List will appear with the browser-safe colors.

Step 3: If you use these colors to paint with, you can save them as a PICT file for conversion to GIF in another program. Highlight the artwork and select Create PICT in the Operations Palette. Make sure dither is left unchecked in the Save window. This ensures that the browser-safe color selection will be preserved.

Working with Color Picker-Based Applications

Certain programs don't let you mix colors by percentages or RGB values. A few such programs include Adobe PageMill, Claris Homepage, and BBEdit, which all rely on the Apple Color Picker to choose custom colors.

Pantone has come to the rescue with a Mac-only product called ColorWeb ■ http://www.pantone.com. Its Internet-safe color-picking system includes two components: a printed swatch set, and a System Color Picker that displays the 216 safe colors inside the Apple Color Picker dialog box.

The Pantone Internet Color Guide looks like a typical Pantone color swatch book, except that it has a web-color spin. It profiles and organizes the 216 browser-safe colors in chromatic order and lists the values for RGB, CMYK, Hexadecimal, and Hexachrome (their proprietary color format for picking printing ink colors).

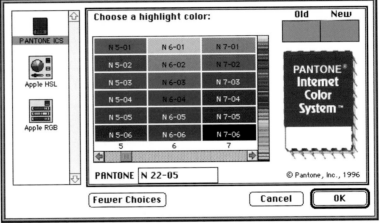

If you install Pantone's ColorWeb software, it will add another entry, called Pantone ICS, into the Apple Color Picker choices. Pantone ICS will enable you to pick from the 216 browser-safe colors.

■ warning

CMYK Is Not Browser Safe

It should be noted that there is no perfectly accurate way with which to convert CMYK values to RGB. The numbers that the Pantone Internet Color Guide cites for CMYK Internet-safe values are ballpark approximations and do not yield browser-safe colors when converted to RGB. The two color spaces—RGB and CMYK—do not share common colors consistently. Some RGB colors are outside of the CMYK color gamut, and there is nothing anyone can adjust for to create a reliable conversion method.

The ColorWeb software is an excellent (Mac-only) tool that offers the capability to pick browser-safe colors in programs that do not support RGB decimal or RGB percentage-based values. Pricing and order information is available at the Pantone web site.

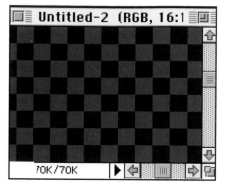

At a magnified view, you can see that Don made a pixel-by-pixel pattern of 3 different browser-safe colors.

At a 1:1 view, the pattern looks like a solid and creates an optical illusion of a color found outside the palette, even though it is still technically browser safe. We call these colors "hybrid" colors within this book.

What Are Hybrid-Safe Colors?

Hybrid-safe colors were invented by Don Barnett and Bruce Heavin when they were working on a prototype web site for DreamWorks Interactive SKG. Their work on that site was never used (although it can be viewed in my second book, *Deconstructing Web Graphics*). If you'd like to see hybrid-safe color in action, look at Don's personal site ■ http://www.cris.com/~Nekton/sources/net_barn.htm.

Don Barnett wanted to use colors that didn't shift or dither in the 256-color environments, but he didn't like any of the 216 colors he had to choose from. He came up with the idea of forming a pre-dithered pattern—on a pixel-by-pixel basis—of multiple browser-safe colors. This created an optical mixture of colors, tricking your eye into thinking it was a new color outside of the 216 limited palette.

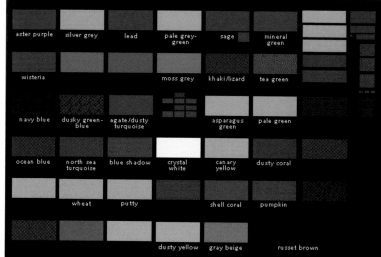

This page of hybrid colors was created by Don Barnett and can be found at ■ http://www.cris.com/~Nekton.

HTML for Hybrid Colors

Hybrid color files are a different story from swatches and GIFs. They must be loaded into the <BODY BACKGROUND> tag of an HTML document.

Here is the basic, most rudimentary HTML you would need in order to load hybrid color files into the background of your web pages:

```
<HTML>
<BODY BACKGROUND="hybrid.gif">
</BODY><HTML>
```

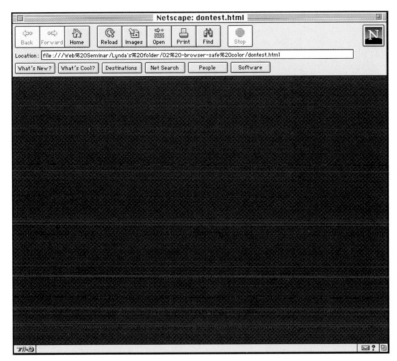

On the left is the source file for the HTML. It is repeated unlimited times, depending on how big the browser window is. To the right is the final screen in Netscape, filled repeatedly with the browser-safe seamless tile. For more information on seamless tiles, see Chapter 8, "Background Tiles."

Hybrid Color Background Tile Creation in Photoshop

By checkerboarding or alternating color pixels, you can mix new colors that create the illusion of colors found outside the 216 limit. There are tens of thousands of browser-safe color combinations possible. Hundreds of hybrid-safe color combinations are located on the CD-ROM of my third book, co-written with Bruce Heavin, called *Coloring Web Graphics*. We used the same technique described in this chapter to create those palette sets.

If you want to make your own hybrid color combinations, it is possible to make them in any paint program. Unfortunately, with the exception of Photoshop, most paint programs don't let you preview the results until you've created an HTML document and look at the results in a web browser.

The object is to make a repeating pattern of pixels. There are two types of patterns that work the best: horizontal lines and checkerboards. The reason for this is that at a 1:1 ratio, these patterns are the least obvious

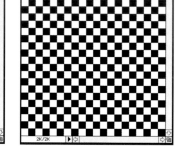
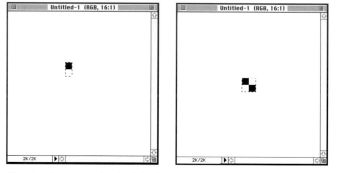

Close-up views of the two types of patterns used for hybrid tile creation.

Creating the pattern for the hybrid tiles can be created with two or four selected pixels, and then defining a pattern based on these selections.

In Photoshop, creating these patterns can be done with a few simple pixels.

Step 1: Using the smallest Pencil Tool, inside a magnified document, create the base art for the pattern tile. Use the Marquee Selection Tool to select either two or four pixels.

Step 2: Under the Edit menu, choose Define Pattern.

Step 3: Create a larger document. Make sure it's an even number of pixels so that the tile will repeat properly in a browser without any erroneous lines or glitches. Under the Edit menu, choose Fill. In the Fill dialog box, select Fill with Pattern.

Coloring Hybrid Tiles in Photoshop

Once you have black-and-white color tiles (or any other color combination), you can recolor the tile easily.

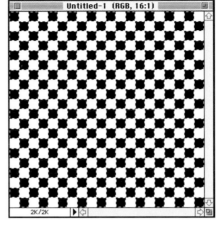

Step 1: Set the Magic Wand Tool to a tolerance of 1. This ensures that it will select only one color. Select a single pixel of either black or white. If the tile is two colors other than black and white, select one of those colors.

Step 2: Under the Select Menu, choose Select Similar. This selects everything in the image that has the same color you originally chose. It's now easy to fill this selection with any color you want, using the Edit, Fill menu. To fill the opposite color, choose Select, Inverse, which reverses the selection, and then proceed to fill with another color.

■ **tip**

Photoshop Shortcuts

A shortcut for filling a selection is to select a color so that it appears in your foreground color toolbar. On Macs, choose Option+Delete; on PCs use Alt+Delete.

A shortcut for filling with a pattern is Shift+Delete on the Mac and on the PC.

Custom Palettes for Shockwave Documents

Macromedia Director is an interactive authoring tool that has a huge installed user base. In the first quarter of 1996, Macromedia released Shockwave, a plug-in that makes Director projects viewable from the web. Since then, Director-based projects have become a common file type on the web.

It's possible to assign custom palettes to Director documents. Information on this process is available from: ■ http://www.macromedia.com/support/technotes/shockwave/developer/shocktechnotes/palettes/colpalette.html. Director (versions 5.0 and above) even ships with a 216 palette, which is located under the Xtras pull-down menu. The file is called Palette.cst on Macintoshes and PALETTES on Windows.

Director 5 ships with a series of palettes, including a broswer-safe palette called Netscape.

Previsualizing Tiles in Photoshop

Working with the Fill with Pattern feature in Photoshop, it's possible to previsualize tileable patterns before sending them to the web browser for the world to see. We'll work with Don Barnett's artwork—shmancy.gif, available from ■ ftp://luna.bearnet.com/pub/lynda/—to show how this is done.

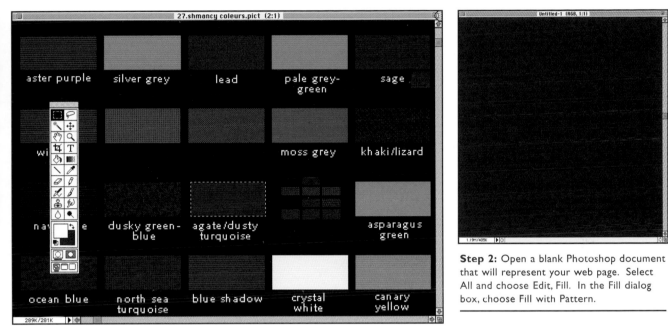

Step 1: Zoom into the file to accurately select the rectangular swatch. Under the File menu, choose Define Pattern.

Step 2: Open a blank Photoshop document that will represent your web page. Select All and choose Edit, Fill. In the Fill dialog box, choose Fill with Pattern.

Introduction

Getting Started in Web Design

Understanding the Web Environment

Web File Formats

Low-Bandwidth Graphics

Hexadecimal Color

Browser-Safe Color

Transparent Artwork

Background Tiles

Rules, Bullets and Buttons

Navigation-Based Graphics

Web-Based Typography

Scanning Techniques for the Web

Layout and Alignment Techniques

Animation

Sound

Interactivity

HTML for Visual Designers

Glossary

Design Resources Appendix

Index

7

Transparency

Transparency is another word for "mask," and masks are often used in computer graphics to make artwork appear in irregular shapes rather than as squares and rectangles. A computer image file by definition is automatically saved in a rectangle. In my humble opinion, way too much artwork on the web is in the shape of rectangles—buttons, pictures, splash screens, menu bars—ugh. Mastering transparency is the only escape!

There are two types of transparency—that which involves masking and that which involves trickery. The easiest way is the trick method, which is easy to explain. Let's say you have a circle and you want it to look like it's free-floating even though it must be inside a rectangular shape. Make the background behind the circle the same color as your web page. If you put the two together, there should be no obvious rectangular border. Seems simple? It is.

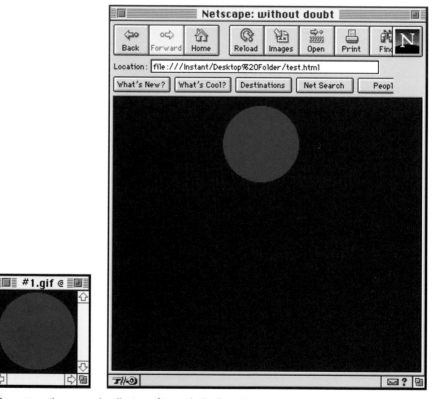

You can easily create the illusion of irregularly shaped images by making the foreground artwork include the same color as your target background on your web page.

But there's a snag. Making foreground and background images on the web that match takes an extra bit of education. This chapter teaches you how to set exact background colors (assuming your end viewer has not changed his or her preferences to override color choices) using two HTML-based techniques. One involves using hexadecimal code to set a specific background color, and the other requires setting up the HTML to use a solid pattern tile. Step-by-step examples will help you understand these two techniques and will show you how to make the irregularly shaped artwork lay on top of colored backgrounds.

It's kind of scary for web designers who count on background colors they pick to achieve the illusion of irregularly shaped images because end viewers can check "Always Use Mine," which will override the color choices you've specified! If you want to view sites as designers intended them to be seen, make sure "Let Document Override" is always checked instead.

Creating Background Color the Hexadecimal Way

This technique was covered in Chapter 5, "Hexadecimal Color," but will be reviewed here for the purposes of creating the illusion of transparency. This first example demonstrates how to include irregularly shaped artwork using the <BODY BGCOLOR> tag.

Step 1: Create artwork that is in an irregular shape. This technique works especially well on images that include anti-aliasing, soft edges, glows, or drop shadows.

Step 2: Use the eyedropper to find out the RGB values of the image. Hint: If you use the browser-safe color charts in Chapter 5, "Hexadecimal Color," you'll find the hex and RGB colors easily.

Step 3: Next, write the following HTML. This code tells the background to be light yellow, by using the hexadecimal code FFFFCC, and inserts the Jamie image on the same page:

```
<HTML>
<HEAD><CENTER><TITLE>Jamie
the flower girl</TITLE>
</HEAD>
<BODY BGCOLOR=#FFFFCC TEXT="993333"
LINK="FF9933" VLINK="FF9933">
</BODY> <P>
<CENTER><IMG SRC="jamie.gif">
</CENTER>
<P>
</HTML>
```

Step 4: Now you can view the final result. No transparency software was used to achieve this result!

Creating Background Color Using Solid Patterns

Another way to color the background of a web page is to use a solid color swatch within the background pattern tag, <BODY BACKGROUND>. This tag is more commonly used with artwork that has an image in it, such as a marble texture. The <BODY BACKGROUND> tag takes whatever art you tell it to use and repeats the artwork tiles so that they fill the entire web page.

For instructions on how to make image-filled types of pattern tiles, refer to Chapter 8, "Background Tiles." We are going to use the same HTML technique that Chapter 8 describes in detail, but our source image for the pattern tile is going to be made out of a solid color instead. As it is repeated over the page, this tile will produce a solid background, identical in appearance to what was demonstrated using the hexadecimal method previously mentioned.

You can actually use both the BGCOLOR and BACKGROUND attributes inside the same BODY tag, which ensures the safest results with this technique. Here's an example of how the code would look:

```
<HTML>
<HEAD><CENTER>
<TITLE>Jamie the flower girl</TITLE>
</HEAD>
<BODY BGCOLOR=#FFFFCC BACKGROUND="yellow.gif"
TEXT="993333" LINK="FF9933" VLINK="FF9933">
</BODY>
<P>
<CENTER><IMG SRC="jamie.gif">
</CENTER>
<P>
</HTML>
```

An advantage to using the <BODY BACKGROUND> method is the background color will not be changed in the event your end users have altered their preferences. Another effect you can create is to set up a background color that is a transition effect that precedes a solid color background tile. For example, some people set their hex background to load first with white and then change to black once the solid background tile is loaded for an eye-catching flashing effect.

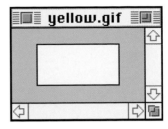

Here's an example of a Photoshop file that is filled with the same solid yellow used in the last example. If this image were used as the <BODY BACKGROUND> file, the HTML could not be overridden if users changed the background color defaults in their browser preferences.

■ **tip**

JPEG or GIF?

It doesn't matter whether your images or tiled background patterns are saved in JPEG or GIF file format. Those decisions should be based on the principles described in Chapter 4, "Low-Bandwidth Graphics." One thing to caution you about: If you are going to use a solid background image and want it to match your solid foreground image, you must use a JPEG background and JPEG foreground, or a GIF background and a GIF foreground. In other words, the file type must match or you will get uncontrollable color shifts between the elements.

Transparent GIFs

If transparent GIFs (TGIFs) are an unfamiliar term to you, don't worry. I know of no other application for transparent GIFs other than the web, so they're relatively new to everyone. Transparent GIFs are used to create the illusion of irregularly shaped computer files by assigning one color in a graphic to be invisible. This process is also called masking.

Transparent GIFs, technically referred to as GIF89a, support masking. Not all imaging programs let you save graphics in the GIF89a format, so details on how to use the various helper applications, online services, and programs that support it are included later in this chapter, in the section "Transparent GIF Software."

When working with transparent GIFs, there are two things to keep in mind: first, how to make art properly for one color masking transparency and second, how to use the programs that let you save the artwork in this file format.

■ tip

HTML for Transparent GIFs

The HTML for transparent GIFs is identical to the HTML for any other type of GIF or JPEG. The <IMG SRC> tag is all that's needed.

For an unlinked transparent GIF graphic, the HTML would look like this:
<IMG SRC="transgif.gif">

For a linked transparent GIF graphic, the HTML would look like this:
<A HREF="http://www.destination_ domain_name.com">
<IMG SRC="transgif.gif"></A>

More information on HTML and previewing web files from your hard drive can be found in Chapter 17, "HTML for Visual Designers."

When to Use Transparent Artwork

I recommend using Transparent GIFs only on web pages that have pattern backgrounds (see Chapter 8, "Background Tiles") because creating the illusion of transparency is very simple using solid colors. Establishing transparency in a GIF adds a lot of extra steps in production, so there's no reason to do that when there's an easier way.

The reason I recommend transparency with pattern background tiles is because you can't reliably match a foreground image to a background tile in standard HTML. (This problem is described in more detail in Chapter 13, "Layout and Alignment Techniques.") If you want to put irregularly shaped artwork over patterned backgrounds, you'll have to use transparency.

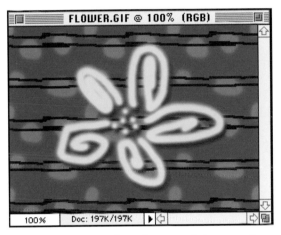

This image was created as a foreground element and was precomposed against a patterned background while in Photoshop.

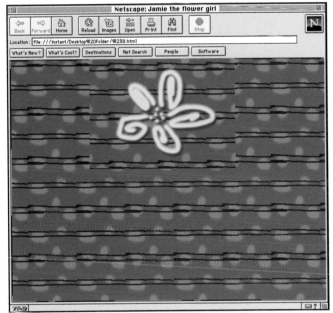

The same image is laid on top of the tiled background. Notice that it is misaligned. You can try to align a foreground image with a complex pattern to the identical background pattern, but they won't line up. And to make matters worse—the alignment is different on a Mac and PC!

Making Clean Transparent Artwork

The key to producing effective transparent GIFs is ensuring your art is produced correctly. We need to begin by first going through a short primer on aliased versus anti-aliased artwork. *Anti-aliasing* is the process of blending around the edges of a graphic to disguise the jaggy square nature of the artwork.

Many of the transparent GIFs I see on the web have ugly residual matte lines, usually in the form of white or black edges. These matte lines can be traced back to the way in which the image was anti-aliased.

On the web, anti-aliasing is not always the best approach. Creating clean transparent GIFs is one of those exceptions where aliased graphics create the least amount of problems.

The anti-aliased blended edge is precisely what causes fringing problems once the graphic is converted to transparent GIFs. Because transparent GIFs drop only one color out of your image, you will see all the remaining colors along the blended edge of anti-aliased artwork, even when what you really want is for all of them to disappear. There is no way to avoid this unless GIF file formats supported masking for more than one color. (Photoshop and PICT file formats, for example, let you mask with 256 levels of transparency, whereas transparent GIFs let you mask with only one.)

Because working with aliased graphics is more foreign to experienced computer designers than not, I've devoted a few sections of this chapter to offer instruction in Photoshop for working with aliased tools.

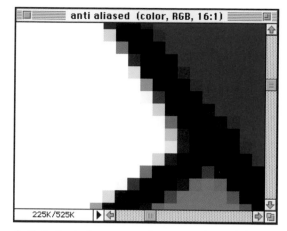

Anti-aliasing is the process where one color and shape blends to another, in order to hide the jagged square pixel nature of computer graphics.

Here is an example of a transparent image with an unwanted white halo. This is because the artwork was created anti-aliased against white. Most well-trained digital artists would never think to work without anti-aliasing. We've been conditioned to make everything look as smooth and perfect as possible. Anti-aliasing was designed to hide the fact that computer graphics are made of square, jagged pixels. Computer screens are a pixel-based medium, so our compulsion to hide this fact in print and other media is not always appropriate for computer screen-based design, such as the web and other multimedia delivery systems like CD-ROMs. Low-resolution web graphics are much more forgiving with aliasing than their print graphic counterparts.

Photoshop Tips for Creating Aliased Images

The following sections demonstrate how to create artwork for transparent GIFs with aliased edges. Photoshop was designed as a sophisticated graphics editing program, and working there with aliased tools is foreign to most designers. Understanding which types of tools are appropriate for the job and how to configure them so that they don't anti-alias is key to mastering clean-edged TGIFs. There are a few different types of graphics we'll study: illustrations, scanned illustrations, and scanned photographs.

Creating Illustration-Based Artwork for Transparent GIFs

If you're an illustrator, you're used to creating artwork from scratch. It's best to start with the correct tools for the job—and they'll most likely be tools you don't normally use. Most paint programs default to working with anti-aliased brushes and fill tools. To create aliased graphics in Photoshop, you want to use the Pencil Tool and the Paint Bucket Tool to draw and fill shapes with.

These are the aliased graphic tools: the Lasso, the Magic Wand, the Paint Bucket, and the Pencil.

While creating your illustrations, be sure to fill the areas that are going to go transparent with a different color. Here's an example of how my logo was prepared properly for converting to a transparent GIF. I used an aliased pencil tool with my pressure sensitive tablet to achieve the handwritten font.

It looks like my logo is set against black, but the black is there only so it would be easy to identify when I made this graphic transparent.

Once my logo was made transparent, and put against a background, no one ever has to know it was created against black. It has no residual matte line around it because the artwork is aliased.

The techniques reviewed here, using aliased bucket and pencil tools, work great if you're creating flat illustration artwork directly in the computer. But what if you're not? The next section addresses other techniques for converting graphics to TGIF.

Turning Prescanned Illustrations into Aliased Art

Sometimes, the source material supplied for web page art has already been scanned and is already anti-aliased. This might be the case with a company logo or something you're bringing in from a clip art book. When working with existing anti-aliased artwork, you can convert the image to being aliased by changing the mode from RGB to Bitmap.

Go to the top menu bar to Image, Mode, Bitmap and set the Threshold setting to 50%. Changing to this mode strips away all the anti-aliasing from the image. You can convert back to RGB mode and access colors in the document, but the lines will remain aliased. There's an example of this Photoshop technique on my Windows 95-equipped PC using Yeryeoung Park's wonderful original sketches for the HotHotHot site ■ http://www.hothothot.com—check out the great use of aliased artwork on the site.

Here are the steps used to convert a scanned image to an anti-aliased image:

Step 1: Open the original scan.

Step 2: Go to Image, Mode and change it to Bitmap. By using the Threshold 50% setting, it equalizes all the grays and makes a black-and-white aliased image.

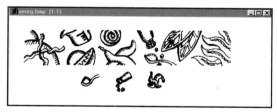

Step 3: Yeryeoung used the pencil and paint bucket tools to create aliased fills for the artwork.

Here are the final (aliased) results at HotHotHot ■ http://www.hothothot.com.

Photographic Source Art for Transparent GIFs

Another common situation is where you have photographs or existing color illustrations with anti-aliased edges that you want to change to transparent GIFs. You don't have to change the interior of your graphic to be aliased, just the edges. For best results you can work large and use the Magnifying Glass Tool to zoom way in to accurately erase the edge using the aliased "block" Eraser Tool. You also can use the aliased Lasso Tool to select the parts you want to delete. Just make sure the anti-aliased box is unchecked! The edge will look terrible in Photoshop, but will look much better on the web!

Here's a step-by-step demonstration of how I would make my daughter's baby head float freely on a web page:

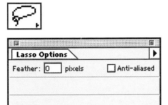

Step 1: Scan the photo. Remember to use the correct scale for the web—72 dpi, RGB color, and small dimensions! Jamie's photo was scanned in at 72 dpi, 3x4 inches.

Step 2: Select the Lasso Tool, with the Anti-aliased box unchecked in the Options.

Step 3: I traced around the shape of her head using the Lasso Tool. Next, I inverted the selection by going to the menu item Select, Inverse. Choosing Edit, Fill, Normal, Foreground, 100%, I filled the outside with white. This image, by itself, against white looks jaggy and horrible around the edges.

Step 4: Next the image is saved as a transparent GIF and put on a web page (see the next two sections for instructions on this). Notice how the image looks perfectly acceptable once laid over a pattern background? Also notice the lack of matte lines.

The preceding examples show the correct method to prepare photo-based source material properly for TGIFs. The following examples show what can (and does!) go wrong with transparent GIFs. As you look at these examples, you should understand why they didn't work successfully and know how to prepare artwork so that this doesn't happen. The next section will discuss techniques to deal with glows, soft-edges, and drop shadows using GIF transparency.

This is what would have happened had I not chosen to cut Jamie out with aliased tools.

If you really want to get down and ugly, make a transparent GIF out of artwork that has a glow around it!

How to Deal with Glows, Soft Edges, and Drop Shadows with GIF Transparency

Because of the problems anti-aliasing introduces, artwork with glows, soft-edges, and drop shadows can look awful as transparent GIFs. One popular solution is to build artwork against the same color background that it will be seen against in the web browser. The artwork will look terrible when you make it, but it will look fine once laid against the final background in a web browser.

aliased

anti-aliased

with shadow

with glow

This figure shows four types of edges for artwork: aliased, anti-aliased, with a shadow, and with a glow.

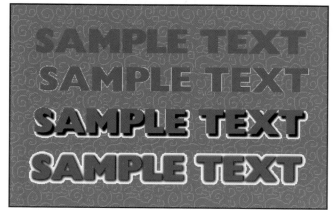

When the different examples of edges are made into transparent GIFs using one-color transparency, notice how every example except the aliased top version picked up the background color they were made against. That's because the images with soft edges picked up parts of the white background color they were created against. This created an unsightly problem, which is commonly called a halo, fringe, or matte line.

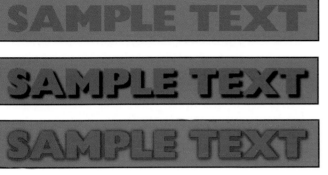

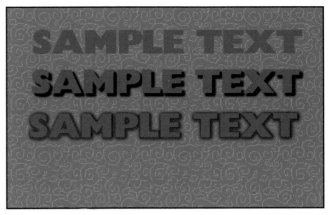

Here's an example of the identical artwork with anti-aliased, shadowed, and blurry edges against the same color background of the target web page.

The end result looks quite acceptable now. Look ma, no matte lines!

When the transparency is set, the files look pretty terrible. They won't look good again until they are laid over a green background. If prepared this way, you will correct their predisposition to favor any other color, which will eliminate unwanted fringes, halos, and matte lines.

■ tip

Transparent GIF URLs

Here are some useful URLs to track down transparency tricks and tips:

Online Transparent GIF creation
■ http://www.vrl.com/Imaging/invis.html

Thomas Boutell's WWW FAQ on Transparency
■ http://sunsite.unc.edu/boutell/faq/tinter.htm

Chipp Walter's Excellent GIF transparency tutorial
■ http://204.96.160.175/IGOR/photosho.htm

Transparent GIF Software

There are lots of popular software packages that support GIF transparency. It's impossible to cover all of them in this book, but I've included instruction for a few different packages that support TGIFs.

Cross-Platform

Adobe Photoshop GIF89a Export Plug-In

Current versions of Photoshop ship with a GIF89a plug-in that supports transparency and interlacing. This plug-in works on Mac and Windows versions of Photoshop. This plug-in is preinstalled in current versions of Photoshop. If you don't have it, you can download the plug-in from these locations:

■ Mac: http://www.adobe.com/supportservice/custsupport/LIBRARY/2eb2.htm
■ Windows: http://www.adobe.com/supportservice/custsupport/LIBRARY/2f22.htm

Here's a step-by-step tour through Photoshop's GIF89a plug-in features:

Step 1: Place the GIF89a Export plug-in in your plug-in folder. Make sure that Photoshop is closed. The plug-in will not be effective until the next time Photoshop is opened. Note that current versions of Photoshop ship with this plug-in, so you do not need to install it yourself.

Step 2: Open the document you wish to make transparent.

Step 3: Convert the file from RGB to Index Color. Go to Mode, select Index, and leave it at its defaults. Or you can practice some of the principles described in Chapter 4, "Low-Bandwidth Graphics." Test the image in 100 colors, or 50, or whatever works. You can decide how low to take the bit depth, and the lower you take it, the smaller the file size will be.

Step 4: After the image is indexed, make a selection and choose Save Selection. The selection will be saved into channel 2.

Step 5: Under File, select Export, GIF89a. The transparent color can be based on Selected Colors or #2. By saving a selection in step 4, I created a channel in the document, called channel #2. If I choose to use the #2 mask, I do not have to base the selection on color at all.

Step 6: The selection based on channel #2 is previewed, allowing me to check it before I click OK to save the file.

This example shows transparency based on a selection, not a color.

This plug-in worked great for a photo. Let's try a selection based on color for the next example.

Step 1: Open an image and convert it to Index Color mode.

Step 2: Under File, select Export, GIF89a. This time we'll base the selection on Selected Colors. Using the Eyedropper Tool, click on the areas you want transparent. The preview shows you what you need to see. When finished selecting with the Eyedropper, click OK to save.

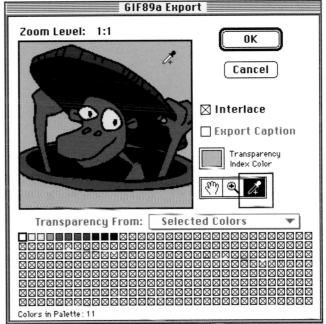

If you have not defined a selection, you can select the color you wish to set as the mask by following the preceding instructions. This example shows transparency being set based on color.

Fractal Design Painter 4.0

Painter 4.0 offers great support for transparent GIFs. You can save an image as a GIF either by selecting the background color or by using one of its floater selections as a defined region for the mask. Open a document (any file format that Painter supports) and convert it to Index Color in the saving process.

Painter is a complicated program to use, and I unfortunately lack the space in this chapter to walk new users through its interface. For those readers who already use Painter, here are the steps for working with its transparent GIF features:

Step 1: Using Painter's Type Frisket Tool and converting it to a Floater, you can identify a masking region for the transparent GIF. **Step 2:** In the save as GIF Options, choose to Output Transparency.

Step 3: Output transparency does a great job of making a selection based on shape rather than a background color. Here's an example of a preview of the image with the type mask in effect.

Transparency Resources

For those of you who like to work while you're online, transparent GIFs can be made directly on the web! There are several sites that will convert a regular GIF into a transparent GIF while you wait. These sites look for an URL that includes a GIF image and will convert the image to the GIF89a format. Some sites let you choose black, white, or an RGB value to go transparent, and others let you click on the image to choose the spot.

To use the online transparency service, you'd have to give the URL of your image, not the URL of an HTML document. A correct URL would look like this:

■ http://www.myprovider.com/mysitename/imagetoconvert.gif

Remember, your artwork must be loaded on a server and be a valid URL. For instructions on how to load your art to a server, check out Chapter 17, "HTML for Visual Designers."

Here's an example of what online transparency software can do.

■ **tip**

URLs for Online Transparency:

Fefe's Transparency Apparatus
■ http://www.inf.fu-berlin.de/~leitner/trans/english.html

Caltech Logo Tutorial
■ http://www.caltech.edu/www/logoinfo.html

TransWeb
■ http://www.mit.edu:8001/transweb.html

GIF Transparentifier
■ http://olympia.ucr.edu/~davec/trans.html

Macintosh

Transparency

A popular Mac freeware application is Transparency, by Aaron Giles. It can be downloaded from ■ ftp.uwtc.washington.edu/pub/Mac/Graphics/. It lacks bells and whistles, but hey, the price is right!

To use, launch the program and open a GIF file. The file must already be saved as GIF to work. Hold your mouse down on the color you want to make into the invisible background and save the file.

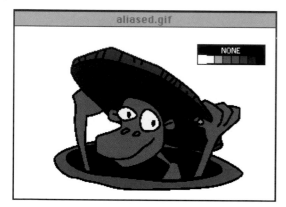

Here's an example of a picture being edited with the freeware application Transparency.

DeBabelizer

Many multimedia developers already sing the praises of De-Babelizer, and its web support is no less impressive. One of the best features about this program is its capability to batch process. (Batch processing is when multiple files are processed at one time.) This capability allows you to take a folder of images and convert them all at once to a specific palette or make them all go transparent as GIF89a's. It's a must-have tool for web designers doing volume image processing (what might be required when putting a mail-order catalog online, for example). Batch processing a series of GIFs in DeBabelizer is no easy task due to its unusual interface. Here's what you do:

Step 1: Put all the images you want to convert to transparent GIFs in one folder. If the images need to be converted to 8-bit first, include steps 3 and 4. Otherwise, skip and progress from step 2 to step 5.

Step 2: Choose the menu commands File, Batch, Save. Click on the New button in the Batch Save dialog box that appears. Locate the folder you want to batch, click on it, and press the Append button. Then click Save. You now have the folder saved as a batch that can be group processed.

Step 3: Choose File, Batch, Super Palette and click Do It. The program will make a custom, adaptive palette (for more information on adaptive palettes, see Chapter 3, "Web File Formats") of all the images in your folder.

Step 4: Choose File, Batch Save, Do Script, Dither to Super Palette. This converts all the images in your folder to the adaptive palette.

Step 5: Next, open one of the images from your folder that's been converted to this new palette and go to the Palette menu.

Step 6: Choose Options, Dithering and Background Color. Check the Color Index radio button in the Dither Options & Background Color dialog box that appears. Use the Eyedropper Tool to select the color you want to make transparent in your image.

Step 7: Next, go to the File menu and Choose Batch, Save. Once this dialog is open, choose GIF89a as the file format. When you click the Do It button, it will convert the entire folder of images to transparent GIFs, dropping out the color you identified as the background color.

DeBabelizer lets you set up scripts, such as Dither to Super Palette (create a common CLUT from a series of images). Its interface is crowded and awkward, but you have to love what it does! A Windows version should be out by the time this book is published.

DeBabelizer offers a lot of different dithering and file reduction methods.

Windows

LView

Download LView from: ■ ftp://gatekeeper.dec.com/pub/ micro/msdos/win3/desktop/lview31.zip. It's shareware, costs $30 to register, and is written by Leonardo Haddad Loureiro (mmedia@world.std.com). To use, open your image, and under Options, choose Background color. The 256-color palette of that image opens. Choose white, black, or a specific color for your transparent selection. After you've made a selection, save as a GIF89a and you are done. You can also select Interlace from the Options menu if you want to interlace the file.

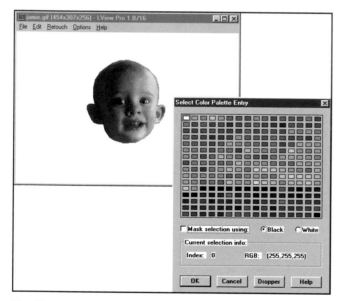

The LView interface with the color table for this image open to select a transparent color from.

GIF Construction Set

The GIF Construction Set—available from ■ ftp://ftp north.net/pub/alchemy—also makes transparent GIFs. If you open your GIF file, a script window appears. Under the Insert menu, select Control. This adds a Control command to the script window. Double-click on the word Control in the script window and a new window appears. When the transparent colour (French Canadian company and spelling) check box is marked, you can click on the colored square and the 256 palette of the image opens. From there, select the correct color, save as a GIF89a, and fait accompli!

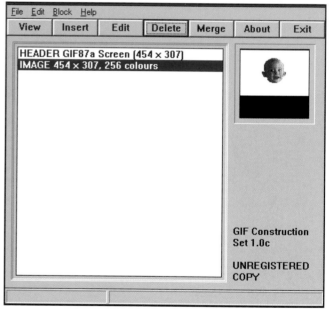

A sample of the GIF Construction Set interface. By adding a Control comment, the color table of this image will appear to allow you to select a color.

Paint Shop Pro

The very popular and reasonably priced Paint Shop Pro (version 3.11 and above) enables you to save TGIFs. You can download version 3.11 from ■ ftp://ftp.winternet.com/users/jasc/psp311.zip. The software can be used free for 30 days and then must be regis-tered for $69.00. It does much more than saving GIFs—this is a full-bodied paint program that's offered for a fraction of the price of Photoshop (with not as much power, of course).

Open the file and determine whether you want white, black, or another color to be transparent. If you want another color, go to the Colors menu and select Edit Palette. Click around to locate the number (1–255) of the color. Next, go to Edit, do a Save As, and choose GIF-CompuServe as the file format. From the submenu that appears, choose either an interlaced or noninterlaced 89a. To set the color, click on the Options button, select the Set the Transparency Value to radio button, and enter the numeric value you found when you were in the Edit Palette mode. Where's the Eyedropper Tool when you need it?

The GIF Transparency Options dialog box requests numeric values, instead of allowing designers to pick color from a palette or use an eyedropper.

8-Bit Transparency with PNG

As you've just seen, GIF transparency is limited and crude. There are workarounds, but who wants workarounds? If you want real transparency, you might want to work with the PNG file format instead of GIF for transparency.

PNG files can be saved with 8-bit masking channels, otherwise known as alpha channels. This next exercise will walk you through making a simple alpha channel in Photoshop.

Step-by-Step Alpha Channel Creation for PNG

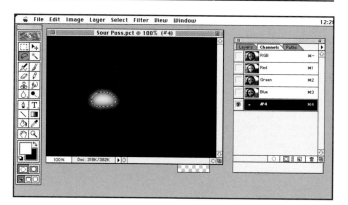

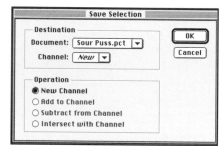

Step 1: In this example, I selected Jamie's eye using the Lasso Tool with a 20-pixel feather. Once the selection was completed, I chose Save Selection under the Select menu.

Step 2: The Save Selection dialog will appear. Click OK.

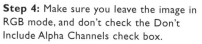

Step 3: If you switch the Layers Palette over to Channels and click on #4, you should see the 8-bit masking channel fill the screen. This mask will be used by the file format to cut away everything that is black. Everything that is white will be preserved, and the gray areas caused by the feather will create partial transparency.

Step 4: Make sure you leave the image in RGB mode, and don't check the Don't Include Alpha Channels check box.

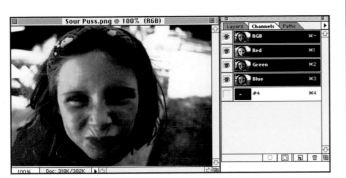

Step 5: Open the PNG file and check the Channels Palette to see if it worked. It did!

Here's my finished home page with Jamie's menacing eye. This is the type of transparency possible with PNG. Because PNG required a plug-in when I wrote this chapter and was not supported by any browser, I had to use the <EMBED> tag to insert this into my HTML. In order to view this page, I used the plug-in from ■ http://iagu. on.net/jsam/png-plugin/.

PNG File Size

In spite of all the hype surrounding PNG, its file sizes are often bigger than JPEG or GIF. Be sure to check out the Image Compression Chart in Chapter 4, "Low-Bandwidth Graphics."

The PNG image with the alpha channel is 342k. Without it the image would be 308k. These images are too big by web standards. The only time PNG compared favorably to GIF or JPEG was when it was saved in 8-bit mode or lower bit depths. In order to save the alpha channel, the file has to be saved in 24-bit, so those file savings are not present when transparency is used.

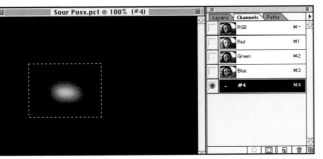

Here is the 342k PNG image with the alpha channel—it's a bit too large by web standards.

One solution to lower the file size would be to crop the image. I looked at the alpha channel while cropping, to make sure it was cropped properly.

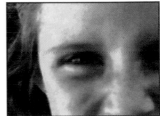

Here's the final, cropped PNG, with alpha channel, weighing in at 42.6k.

Introduction

Getting Started in Web Design

Understanding the Web Environment

Web File Formats

Low-Bandwidth Graphics

Hexadecimal Color

Browser-Safe Color

Transparent Artwork

Background Tiles

Rules, Bullets and Buttons

Navigation-Based Graphics

Web-Based Typography

Scanning Techniques for the Web

Layout and Alignment Techniques

Animation

Sound

Interactivity

HTML for Visual Designers

Glossary

Design Resources Appendix

Index

8

BROWSER SAFE COLOR
33FF

Web 224 typography

Photoshop

INDEX
<STRONG>
Width="500"
.Gif
.Jpg
.Png

TRANSPARENCY

Height="600"

</A>

10.2

Imaging Methods
Extending HTML
Web file formats
bgcolor="FFFFCC"

link="cyan"

  BODY

<Img src="

Image compression
Limited palettes
IMAGE OPTIMIZATION
216 Colors

GRAPHY

Animation, sound and

LYNDA.COM

www.Design

Introduction
Getting Started in Web Design
Understanding the Web Environment
Web File Formats
Low-Bandwidth Graphics
Hexadecimal Color
Browser-Safe Color
Transparent Artwork
Background Tiles
Rules, Bullets and Buttons
Navigation-Based Graphics
Web-Based Typography
Scanning Techniques for the Web
Layout and Alignment Techniques
Animation
Sound
Interactivity
HTML for Visual Designers
Glossary
Design Resources Appendix
Index

Font

9

BROWSER

Web 10 224 typography

Photoshop

INDEX

Width = "500"

STRONG

.gif
.jpg
.png

Image compression
Limited palettes
IMAGE OPTIMIZATION
216 Colors

TRANSPARENCY

Height = "600"

</A>

1024

<center

Imaging techniques
Extending HTML
Web file formats
bgcolor="FFFECC"

Animation, sound and

alink="cyan"

LYNDA.COM

<center> BODY

www.Design

Introduction

Getting Started in Web Design

Understanding the Web Environment

Web File Formats

Low-Bandwidth Graphics

Hexadecimal Color

Browser-Safe Color

Transparent Artwork

Background Tiles

Rules, Bullets and Buttons

Navigation-Based Graphics

Web-Based Typography

Scanning Techniques for the Web

Layout and Alignment Techniques

Animation

Sound

Interactivity

HTML for Visual Designers

Glossary

Design Resources Appendix

Index

10

<H1>
<P>
Web
typography
<A>
<STRONG>
.Gif
.Jpg
Png
<img src="
Image compressio
Limited palettes
IMAGE OPTIMIZATION
216 Colors
Width ="500
Height ="600
</A>
10.2
<center>
Extending HTML
Web file formats
bgcolor="FFFFCC
alink="cyan"
Animation, Sound and
LYNDA.COM
</center>
BODY
33
www Design

Navigation Issues in Web Design

Navigation issues are not present in print design; everyone knows how to navigate through a book or magazine—just turn the pages. But with the web's ability to link graphics and text comes the need to understand a bit about navigation. How does one offer visual design direction to help guide others to information?

Some of the navigation issues that this chapter covers are

- Storyboarding
- Programming text and images to link
- Turning off borders of linked images
- Creating navigation bars
- Creating imagemaps
- Creating frames

Creating links for text and images involves HTML. Creating images that look like navigational buttons involves design. Creating single images that link to multiple URLs involves design and HTML. Web navigation brings this all together as one artform that combines design, programming, and organizational skills.

Storyboarding

Everybody creates storyboards differently in this business. Some people scribble their site's navigational structure on napkins whereas others make beautiful presentation boards that sell their design as well as their site's organizational structure. As much as you'd probably like to be told exactly how to make the best storyboard, you won't find me being dogmatic about any one way to do so.

The thing to keep in mind is that sites often grow. They are fluid. They evolve. This is not true of print or multimedia. The web is its own medium when it comes to planning, storyboarding, navigating, and designing.

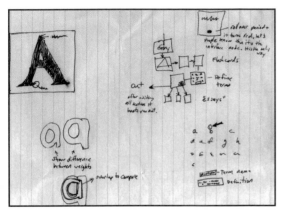

Steven Turbek's storyboard helped him work out the logistics of the Shockwave interface he designed for typoGRAPHIC ■ http://www.razorfish.com/typo.

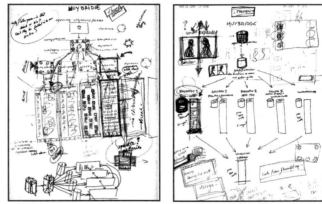

Storyboards for the Muybridge site at Discovery Channel Online ■ http://www.discovery.com helped the site designers figure out their navigational structure prior to working on the computer.

■ **tip**

Storyboarding Your Site

An excellent resource for flowcharting and brainstorming the content of your site is

Web Concept & Design
Publisher: New Riders
Author: Crystal Waters
Retail Price: $39.95 ■ ISBN: 1-56205-648-4

Hot Images and Text

The meaning of hot for the web is no longer restricted to what is new or popular. When an image is hot, it means that it will send the viewer somewhere else after it's clicked. A hot button can link a viewer to another image, page, site, or external file, depending on how the link is programmed.

A single image can be programmed to be hot if it has been placed on the page by using HTML tags that link to an outside URL. There are two types of hot images: those single images that are linked to one outside URL and single images that have been divided into regions by using imagemap tags to direct viewers to multiple URLs.

If an image is static (has no linking HTML tags), it's called an *inline* graphic. Inline means it's embedded as part of your page and requires no outside helper application to view. **When a graphic is hot, it is sometimes referred to as a map, link, hyperlink, or interactive button. All these words describe the same thing; clicking on such an image will transport you elsewhere.**

This chapter reviews the two types of hot images: linked graphics and imagemap-based graphics. You'll learn how to do both as well as how and when to use one type of hot graphic over another.

Identifying Hot Images

Images that are hot have certain visual markings that are different from static inline graphics. Typically, if a border appears around an image, it indicates that it is a linked graphic. This border defaults to a blue color in most browsers. If your audience has had any experience on the web, they will be trained that any time they encounter a border around an image, it means it can be clicked on as an active link.

There are some instances where a hot image will not have a telltale border around it. If you'd prefer that your hot graphic be without one, this chapter will describe how to program the border to be "invisible." **The only way a viewer will know to click on these types of borderless hot images is if your graphic invites them to bring their cursor closer.** In most browsers, after the viewer's cursor passes over a hot spot, it changes from a pointer to the hand cursor shown. This indicates, just like the border symbol, that an image is a clickable button instead of a static inline graphic.

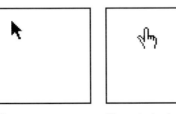

The arrow cursor signifies that there is no link.

The pointing hand cursor indicates that the text or image is linked (hot).

Creating Linked Images and Text

The easiest way to create a link that connects one graphic to another web source is to use the <A HREF></A> tag with an <IMG SRC> tag nested inside. This combination of tags automatically defaults to putting a border around the graphic. Here's an example of this standard HTML code:

```
<HTML>
<A HREF="http://www.lynda.com>
<IMG SRC="lyndadraw.gif">
</A>
</HTML>
```

A linked image often has a tell-tale blue border, and the cursor will change to a pointing finger when viewed in browsers.

Turning Off Image Borders

Sometimes that pesky blue border around an image is totally wrong for the page it was designed for. If you've gone to a great deal of trouble to make an irregularly shaped image float freely on a background (using the techniques described in Chapter 7, "Transparent Artwork"), you aren't going to want to ruin the illusion you worked so hard to achieve by having a glaring rectangular shape around your graphic.

Here's the code to eliminate the border:

```
<HTML>
<A HREF="http://www.lynda.com>
<IMG SRC="lyndadraw.gif" BORDER=0>
</A>
</HTML>
```

Here's an example of a linked image with no border. The border was turned off within the HTML, but the pointing finger cursor will still appear when the mouse rolls over the linked image.

Just as you can make the border disappear, you can also make it appear stronger. The following Netscape-specific code gives a thicker border to the image:

```
<HTML>
<A HREF="http://lynda.com>
<IMG SRC="lyndadraw.gif" BORDER=5>
</A>
</HTML>
```

This linked image has been programmed to have a thicker border.

Sometimes your page has a specific color theme and the standard blue rectangle doesn't fit in. You can also change the color of your borders if you program the links on your page to include hexadecimal values inside the <BODY LINK> tag (see Chapter 5, "Hexadecimal Color"). This code changes the border color of the current image:

```
<HTML>
<BODY LINK="FFCC00">
<A HREF="http://www.lynda.com>
<IMG SRC="lyndadraw.gif" BORDER=5>
</A>
</BODY>
</HTML>
```

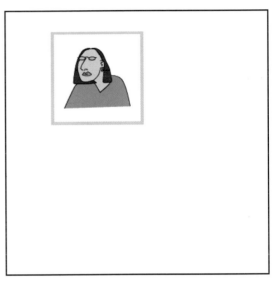

This image has a different color border programmed using hexadecimal color values.

Creating Navigation Bars

Navigation bars can be made out of text or images or both. They provide entrance ways to your information. The same HTML tags that were just reviewed apply to navigation bars. Examples follow.

This is the code to the navigation bar at the bottom of my page.

```
<A HREF=/>home</A>
  ¦ <A HREF=/dwg/links.html>links</A>
  ¦ <A HREF=/dwg/multigif.html>a-gifs</A>
  ¦ <A HREF=/hex.html>color</A>
  ¦ <A HREF=/books.html>web design books</A>
  ¦ <A HREF=/dwg/wds.html>classes</A>
<BR>
<A HREF=/articles.html>articles</A>
  ¦ <A HREF=/dwg/vi.html>inspiration</A>
  ¦ <A HREF=/dwg/mw.html>macworld</A>
  ¦ <A HREF=http://www.weinman.com/>family</A>
  ¦ <A HREF=/webdesign.html>list</A>
<BR>
<A HREF=/dwg/mg.html>motion graphics</A>
  ¦ <A HREF=http://www.cgibook.com/>cgi</A>
  ¦ <A HREF=/guestbook/>guestbook</A>
  ¦ <A HREF=/bookstore/>bookstore</A>
  ¦ <A HREF=/email.html>e-mail</A>
```

```
home | links | a-gifs | color | web design books | classes
    articles | inspiration | macworld | family | list
  motion graphics | cgi | guestbook | bookstore | e-mail
```

This is what my navigation bar looked like at the time this chapter was written, using straight HTML text. I have so many categories that I decided against icons on my site.

The following HTML for a navigation bar that includes images and text is slightly more complex as it involves tables for placement and font sizing tags.

```
<TABLE BORDER=0 CELLPADDING="3" CELLSPACING="0">

<TR><TD ALIGN=center>
<A HREF="art.html">
<IMG SRC="elk.gif" ALIGN=middle
BORDER="0" ALT="Art">
</A></TD><TD ALIGN=center>
<A HREF="artists.html">
<IMG SRC="horse.gif" ALIGN=middle
BORDER="0" ALT="Artists">
```

```
</A></TD><TD ALIGN=center>
<A HREF="life.html">
<IMG SRC="buffalo.gif" ALIGN=middle
BORDER="0" ALT="Life">
</A></TD><TD VALIGN=top ALIGN=center>
<A HREF="info.html">
<IMG SRC="round.gif" ALIGN=middle
BORDER="0" ALT="Info">
</A></TD><TD ALIGN=center>
<A HREF="us.html">
<IMG SRC="sunbird.gif" ALIGN=middle
BORDER="0" ALT="Us">
</A></TD></TR>

<TR><TD ALIGN=center><A HREF="art.html">
<IMG SRC="spot.gif" ALIGN=middle ALT="." BORDER=0>
</A></TD><TD ALIGN=center>
<A HREF="artists.html">
<IMG SRC="spot.gif" ALIGN=middle BORDER="0" ALT=".">
</A></TD><TD ALIGN=center>
<A HREF="life.html">
<IMG SRC="spot.gif" ALIGN=middle ALT="." BORDER=0>
</A></TD><TD ALIGN=center>
<A HREF="info.html">
<IMG SRC="spot.gif" ALIGN=middle ALT="." BORDER=0>
</A></TD><TD ALIGN=center>
<A HREF="us.html">
<IMG SRC="spot.gif" ALIGN=middle ALT="." BORDER=0>
</A></TD></TR>

<TR><TD ALIGN=center><FONT SIZE="+2"><TT>
<A HREF="art.html">Art</A></TT></FONT></TD>
<TD ALIGN=center><FONT SIZE="+2"><TT>
<A HREF="artists.html">Artists</A></TT></FONT></TD>
<TD ALIGN=center><FONT SIZE="+2"><TT>
<A HREF="life.html">Life</A></TT></FONT></TD>
<TD VALIGN=top ALIGN=center><FONT SIZE="+2"><TT>
<A HREF="info.html">Info</A></TT></FONT></TD>
<TD ALIGN=center><FONT SIZE="+2"><TT>
<A HREF="us.html">Us</A></TT></FONT></TD></TR>
</TABLE>
```

This navigation bar was designed by Ann E. Fullerton and can be found at ■ http://www.nativespirits.com. This code is much more complex because it involves all kinds of tricks we haven't gotten to yet. (Hint: See Chapter 13, "Layout and Alignment Techniques," and Chapter 11, "Web-Based Typography.")

My brother's site at ■ http://www.weinman.com/wew/ takes the navigation bar idea a step further and uses text and images complete with a "rollover" technique. This navigation bar is attractive, but most end users won't know what the icons mean.

You don't know what categories the icons represent until your cursor rolls over the artwork, which brings up the text underneath. This was done by using JavaScript with two GIF files, one with the text and the other without.

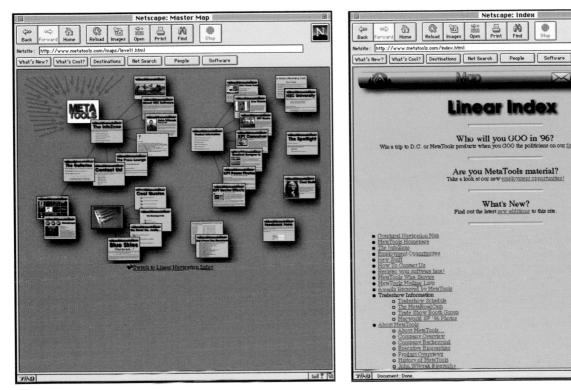

MetaTools has two types of navigation systems on its site: this one which is image-based...

...and this alternative, text-based page.

The Miraculous Server Include Tag

My brother (author of *The CGI Book*) is a long-time programmer who impresses me constantly with his acumen
for this HTML stuff. He hosts my site at ■ http://
www.lynda.com and taught me about the server
include directive.

What is a server include directive? It requests an external file and nests it inside an HTML document. This means
that you can put your navigation links in a single file and
have multiple HTML pages request the single file. This is
so awesome because if you add a category to your site,
you have to update only one page. We use this tag on
every HTML document on my site.

**Which leads me to another good point. It's good
to have all your links accessible from any page on
your site. What good is a navigation bar if it isn't
on a page? Someone might bookmark your page
and not know whose site he or she has stumbled
upon. It happens, trust me!**

Here's the directive within the requesting HTML file that
tells the page to grab the server include file.

```
<!--#include virtual="/menu.incl" -->
```

And here's the menu.incl document.

```
<A HREF=/>home</A>
  ¦  <A HREF=/dwg/links.html>links</A>
  ¦  <A HREF=/dwg/multigif.html>a-gifs</A>
  ¦  <A HREF=/hex.html>color</A>
  ¦  <A HREF=/books.html>web design books</A>
  ¦  <A HREF=/dwg/wds.html>classes</A>
<BR>
```

```
<A HREF=/articles.html>articles</A>
  ¦  <A HREF=/dwg/vi.html>inspiration</A>
  ¦  <A HREF=/dwg/mw.html>macworld</A>
  ¦  <A HREF=http://www.weinman.com/>family</A>
  ¦  <A HREF=/webdesign.html>list</A>
<BR>
<A HREF=/dwg/mg.html>motion graphics</A>
  ¦  <A HREF=http://www.cgibook.com/>cgi</A>
  ¦  <A HREF=/guestbook/>guestbook</A>
  ¦  <A HREF=/bookstore/>bookstore</A>
  ¦  <A HREF=/email.html>e-mail</A>
```

It's really this simple. Just put the menu.incl document on
the server with the HTML files that request it, and you've
got yourself a much more flexible navigation system.

■ **tip**

Recommended Reading

The server include directive can do all sorts of other
things besides provide a flexible navigation bar system.
My brother's book includes a chapter on the subject
and shows how you can use it for a counter and
date/time stamp.

The CGI Book
Publisher: New Riders
Author: William E. Weinman
PRICE: $45.00 ▪ ISBN: 1-56205-571-2

What Are Imagemaps?

At many web sites you will see a list of underlined text links on a page (often referred to as a hotlist). This is simply a list of multiple URLs assigned to multiple text objects. Instead of using multiple text links, however, the list of URLs can be attached to a single image object. Such an object is called an imagemap, which is a fancy way of presenting a list of links. This takes a little longer to download than a hotlist because of the added time required by the graphic to load. Most of the time, it's worth the wait because imagemaps are a more convenient, more visual way to present multiple choices to your audience.

This image works well as an imagemap.

Imagemap software enables you to select regions and assign multiple links to a single image.

Client-Side Imagemaps Versus Server-Side Imagemaps

An imagemap must contain specific information, such as coordinates for regions within a single image that are hyperlinked to multiple URLs.

A client-side imagemap requires that all the information about the imagemap be stored within the HTML document. A server-side imagemap requires that the information about the imagemap be saved within a "map definition file" that needs to be stored on a server and accessed by a CGI script. In general, a server-side imagemap is far more complicated to set up than a client-side imagemap. Server-side imagemaps work very differently on different systems—even on different systems using the same brand of server!

Another difference is how the two types of imagemaps display data within the Netscape browser. A server-side imagemap shows the coordinates at the bottom of the screen whereas a client-side imagemap shows the actual URL at the bottom of the screen, which is much nicer.

Most people prefer client-side imagemaps over server-side imagemaps, but some older browsers still don't support the tags. That's why many webmasters include both types of imagemaps in their documents.

```
http://www.razorfish.com/bluedot/typo/menu.map?105,70
```

Here's an example of a server-side imagemap reading on the bottom navigation bar of Netscape. It shows the position coordinates.

```
http://www.cgibook.com/links.html
```

Here's an example of a client-side imagemap reading on the bottom navigation bar of Netscape. It shows the URL! Much better.

Creating Server-Side Imagemaps

Imagemaps are more complicated to code than creating single linked images using the <A HREF><IMG SRC></A> tag. They are complicated on a number of fronts. Each hot region's dimension in pixels has to be determined and documented. In the case of a server-side map, the dimensions must be stored in an *imagemap definition file*. This definition file is composed slightly differently depending on which kind of server your web site uses.

The server is where your artwork and HTML gets stored. There are two types of servers—NCSA and CERN—and each requires the imagemap definition file code to be slightly different. **This means that you have to ensure that the way you've coded the imagemap is compatible with the type of server your site is stored on. The first step to deciding how to build your imagemap is to call the online service provider with whom you have your Internet account and web site to find out what kind of server they use.**

Do You Really Need an Imagemap?

Carefully analyze whether you really need an imagemap or whether there's some other way to accomplish the same goal. For example, if your image is composed of rectangles, or can be seamed together by using rectangular shapes (or transparent irregular shapes—see Chapter 7, "Transparent Artwork"), it might be easier on your end to load multiple single graphics with independent links than to load one graphic with multiple links.

You will see examples of imagemaps used on opening menu screens all over the web. Sometimes an imagemap is used, even when the menu bar is composed of rectangular shapes. Some sites do this because the one image will load faster than multiple images. This is a valid reason to use an imagemap, but even so, the difficulty of creating and maintaining one might outweigh the performance increase. Other sites do it just because they can. Perhaps it's trendy and shows off a certain amount of web-design machismo? I don't know, but it's another decision you get to make when building your site. I, being the lazy sort, make and use imagemaps only when necessary.

The Four Stages of a Server-Side Imagemap

Let's walk through the imagemap-making process quickly and then break out with more detail. The first step to making an imagemap is to create or choose a graphic as the source for the map. It's easiest to define regions if your graphic has obvious areas, such as a map or illustration, but you can use anything, including photographs and typography.

After you've chosen an image, you will need to create a map definition file: a text file you create that contains information about where the hotspots are located on your image. You can define the regions by using polygons or circles with the location of each region defined by pixels. This information is then composed as a text file specifically prepared for either a CERN or NCSA server.

Next, with a server-side imagemap, a map-processing CGI script is required to instruct the server to recognize the map definition file. Different scripts work for different platforms and servers, and it's best to contact your provider to ask what type of CGI works with their server. Chances are they already use a CGI script that they'll let you have access to and can instruct you on how to use it properly.

The last step is to set up the HTML tags to support the imagemap using the <ISMAP> tag. Now, let's break this down further and walk through the process used to create imagemaps.

<dwg 2>

Starting with the Graphic

First, make sure your source graphic is saved as a GIF (standard, transparent, or inter-laced will all work) or a JPEG. In the file name, don't forget to use the proper exten-sions, .gif and .jpg in lowercase, with no spaces in the name—for example, map.gif.

Defining the Regions of an Imagemap

Manually defining the coordinates of an imagemap can be a hellacious chore. You'd need to plot each point and arrive at the x and y coordinates of each region. Once you col-lected all the data, you'd need to write a text file for the server (slightly different ones for NCSA and CERN servers). This type of grunt work would have been best handled by a helper app, and we're lucky that several have cropped up that do the repetitive chore well. This chapter will show you how to work with two helper apps: WebMap for Mac imagemap authoring and MapEdit for PC imagemap authoring.

Here's an example of what a map definition file looks like for an NCSA server:

```
#
# Created by WebMap 1.0
# Wednesday, November 27, 1996 at 8:52 PM
# Format: NCSA
#

poly http://www.stink.com/films/
252,43 275,26 309,21 333,23 340,42
313,68 268,78 248,68 246,48 252,43
poly http://www.stink.com/images/
297,87 343,85 363,103 354,130 311,
142 277,134 264,118 273,98 297,87
poly http://www.stink.com/sketches/
302,152 331,153 349,170 339,193 303,
197 277,186 277,172 289,159 302,152
```

Here's an example of what a map definition file looks like for a CERN server:

```
#
# Created by WebMap 1.0
# Wednesday, November 27, 1996 at 8:52 PM
# Format: NCSA
#

poly http://www.stink.com/sketches/
302,152 331,153 349,170 339,193 303,
197 277,186 277,172 289,159 302,152
poly http://www.stink.com/images/
297,87 343,85 363,103 354,130 311,
142 277,134 264,118 273,98 297,87
poly http://www.stink.com/films/
252,43 275,26 309,21 333,23 340,42
313,68 268,78 248,68 246,48 252,43
```

Using WebMap

WebMap is shareware imagemap software written by Rowland Smith. The evaluation version of WebMap is available at the following URL: ■ http://www.city.net/cnx/software/webmap.html.

Launch WebMap. Open your file, and the graphic will appear in a window.

Use the toolbar containing the circle, rectangle, and free polygon to draw the shape of each region. After you've defined the area, click on the region and double-click on the [Undefined] list to the right. Enter the URL you wish to link to with an absolute path name (must include http://www).

When you're finished making and naming the regions, define a default URL by going to the Edit menu and selecting Default URL. This should be the name of the URL that the imagemap resides on. If your shape is irregular, the default URL should be where the file leads the viewer if he accidentally clicks off one of your defined regions.

Once you've done these things, go to the File menu and select Export as Text, choosing an NCSA or a CERN script depending on which type of server your site is on. The imagemap definition file must end with a .map extension. Typically, your map definition file and map graphic reside in the same folder on your server. Be sure to check this out with your web administrator.

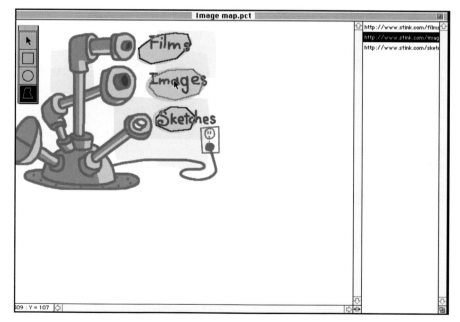

In WebMap, drag the Free Polygon Tool around the region you want to assign a link. The URLs for each link are typed in for the selected region.

Using MapEdit

MapEdit is shareware imagemap software written by Thomas Boutell. You might recognize his name as the author of the PNG file format (see Chapter 3, "Web File Formats"). MapEdit can be downloaded from ■ http://www.boutell.com/mapedit/.

Begin MapEdit by pulling down the menu bar to File, Open/Create to open your file. You'll be asked to locate the map file (map definition file) in advance and to load the graphic that you want to plot at the same time. If you haven't already started a map file, you can name it here now. You also need to decide at this point whether you want to write an NCSA script or a CERN script by checking the appropriate Create Type/NCSA/CERN radio button.

After you specify the map file name, the GIF, JPEG, or PNG file name, and the script type, choose OK to display the image in Map-Edit. Choose Tools, Polygon and drag around the appropriate shape.

When you want to close a polygon path, click the right mouse button. This displays the Object URL dialog box in which you must identify which URL the area you've just defined is linked to. Be sure to use an absolute path name (http://www...) as opposed to a relative path name (/my folder/myWebsite).

When finished, you can set the default URL by going to Edit, Default URL. Enter the absolute URL of the site your map is sitting on. This sets the default address to keep your viewers on this page in case they click off a defined region of your imagemap. When finished, choose File, Save As to display the Save As dialog box, and the name of your map definition file is automatically inserted.

As before, the finished files all need to be stored in the same folder on your server. Check with your web systems administrator for exact instructions.

Using MapEdit, you choose from an assortment of polygon tools to define the imagemap. Every imagemap software program is slightly different, but almost all of them offer intuitive drawing tools and create the server-side scripts automatically for you.

Writing HTML to Support Server-Side Imagemaps

The deconstruction to server-side imagemap follows:

```
1  <A HREF="http://www.domain.nam/cgi-
   bin/filename.map">
2  <IMG SRC="imagename.gif"
3  BORDER=0
4  ISMAP>
5  </A>
```

1   This establishes the anchor or destination of the links for the image map. Because the map definition file is included in the absolute path, the HTML will reference the imagemap coordinates and the CGI script.

2   This tag defines the name of the image to which the imagemap will be applied.

3   Whenever there's an **<A HREF>** tag, it automatically generates a default blue border around the graphic. The **BORDER=0** tag will turn off the border.

4   The **ISMAP** command must be included at the end of a server-side imagemap tag.

5   The **</A>** is required to end the **<A HREF>** tag.

The HTML document must now be loaded to the server, with the GIF or JPEG and the imagemap definition file map with the .map extension. Unlike most HTML, there is no way a server-side imagemap can be tested from your local hard drive. You must upload the proper files to the server, or the imagemap will not work.

Creating Client-Side Imagemaps

Creating client-side imagemaps is slightly easier than server-side imagemaps because you don't need a CGI or a separate map definition file. The steps for creating a client-side imagemap follow.

Step 1: Get the coordinates for your image. It's possible to get these coordinates in many WYSIWYG HTML editors, and the two programs mentioned here: MapEdit and WebMap. MapEdit will automatically generate the image-map coordinates in a client-side configuration. WebMap will not, but you can use a converter and have it restructure the data in the necessary fashion. Here's a converter that will help:

■ http://hyperarchives.lcs.mit.edu/HyperArchive/Archive/text/html/map-convert-10-a.hqx

Step 2: The coordinate information needs to be configured differently for a client-side imagemap than for a server-side imagemap. Here's an example of what the client-side coordinate data would look like. Compare it to the server-side map definition above, and you'll see it's the same information, just presented in a different order:

```
1  <MAP NAME="imagemap">
   <AREA SHAPE="polygon" COORDS=
   "302, 152, 331, 153, 349, 170, 339, 193, 303,
   197, 277, 186, 277, 172, 289, 159, 302, 152"
2  HREF="http://www.stink.com/sketches">
3  <AREA SHAPE="polygon" COORDS=
   "297, 87, 343, 85, 363, 103, 354, 130, 311,
   142, 277, 134, 264, 118, 273, 98, 297, 87"
   HREF="http://www.stink.com/images/">
   <AREA SHAPE="polygon" COORDS=
   "302, 152, 331, 153, 349, 170, 339, 193, 303,
   197, 277, 186, 277, 172, 289, 159, 302, 152"
   HREF="/www.stink.com/films/">
4  <IMG SRC="imagemap.gif" WIDTH="400" HEIGHT="300"
5  BORDER=0
6  USEMAP="#imagemap" ISMAP>
7  </MAP>
```

Everything within the client-side imagemap information gets stored within the HTML. The code for the server-side imagemap was very short. The code for the client-side imagemap is longer because it includes all the coordinate data within.

1 The map name is something that you define. It can be any name but must match what is used in the **<USEMAP>** tag.

2 The **<HREF>** tag instructs the imagemap to load the referenced HTML.

3 This part of the code defines which shape the imagemap forms.

4 Unlike the CERN and NCSA server-side map definition example, on a client side example no **<A HREF>** tag is necessary. The image for the map is told to display via the **<IMG SRC>** tag.

5 Just like the server-side example, the **BORDER=0** tag turns off the default blue border. It's not necessary to turn the border off, but it often ruins the illusion of irregular shaped regions if you leave it turned on.

6 The **<USEMAP>** tag specifies the name of the client-side imagemap file to use. The **#** character must always precede the map name.

7 The **</MAP>** tag is required to end the client-side imagemap.

Using Server-Side and Client-Side Imagemaps Together

Many people use both server-side and client-side maps. This enables viewers from any browser to be able to use the imagemap.

Here's the code necessary to combine both types of imagemap features:

```
<A HREF="http://www.domain.nam/cgi-bin/filename.map">
<IMG SRC="funkmachine.gif" border=0 ISMAP>
</A> USEMAP="#imagemap">
<MAP NAME="imagemap">
<AREA SHAPE="polygon" COORDS=
"302, 152, 331, 153, 349, 170, 339, 193, </MAP>
303, 197, 277, 186, 277, 172, 289, 159, 302, 152"
HREF="http://www.stink.com/sketches">
<AREA SHAPE="polygon" <IMG SRC="../credits/credits_
b.GIF" WIDTH=160 HEIGHT=116 COORDS=
"297, 87, 343, 85, 363, 103, 354, 130,
ALT="credits" BORDER=0 311, 142, 277, 134,
264, 118, 273, 98, 297, 87"
USEMAP="#credits_b" ISMAP></A>
HREF="http://www.stink
.com/images/"><MAP NAME="credits_b">
<AREA SHAPE="polygon" COORDS=
"302, 152, 331, 153, 349, 17, 339, 193, 303,
197, 277, 186, 277, 172, 289, 159, 302, 152"
<AREA SHAPE="rect" COORDS="2,73,128,97"
HREF="/www.stink.com/films/">
</MAP>
</HTML>
```

Importance of the <ALT> Tag

The <ALT> tag provides alternative information to images that can be read by text-based browsers. Let's say that visitors to your site arrive with browser software that does not recognize imagemaps. Or they've turned off their images because they're in a hurry? Or your end viewer is disabled (yes, visually impaired people can and do use the text-based web; there are devices that can "read" the pages to them). All these situations can be accommodated by adding one simple <ALT> tag to your HTML.

Using our example one more time, here's where the tag would be included:

```
<A HREF="http://www.domain.nam/cgi-bin/filename.map">
<IMG SRC="imagename.gif"
ALT="this is an image of my bla bla"
BORDER=0
ISMAP>
```

Importance of <WIDTH> and <HEIGHT> Tags

By adding <WIDTH> and <HEIGHT> tags to images within HTML, you are giving the browser information about the size of your graphic. This is a good thing, for a couple of reasons. First of all, the browser doesn't have to calculate the image size because you've supplied the information for it, which saves time. It allows the text to load before the images, which can be a good thing with large images. Audiences will get something to look at while they're waiting! MSIE actually requires that you use the <WIDTH> and <HEIGHT> tag attributes or the client-side imagemap tags don't even work.

Here's the way to implement the <HEIGHT> and <WIDTH> tag attribute.

```
<A HREF="http://www.domain.nam/cgi-bin/filename.map">
<IMG SRC="imagename.gif" WIDTH=350 HEIGHT=200
ALT="this is an image of my bla bla"
BORDER=0
ISMAP>
```

The values you put inside the <WIDTH> and <HEIGHT> tags reflect how large the image is, measured by pixels. You can even resize an image if you put values that are larger or smaller than the image! Basically, the browser uses your information for the image size instead of looking to the image itself for size information.

■ **tip**

Imagemap Tutorial URLs
■ http://www.ihip.com/
■ http://www.spyglass.com/tech spec/tutorial/img_maps.html

Imagemap Software Tools
MapEdit (Windows, PC, and Unix)
■ http://www.boutell.com/mapedit/

MapThis! (Windows)
■ http://galadriel.ecaetc. ohio-state.edu/tc/mt/

WebMap (Macintosh)
■ http://home.city.net/cnx/ software/webmap.html

Glenn Fleishman's Server-Side to Client-Side Online Converter
■ http://www.popco.com/ popco/convertmaps.html

Frames for Navigation

What are frames? Frames offer the capability to divide a web page into regions, so that each region functions as its own web page. This means parts of a page can change, while other regions of the page remain static. Frames are perfect for navigation bars that will not change from page to page, while other content can be set to change independently.

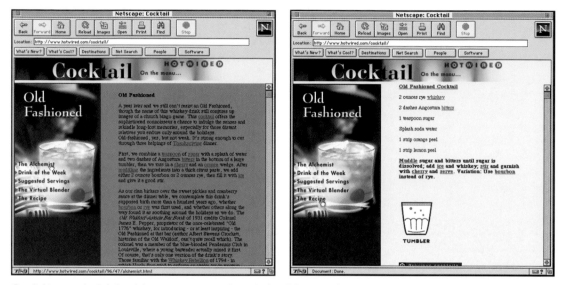

By clicking on the left-hand frame, content in the right-hand frame updates independently. These examples are from ■ http://www.hotwired.com/cocktail/. A case study of this site is in my second book, *Deconstructing Web Graphics*.

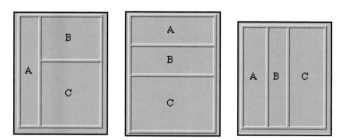

Examples of frame configurations from the excellent tutorial site in Japan: HTML for Angels—■ http://ncdesign.kyushu-id.ac.jp/html/ Normal/frame.html.

Frames sound great in theory, but there are some noteworthy snags. Many site designers insert existing web pages that were originally designed for full-screen browsers into cramped small-frame regions. This forces the end viewer to scroll through graphics and text inside smaller windows than the pages were originally designed for. Real estate on a web page is already a precious commodity, and breaking apart a small screen into multiple small screens can do more damage to your presentation than good. My recommendation is that you use no more than three frame regions to a page, so that your audience isn't frustrated by having to scroll through small windows.

HTML for Frames

The HTML for frames is often difficult to understand because it, by nature, includes other "nested" HTML documents. The first document in this example is named Framed.html and displays three frame regions. The content of those frames is actually contained in three other HTML documents that this document references. The three other files are named header.html, menu.html, and info.html.

framed.html: This is the opening page of the sample frameset.

```
<HTML>
<HEAD>
<TITLE>Framed!</title>
</HEAD>
```
1 `<FRAMESET ROWS="108,*">`
2 `<FRAME SRC="header.html" MARGINWIDTH=0 MARGIN-`
`HEIGHT=0 NORESIZE SCROLLING="no"`
`    NAME="header">`

3 `<FRAMESET COLS="200,*">`
4 `<FRAME MARGINWIDTH=10 MARGINHEIGHT=10`
`SRC="menu.html" NORESIZE SCROLLING="no"`
`    NAME="menu">`
5 `<FRAME MARGINWIDTH=10 MARGINHEIGHT=10`
`SRC="info.html" NAME="info">`
6 `</FRAMESET>`
`</FRAMESET>`
7 `<NOFRAMES>`
8 `<BODY>`
`    If you had frames, you'd be home by now.`
`</BODY>`
9 `</NOFRAMES>`
`</HTML>`

1 **<FRAMESET>** defines the parameters of the frames. This document has two nested framesets. The first defines two rows. Rows are horizontal areas, one on top of the other. The top will be for the header, and the bottom row will have another **<FRAMESET>** with two columns.

The first row is 108 pixels high. Netscape uses 8 of those pixels for the frame itself, and the graphic is 100 pixels high. Frame sizes can also be defined in terms of percentages (25%) instead of pixels. When you are using a graphic with a known size, it is more useful to define the size of the frame in terms of pixels.

The second row is defined with a *, which lets the browser use the rest of the space at its own discretion. It will take up whatever space is left after the 100 pixels of the first row are allocated.

2 The **<FRAME>** tag is used to specify the contents of an individual frame. The **SRC=** attribute specifies header.html as the initial content of the frame; **MAR-GINWIDTH** and **MARGINHEIGHT** declare the margin sizes (zero in this case, to put an image right up to the borders); **NORESIZE** tells the browser to disallow resizing by the user; **SCROLLING="no"** gets rid of any scrollbars; and **NAME="header"** names the frame for use by **<TARGET>** tags later on.

3 The second row has another **<FRAMESET>** tag instead of a **<FRAME>** tag. This is for splitting the row into columns. Two columns are defined: the first column will take up 200 pixels on the left side of the row, and the second column will take the remaining lateral space in the row.

4 Each **<FRAME>** tag defines the next undefined frame specified in the immediately preceding **<FRAMESET>** tag. This one is for the first column from the **<FRAME-SET>** in #3 . . .

5 . . . and this one is for the second column from the **<FRAMESET>** in #3.

6 **<FRAMESET>** requires an ending **</FRAMESET>** tag to tell the browser that it is done defining frames.

7 Everything between **<NOFRAMES>** and **</NOFRAMES>** will be ignored by a frames-capable browser. The content within this section is what will be seen by people whose browsers cannot render frames.

8 The **<BODY>** tag is required in the **<NOFRAMES>** section. You can use it as you would in a normal HTML document.

9 This ends the **<NOFRAMES>** section.

header.html: This document is nested within the top frame of framed.html.

```
      <HTML>
1     <HEAD><TITLE>Hey! I thought I
      was in a frame!</TITLE></HEAD>
2     <BODY BGCOLOR=33cccc>
3     <IMG SRC=title.gif WIDTH=600 HEIGHT=100>
      </BODY>
      </HTML>
```

1 Because each HTML document could end up on someone's screen outside of a frame, it's a good idea to give it a title anyway.

2 When you give a framed document a background color, the background of the frame takes on the color. This document has a background color that is the same as the background of the title graphic. That way, if someone's screen is bigger than our graphic, it blends seamlessly.

3 The whole body of the document is just the image.

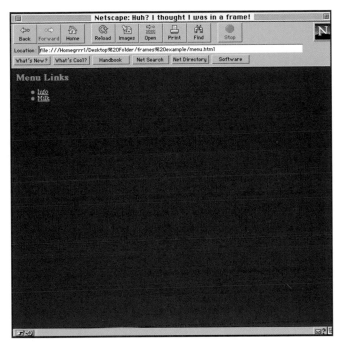

menu.html: This document is nested within the left frame of framed.html.

info.html: This document is nested within the right frame of framed.html.

```
<HTML>
<HEAD>
```
1
```
<BASE TARGET=info>
<TITLE>Huh? I thought I was in a frame!</title>
</HEAD>
<BODY BGCOLOR=000066 TEXT=00ccff LINK=00ffcc
VLINK=00ffcc ALINK=00ccff>
<H2>Menu</H2>
```
2
```
<MENU>
   <LI><A HREF=info.html>Info</A>
   <LI><A HREF=milk.html>Milk</A>
   <LI><A HREF=blue.html>Blue</A>
   <LI><A HREF=light.html>Light</A>
   <LI><A HREF=monster.html>Monsters!</A>
</MENU>
</BODY>
</HTML>
```

1 The **<BASE>** tag has a target attribute so that all the hyperlinks load in the frame named "info".

2 The **<MENU>** tag is used to create a menu in the left-hand frame. Be sure to keep all your menu text as short as possible so that it fits in the frame.

Alternatively, you could create a vertical imagemap designed to fit precisely in the frame.

```
<HTML>
<HEAD>
```
1
```
<TITLE>Info!</TITLE>
<BODY BGCOLOR=cccc99>
```
2
```
<H2>Info</H2>
<P>Frames can be a useful tool, when used carefully.
</BODY>
</HTML>
```

Each of the documents in the right-hand frame is structured as a normal HTML document. It's important to keep the amount of text to a minimum so that it fits nicely in the limited space of the frame.

1 The **<TITLE>** tag describes the document, for people who might load it outside of a frame.

2 All the HTML in the document is designed just as you would a document that was not going in a frame.

Floating Frames

Microsoft Internet Explorer (MSIE) introduced floating frames, which enable the browser to position a frame in the middle of the browser window instead of limiting its position to divided regions, as in the case with standard frame tags. MSIE honors a new tag, <IFRAME>, that instructs the browser to float the frame. For step-by-step instructions, visit

■ http://www.microsoft.com/WORKSHOP/AUTHOR/NEWFEAT/IE30HTML-F.HTM

Floating frames are great, but unfortunately at the time this chapter was written, they were supported only by MSIE.

These screens can be found on the MSIE site as examples of floating frames. By clicking on the bottom navigation bar, the only part of the page that changes is inside the middle window. When floating frames are widely implemented, this type of navigation will be welcomed by many site designers.

■ **note**

Extra Frame-Related HTML Attributes

There are a few other frames-related tags that have not been reviewed here.

If the image inside a frame is bigger than the browser window, a scrollbar automatically appears. If you want to turn that scrollbar off, you could add the code: **SCROLLING=NO**

When creating links for frames or client-side imagemaps, you can set a TARGET attribute to instruct the link to target another browser window besides the one its in. Here's a list of TARGET attributes.

TARGET="_self" is the default way frames work, even without this tag. It means that the linked reference will appear inside the same frame that is already visible.

TARGET="_blank" will open a new browser window, while leaving the old one behind it.

TARGET="_top" takes you to the referenced URL without keeping it inside your frameset.

TARGET="_parent" removes all the frames on your page, and shows you the referenced link in its own window.

Aesthetic Cues for Navigation Graphics

Many designers, myself included, have grown weary of predictable beveled 3D buttons on web pages. The truth is, however, that beveled 3D buttons give a universally accepted visual cue that a graphic has linking properties. If you're tired of the 3D look, however, there are other signals that imply a linked image. Drop shadows are often used, as are colored shapes. A sample gallery of navigation-style graphics follows. These were created by Bruce Heavin, using the illustration he made of me, and Alien Skin's Black Box Photoshop filters (■ http://www.alienskin.com). The Alien Skin filters are Mac- and PC-compatible Photoshop filters that save a lot of time and fussing with complicated alpha channel operations.

Cutout Filter

Drop Shadow Filter

Carve Filter

Cutout to Background Filter

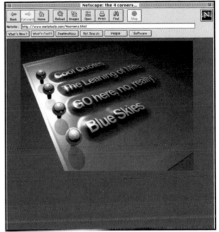

Glass Filter

Glow Filter

Inner Bevel Filter

Outer Bevel Filter

The MetaTool's site has a lot of playful linked graphics ■ http://www.metatools.com/.

Carve Filter

Cutout to Background Color Filter

Cutout to Image Filter

Drop Shadow Filter

Glass Filter

Outer Bevel Filter

Inner Bevel Filter

Glow Filter

Bruce worked with the image of me, using a circular selection and a selection in the shape of his illustration's contour.

■ note

Rollovers Versus Buttons

It's true that buttons with 3D effects look clickable, but after seeing so many on the web and in multimedia, these conventions grow tiresome and predictable. An alternative graphic approach would be to create rollover-style buttons, where the buttons behave responsively with a different graphic or sound when the end user's cursor passes over. Rollovers are not possible in straight HTML-based pages; these techniques are discussed in-depth in Chapter 16, "Interactivity."

Introduction
Getting Started in Web Design
Understanding the Web Environment

Web File Formats
Low-Bandwidth Graphics
Hexadecimal Color

Browser-Safe Color
Transparent Artwork
Background Tiles
Rules, Bullets and Buttons
Navigation-Based Graphics

Web-Based Typography

Scanning Techniques for the Web

Layout and Alignment Techniques
Animation
Sound

Interactivity
HTML for Visual Designers
Glossary
Design Resources Appendix
Index

BROWSER SAFE COLOR
33FF

Web Safe typography

otoshop

0033

<TAB>

<A>

<INDEX>

Width="500"

<img src="

<STRONG>
.Gif
.Jpg
.Png

Image compression
limited palettes
IMAGE OPTIMIZATION
216 colors

PARENCY

</A>

Height="600"

<H>

10.2

<center>

GRAPHY

Imaging techniques
Extending HTML
Web file formats
bgcolor="FFFFCC"

Animation, sound and

@link="cyan"

LYNDA.COM

33

<center> BODY
Animation

www Design

Web-Based Typography

There is a fundamental controversy associated with web design. You have your HTML purists and programmers, and you have your design purists and nonprogrammers, and often they do not agree or find common ground. Visual design is about control. Typography is an incredibly powerful visual design medium, but good typography requires much more control than HTML currently affords. HTML is about display flexibility and cross-platform distribution of information. HTML and browser support of specific tags are the vehicles by which web pages are delivered, and design is the vehicle by which they are delivered artistically.

This chapter was written to help each side of the design and programming fence understand the other. It will help designers learn tricks to make web typography look as good as it can and will help programmers understand what designers want from HTML.

This chapter covers the following topics:

- Type principles and definitions
- Aesthetic considerations
- HTML type
- Type alignment tricks
- Font usage in HTML pages
- Images as type
- Anti-aliased type versus aliased type
- Mixing type images and HTML

Short Glossary of Key Typographic Terms

In order to understand what kind of type control designers want, let's first examine some type principles and definitions. Here's a short glossary of typographic terms, using HTML-based examples.

Images   Stories   Links   Clients   Books   Web   Shockwave

bruce@stink.com

Serif: A serif typeface has a stroke attached to the beginning or end of one of the main strokes of a letter. Many people believe that this style of type is easiest to read as body copy. The default font in most browsers is a serif typeface: Times Roman on Macs and Times New Roman on PCs.

summer 96 | winter 96 | fall 95 || credits || survey | subscribe | mail | menu

Sans serif: A sans serif typeface has no slab attached. Sans serif typefaces on the web require special tags, requesting that your end user use a graphic picture of type instead of HTML. This sans serif type is specified with the <FONT FACE> tag, described fully later in this chapter.

home | links | a-gifs | color | web design books | classes
articles | inspiration | macworld | family | list
motion graphics | cgi | guestbook | bookstore | e-mail

Monospace: A monospace font takes up the same amount of horizontal width per character. This navigation bar is set in Courier using the <PRE> tag. Monospace typefaces can be specified with the <PRE>, <CODE>, or <TT> tags.

regular leading regular leading regular leading regular leading regular leading regular
regular leading regular leading regular leading regular leading regular leading regular
regular leading regular leading regular leading regular leading regular leading regular
regular leading regular leading regular leading regular leading regular leading regular
regular leading regular leading regular leading regular leading regular leading regular

Default leading: Leading (pronounced ledding) is the space between lines of type. The origins of the word leading came from early days of typography when lead type was used. Blank pieces of lead were used between each row as spacers. This is standard leading in HTML using no custom tags.

ing looser leading looser leading looser leading looser leading looser leading looser le

ing looser leading looser leading looser leading looser leading looser leading looser le

looser leading looser leading looser leading looser leading looser leading looser leadi

Looser leading: This looser leading in HTML was created by using the paragraph break tag <P>.

DROP CAPs CAN BE KEWEL

Drop cap: A drop cap is used with all capital letters, and indicates that the first letter of a word is in a larger cap size. This is accomplished in HTML by using the <FONT SIZE> tag.

FOR HOTWIRED MEMBERS
Test Patterns presents pet projects that kept us up nights: MiniMind, KHOT, and the amazing Beta

Small caps: HotWired uses small caps on its front page ■ http://www.hotwired.com/frontdoor/.

---

fe palette, as I so named it, is the actual palette that Mosaic, Ne
within their browsers. The palettes used by these browsers are slic
s. This palette is based on math, not beauty. I didn't and wouldn't
ors in this palette, but Netscape, Mosaic and Internet Explorer did

Body text: The body text, or body copy, of a document is composed by the main block of text.

The Browser Safe Color Palette

By Lynda Weinman

Headline text: A headline is used to break apart information. It can do so by being larger in size, a different color, a different font, an underline, or bold or different visual treatment, which will cause it to stand out.

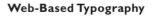
Glossary of Terms Not Possible with HTML

This type of precise typographic control is possible in programs such as QuarkXPress, Illustrator, and FreeHand. This control is not possible within HTML, but we wish it was.

<no baseline shift on brackets>

<with baseline shift on brackets>

Baseline shift: Enables you to change the position of a single character up or down.

---

unkerned kerned

Kerning: Enables you to adjust the letterspacing between individual characters.

---

12 pt. type with 14 pt. leading
12 pt. type with 14 pt. leading
12 pt. type with 14 pt. leading

Leading adjustment: Enables you to specify specific leading with point size measurements.

---

12 pt. type with 20 pt. leading

12 pt. type with 20 pt. leading

12 pt. type with 20 pt. leading

Looser leading adjustment: Enables you to establish specific leading with point size measurements. Here's an example of looser leading with accurate control.

---

this text has default word spacing

this text has word spacing of 125%

Word spacing: Enables you to adjust the space between words.

---

without tracking
with tracking

Tracking: Enables you to adjust the global spacing between letters.

Interesting Typography-Based URLs

For the most amazing type glossary to be found on the web, visit Razorfish's **typo-GRAPHIC** site. The **typoGRAPHIC** site also teaches about the principles of type and using hypertext at its best. Oh, and a little Shockwave, Java, and animated GIF action, too!
- http://www.razorfish.com/bluedot/typo/glossary/
- http://www.razorfish.com/bluedot/typo/

Typofile is an online magazine devoted to type techniques and technology. This site has lots of great tutorials and essays about typography.
- http://www.will-harris.com/type.htm

A short presentation on basic typography by **Paul Baker Typographic, Inc.** includes the use of letter and word spacing, measure, leading, choosing a typeface, and so on.
- http://www.pbtweb.com/typostyl/typostyl.htm

LettError is a two-person virtual design studio. Acclaimed type designers Just van Rossum and Erik van Blokland work from their respective homes in The Hague, The Netherlands. Their goal is to create typefaces that do more than the usual fonts—they create animations, music, typography, web sites, and some graphic design as well. Check 'em out! Be sure to read their rant on embedded fonts in PDF documents.
- http://www.letterror.com/LTR_About.html

Type designer **Thomas Mueller's Liquid Typography** site includes his portfolio and thesis project.
- http://www.razorfish.com/thomas/

■ **note**

HTML Type Versus Graphical Type

There are basically two kinds of typographical elements on the web (or the printed page, for that matter): body type and headline type. Body type, often referred to as body copy, composes the bulk of the written text. Body type is typically smaller and contains the majority of the written content of a web page. Headline type is typically larger and is used to quickly draw the viewer's eye to it, help define a page break, or organize multiple ideas.

You can make body and headline type a couple of different ways on the web. One way involves using HTML and specialized font tags.

The alternative way is to create graphics that have images of type as the visual content instead of pictures. This kind of image-based type is referred to in this chapter as *graphic-based type*. HTML type is ideal for body copy, and graphic-based type is ideal for headlines. This chapter examines procedures for using standard HTML type, adding specialized type tags, and methods for making graphic images with headline type using Photoshop and Illustrator. Understanding some of the aesthetic issues related to type design principles is important before we move toward specific production methods.

Aesthetic Considerations

I think the web is an incredibly great way to gather information. Typically, when I find a page with a lot of text on it though, I'll print the page on my printer rather than sit and read through the text on my screen. Who wants to have the light of the monitor blaring in their face while having a recreational read? Give me crisp type on paper any day over that! I feel the same way about all computer-based text delivery systems, such as CD-ROMS and interactive kiosks. If you want me to read a lot of text, I'd rather do so on paper. As designers, we have to recognize that computer-based presentations pose distinct challenges and not treat our type-ridden web pages the same way as we would print.

So what design principles can you follow to help out your computer-screen-based reader? I advocate breaking up type into small paragraphs. Also, use different weights, such as bold and italics, to make it possible to skim the page easily and catch the important points. Adding hypertext whenever possible (text that links you from one spot to another, which is typically underlined or bold depending on the way the viewer's browser preferences are set) is another way to break up screen text into more digestible portions. The idea is to break up blocks of text as much as possible. Assume your readers are skimming, and make it easy for them to do.

Understand that you're asking a lot of your end viewer to sit and read pages and pages of type on a screen. It's your job to invent ways to hold his interest and to bring out the important ideas. This is possible through using both HTML and graphic-based text. Let's examine HTML first.

■ tip

Printing Web Pages

As if there weren't enough things to think about in web design, here's a new wrench to throw your way. If you intend to have your audience print information from your pages, you should design your pages with that in mind. Many people don't realize that when you set up a dark web page background with white type, for example, that the background is not printed with the file. What results? White type on white paper—or as some might say, nothing!

It's not to suggest that you have to always use light backgrounds with dark type on every page, but if there is a specific page that you know you want your audience to print, make sure you test print it yourself to see whether it's legible!

HTML-Based Typography

The advantages of using HTML for most body type
needs are obvious. First of all, the memory and download time required for using native text is much lower
than that used for graphics. Many sites are text-intensive,
and using HTML-based type is the only choice to present
large quantities of written information in a timely and
efficient manner.

The following examples and code demonstrate how to
use HTML type tags.

Headings

Headings are created using the <H></H> tag. The heading tags always have to be in the <HEAD> part of an
HTML file. Here's some sample heading code:

```
<HTML><HEAD>
<H3>Welcome to this Site!</H3>
<H4>Welcome to this Site!</H4>
<H5>Welcome to this Site!</H5>
</HEAD>
</HTML>
```

Welcome to this Site!
Welcome to this Site!
Welcome to this Site!

Bold

Here are a couple of ways to make type bold:

```
<HTML>
Talk <B>LOUD!</B><P>
Talk <STRONG>LOUD!</STRONG>
</HTML>
```

Talk **LOUD!**

Talk **LOUD!**

Italics

Here are a couple of ways to italicize type:

```
<HTML>
<I> Are you <I>ever going to shut up? </I> <P>
<EM> Are you <EM> ever going to shut up? </EM>
</HTML>
```

Are you *ever going to shut up?*

Are you *ever going to shut up?*

Preformatted

Preformatted text usually shows up in Courier or mono-
type. Here's the code:

```
<HTML>
<PRE> When are you    g    o    i    n    g
to be QUIET?</PRE>
</HTML>
```

When are you   g   o   i   n   g   to be QUIET?

Blinking Text

Use with caution! Many end viewers find this tag annoying.

```
<BLINK> flash news!</BLINK>
```

Changing Font Sizes

Font sizes can be changed by using the <FONT SIZE>
</FONT> tag. Here's how:

```
<HTML>
Do you ever <FONT SIZE=5>listen</FONT>
to direction anymore?
</HTML>
```

Do you ever **listen** to direction anymore?

Drop Cap

Here's the code for creating drop caps:

```
<HTML>
<FONT SIZE=4>D</FONT>ROP <FONT SIZE=4>C</FONT>AP
</HTML>
```

DROP CAP

Small Cap

Use the following whenever you want small caps:

```
<HTML>
<FONT SIZE=1>SMALL CAPS </FONT><BR>
REGULAR CAPS
</HTML>
```

SMALL CAPS
REGULAR CAPS

Centering Text

Text can be centered by using the <CENTER> tag. Use the following code:

```
<HTML>
<CENTER>
I'm in the middle...
</CENTER>
</HTML>
```

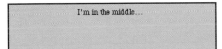

I'm in the middle...

 note

Useful URLs

Netscape has a site that has a style sheet for using the <FONT SIZE> tag as well: ■ http://www.cen. uiuc. edu/~ejk/fontsizes html. Logging on to this site automatically generates an entire range of font sizes by using the font your browser is set to. In addition, here are two helpful style sheets that Yoshinobo Takahas, from Disney Online, shares.

Header Tests (H[1-6])
This is a Header 1
This is a Header 2
This is a Header 3
This is a Header 4
This is a Header 5
This is a Header 6

Font Size (FONT SIZE=[1-7])
This is Font Size 1
This is Font Size 2
This is Font Size 3
This is Font Size 4
This is Font Size 5
This is Font Size 6
This is Font Size 7

Font Size (FONT SIZE=[-2-+4])
This is Font Size -2
This is Font Size -1
This is Font Size +0
This is Font Size +1
This is Font Size +2
This is Font Size +3
This is Font Size +4

Header Tests (H[1-6])
This is a Header 1
This is a Header 2
This is a Header 3
This is a Header 4
This is a Header 5
This is a Header 6

Font Size (FONT SIZE=[1-7])
This is Font Size 1
This is Font Size 2
This is Font Size 3
This is Font Size 4
This is Font Size 5
This is Font Size 6
This is Font Size 7

Font Size (FONT SIZE=[-2-+4])
This is Font Size -2
This is Font Size -1
This is Font Size +0
This is Font Size +1
This is Font Size +2
This is Font Size +3
This is Font Size +4

Fun with ASCII!

ASCII text was a computer art craze in the 1970s, before computer graphics were something individuals could do easily on personal computers. There were no imaging programs that let people work with vector or bitmap artwork like today, so people made artwork with text characters. Many web pages keep the tradition of ASCII art alive. ASCII art can provide a welcome diversion from typical web art fare.

Publishing ASCII art over the web is a brilliant idea. It has all the advantages of speedy HTML-based text delivery and the advantage of working on almost every browser because the only HTML necessary to produce involves the <PRE> tag, which is widely supported.

Case Study: Hollywood Records

The Hollywood Records site at ■ http://www.hollywood rec.com uses ASCII for the low-fi (low-bandwidth) version of its site. An in-depth version of this case study is in my second book *Deconstructing Web Graphics*.

Here's a screen-shot of one of its pages that uses ASCII.

Beginning here and ending on the following page is the HTML source code for the image on the left.

```
<HTML>
<HEAD>
<TITLE>GWEN MARS Press</TITLE>
</HEAD>
<BODY TEXT="#A99A05" LINK="#A99A05"
VLINK="#FFFFFF" BGCOLOR="#001000">
<CENTER>
<PRE>
<FONT SIZE=+0>
<B>
<A HREF="/HollywoodRecords/Bands/GwenMars/
Press/GwenMarsPressM.html">
HI-FI GRAFX</A> /
<A HREF="/HollywoodRecords/Bands/GwenMars/
GwenMarsV.html">SCI-FI VR</A> /
<A HREF="/Note">EMAIL US</A> /
<A HREF="/Help">HELP</A>
<A HREF="/HollywoodRecords/Hollywood
RecordsL.html">HOLLYWOOD RECORDS</A>/
<A HREF="/HollywoodRecords/Bands/
BandRosterL.html"> MUSICIANS</A> /
<HREF="/HollywoodRecords/Bands/
GwenMars/GwenMarsL.html">GWEN MARS</A>
</B>
</FONT>
</PRE>
```

```
<PRE>
                                     . . u o e e u u .

                        z $ $ $ $ R # " " ` ` ` " " " # R $ b L                          . u o d W $ W u

                   : $ $ $ "                              ^ " % .          . o $ R # " " ` ` # $ $ $

                 : $ $ F                                        + "                         8 $ $

              8 $ F                                                              $ $ P

             $ $ "                                                            d $ $ "

            $ $ ~                                                            d $ $ "

           $ $ F                                                           d $ $ "

          t $ $                                                          d $ $ "

          $ $ F                                                        x @ $ P `

         ' $ $ .                                              . @ $ $ "

         9 $ $ .                                    . ~      . @ $ $ #

         9 $ $ .                             . e "      . @ $ $ # `

        z $ $ $ $ &                    . o $ "    u @ $ $ #

      . @ $ $ $ " $ $ $ L           . z $ $ "    z $ $ R "

     : $ $ $ #      ? $ $ $    . o $ $ * "   . d $ $ #

    : $ $ $ "              . o $ $ $ #   z $ $ # `                                        :

   @ $ $ "           u @ $ $ $ P "  u @ * "                                          d

  : $ $ $ L  . o $ $ $ $ $ "  . d $ $ $ N                                      x R

 : $ $ $ $ $ $ $ $ R " `    `     ' # $ $ $ k                          d $ "

 ' * * * * " "                        " $ $ $ $ e u                  . u @ $ $ "

                     " * $ $ $ $ $ $ $ $ $ $ $ $ $ $ # "

                              ` ` `
</PRE>
<FONT SIZE=+2><B><CODE>PRESS INFO</CODE></B></FONT><P>
</PRE>
</FONT>
</CENTER>
</BODY>
</HTML>
```

The Hollywood Records design team worked with a Mac-based program called Gifscii. Gifscii converts GIFs to ASCII. There are a few other products that enable you to work with ASCII artwork. Ascii Paint enables you to paint with ASCII characters: ■ http://www. umich.edu/~archive/mac/graphics/graphicsutil/asciipaint.sit.hqx.

HTML Font Choices

Chances are, the person looking at your web page is using the default settings for whatever browser he or she is viewing the page from. Most browsers default to using a Times Roman font. I've seen sites that include instructions to the viewer to change their default font to some other typeface. I wish them luck! I know very few web navigators who would take the time to change their settings to see an individual page. If you want your HTML type to be something other than Times Roman, don't count on asking your viewers to change their web browser settings as a foolproof method. In fact, I would imagine an extremely low percentage of viewers would actually act on the suggestion. As an alternative, try the <FONT FACE> tag described next.

Font Face Tag

If you want your audience to see your body copy in a font other than their default font settings, there is a new tag to the rescue, developed by Microsoft, called <FONT FACE>. A good explanation of this tag is found at ■ http: //www. microsoft.com/truetype/iexplor/iedemo.htm

The <FONT FACE> tag enables you to specify which font your page will be displayed in. The main caveat is that your end user must have the font you request installed, or the tag will not work.

Microsoft has a free Mac or PC Web Fonts package that you can download from ■ http://www.microsoft.com/truetype/hottopic.htm.

PACK All of the above fonts are included in one file for Windows [newfonts.exe: 712KB, self extracting archive] or Apple Macintosh [newfonts.sit.hqx: 880KB, BinHex].

Arial, **Arial Bold**, *Italic*, ***Bold Italic***
Download Arial for Windows [arial.exe: 397KB, self extracting archive] or Apple Macintosh [Arial.sit.hqx: 346KB, BinHex].

Times New Roman, **Times New Roman Bold**, *Italic*, ***Bold Italic***
Download Times New Roman for Windows [times.exe: 485KB, self extracting archive] or Apple Macintosh [TimesNewRoman.sit.hqx: 420KB, BinHex].

Courier New, **Courier New Bold**, *Italic*, ***Bold Italic***
Download Courier New for Windows [courier.exe: 457KB, self extracting archive] or Apple Macintosh [CourierNew.sit.hqx: 408KB, BinHex].

The Web Fonts package includes Arial, Arial Bold, Arial Italic, Arial Bold Italic, Arial Black, Comic Sans MS, Comic Sans MS Bold, Courier New, Courier New Bold, Courier New Italic, Courier New Bold Italic, Impact, Times New Roman, Times New Roman Bold, Times New Roman Italic, and Times New Roman Bold Italic.

The odds are that—even though Microsoft offers the free Web Fonts Package to Mac and PC users—most of your web audience won't even know about it or take the time to install fonts that don't ship on their system. For that reason, it's safest to go with these basic fonts that ship with every Mac and PC.

PC	Mac
Arial	Helvetica
Courier New	Courier
Times New Roman	Times

Two other problems worth mentioning occur when you add bold tags or header tags to the <FONT FACE> tag. The results might look funky, so here is some sample code to show how to use the <FONT FACE> tag:

```
<HTML>
<FONT FACE ="helvetica, arial"> TESTING,
</FONT> one, two, three.
</HTML>
```

TESTING, one, two, three.

To add size variation, add the SIZE attribute to the tag:

```
<HTML>
<FONT FACE="helvetica, arial" SIZE=5>
TESTING, </FONT> one, two, three.
</HTML>
```

TESTING, one, two, three.

To change the color, add the COLOR attribute to the tag:

```
<HTML>
<FONT FACE ="helvetica, arial" SIZE=5
COLOR="cc3366"> TESTING, </FONT> one, two,
three.
</HTML>
```

TESTING, one, two, three.

■ **warning**

Font Size Differences Between Macs and PCs

No, you are not nuts. If you have a Mac and a PC, you will notice that standard 12-point default fonts look different on each platform. Fonts display larger on PCs than on Macs. Sigh. I know you don't want to hear this, but this is one of the cross-platform discrepancy things that there is no real solution for. Except perhaps to serve different pages to Mac and PC end viewers, which is more than a bit too labor-intensive for most site designers. Remember to always check your pages on both platforms. You can adjust glaring problems accordingly.

A PC screen shot of my site.   A Mac screen shot of my site.

For amusement, I composited the two together in Photoshop by using the Multiply filter. The size differences with the graphic (the man) are nil—but check out the size differences of the type! Mama mia!

Graphics-Based Typography

We've just examined many HTML possibilities; now it's time to move on to graphics-based text. Using graphics for text instead of HTML is where you get the chance to flash your type design aesthetic for the world to see. You'll be able to use any font your heart desires and add special effects to it, such as drop shadows, glows, and blurs. A great advantage to using this technique is that the end users will not have to own the font you used or have it installed on their system. Because it's a graphic, it shows up like any other graphic regardless of what system your end viewers use.

Some of the chapters already presented demonstrate techniques I recommend you combine with your text-based graphics. Using transparency and solid colors that match the background color of your page are two processes in particular that can be employed in combination to achieve some of the effects described here.

■ note

Aliasing Versus Anti-Aliasing

Most digital artists prefer the way anti-aliasing looks, but anti-aliasing is not always the best technique with typography.

Very small type actually looks worse and quite mushy if it's anti-aliased. Think about HTML type, the type on your computer desktop, and the type in a word processor. Very small type sizes (12 pt. and less) do not look good anti-aliased.

yucky mushy small type that's anti-aliased...

This anti-aliased small type looks bad.

no longer yucky mushy small type **because** it's aliased

This aliased, HTML type looks much better.

Using Photoshop for Type Design

Photoshop is the ideal environment to create type and graphic web elements in. Photoshop layers enable you to do all kinds of special type effects for headlines that you can use on the web. Here are some sample type design treatments and instructions to create them. I've used Photoshop 4.0 for these examples, but all of these techniques work in earlier versions of Photoshop as well.

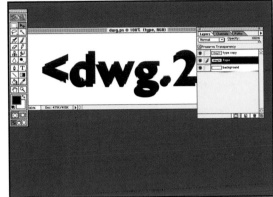

This example demonstrates using the Preserve Transparency feature of Photoshop layers. When checked in the Layers Palette, Preserve Transparency enables you to change the color of the type by painting or filling it. I have a sample browser-safe palette, organized by reds, open to select colors from, which is one of hundreds of artistically organized color swatch sets from the *Coloring Web Graphics* CD-ROM.

Because my type is on a layer, it's easy to copy so I have two versions of the same layer. I filled the bottom layer with black, using the Preserve Transparency feature. I then moved the layer with the Move Tool to create a drop shadow.

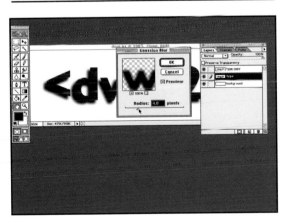

Realistic drop shadows are easy to make in Photoshop. Because my shadow is on a separate layer, adding the Gaussian Blur filter enables me to preview its setting before I commit.

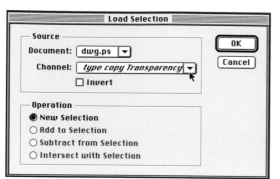

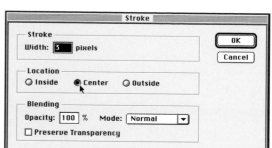

When you leave type separated on separate layers, a mask that is invisible is stored. To load the mask, choose Select, Load Selection and then set the Channel information in this dialog box to Transparency.

By loading the selection, it's possible to then stroke the selection. I chose first to Load the Selection from the transparency of the type layer and then created a new empty layer with the selection still active. By choosing Edit, Stroke, the resulting stroked line went onto an independent layer. When working with type treatments in Photoshop, it should always be your goal to have every element isolated on its own layer so that it can be independently manipulated.

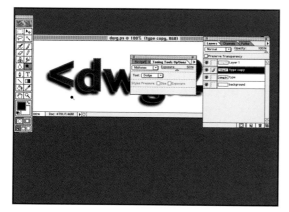

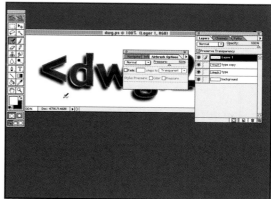

This shows an example of a stroked edge around the type. The chrome-style effect is created with the Dodge and Burn tools. It's possible to create lighting effects with these tools and add more three-dimensional look to the type, if that's the look you're going for.

In this example, using Preserve Transparency, I am able to airbrush highlights into the stroked text layer.

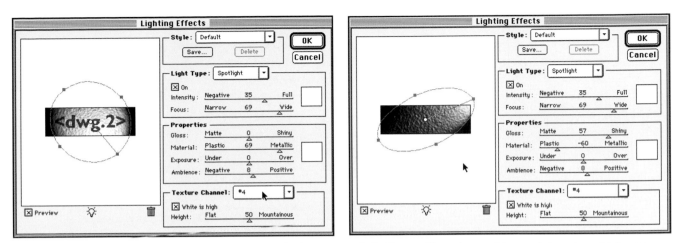

It's also possible to add lighting effects. I show two examples here, one with the Texture Channel set to None and the other with it set to #4. The #4 represents an alpha channel I made by simply adding noise to a black-and-white piece of artwork.

It's possible to make type treatments with lots of Independent layers and lighting effects in Photoshop. Using the techniques of keeping everything on separate layers helps a lot.

This type treatment was made very simple, with a single drop shadow and using the Cloud filter for the upper type layer.

Working with Illustrator Type in Photoshop

Unless I have a very simple logo, I rarely set type in Photoshop. The typesetting tools in Photoshop are limited and disappointing. Photoshop excels in its coloring treatment capabilities. You can't make soft-edged shadows or work with layers and filters as easily in any other graphics program. Illustrator, however, has far more sophisticated and professional type controls, and is a much better type design program. It does such things as type along a path, type within a defined space, size, kern, and adjust tracking, leading, and spacing. The problem is that Illustrator was created as a PostScript program and writes files in formats that the web does not recognize. Here's how to set the type in Illustrator and bring the results into Photoshop so that the type can be utilized on a web page.

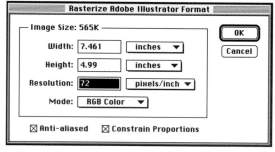

Open a new Illustrator file. Set your type. You'll find all the controls your typesetter heart has been waiting for—sizing, kerning, spacing, superscript, and so on. Look to the glossary for explanations if you aren't familiar with these terms. Once you've got everything set the way you want it, save the file as a default Illustrator 5 document and quit.

Open Photoshop. Open the Illustrator file, and this dialog box appears.

Once you've opened the file in Photoshop, it automatically comes in on its own layer and is a perfect candidate for the techniques described previously.

Here is the final image after it has been touched up with Photoshop. What teamwork!

Writing the HTML to Place Your Text Graphics into the Page

Placing graphics on a web page is addressed in depth in Chapter 9, "Rules, Bullets, and Buttons," and Chapter 10, "Navigation-Based Graphics." The basic way to insert a graphic on a page is to use the <IMG SRC> tag. Here's how to put the drop shadow artwork, created earlier, on a page:

```
<HTML>
<IMG SRC="dropshad.jpeg">
</HTML>
```

If you want to link the drop shadow image to another source, combine the <IMG SRC> tag with an <A HREF> tag. Here's how:

```
<HTML>
<A HREF="http://www.domain.com><IMG
SRC="dropshad.jpeg"></A>
</HTML>
```

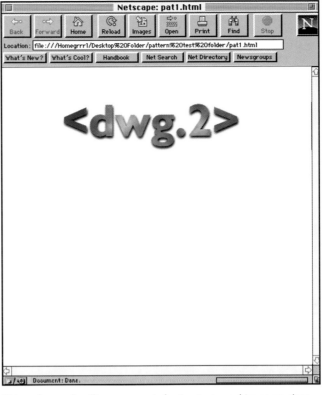

This web page headline was created using text graphics as an alternative to HTML.

Mixing Graphic Type and HTML

If you want to get clever, I've seen wonderful examples of mixing HTML and graphic-based typography. An in-depth version of this case study is in my second book, *Deconstructing Web Graphics*.

Case Study: Alice In Chains

The Alice in Chains site, designed by Mary Maurer and Peter Anton of Sony Music Online, uses mixed HTML and graphic type in a very novel way. Most of the type was set in varying sizes to get a more organic, varied, and erratic look. They used a combination of graphics-based typography tricks and HTML tricks.

This kind of typesetting is impossible to do within Photoshop, which has limited type-handling capabilities. Photoshop allows you to set type in any font within your system but doesn't offer size controls over individual letters.

Mary used QuarkXPress for laying out the typography for the Photoshop files. Because it's impossible to directly import a QuarkXPress file into Photoshop, Mary took screen captures of those files. (A screen capture takes a picture of anything that's on your screen, regardless of what program you're using, and creates a file, which then can be opened in Photoshop.)

Mary also worked with Peter to see whether he could program HTML text to simulate some of her Quark-XPress files. She was quite pleased with the results, which are deconstructed in the following section.

This image uses the font Trixie, by Fonthaus (Fonthaus has a web site at ■ http://home.cityqueue.com/CityQueue/business/fonthaus.html), but each letter is set in a different size. This was done in Quark, and was brought into Photoshop via screen capture software.

The HTML-based text had mixed type sizes, too. This page can be viewed at ■ http://www.music.sony.com/Music/ArtistInfo/AliceInChains/biolane3.html.

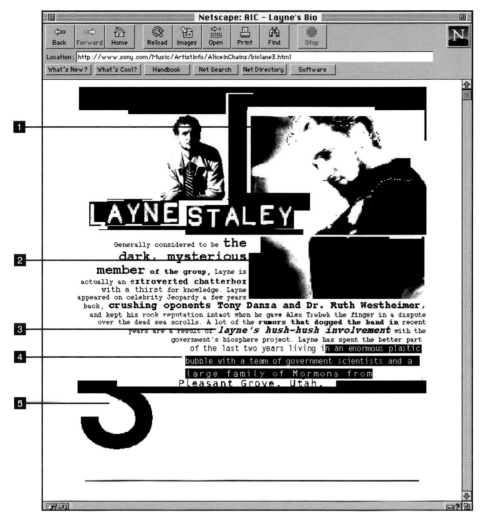

Here's the finished result of the HTML, which is deconstructed on the following two pages.

HTML for Mixed Type Sizes

```
<HTML>
<HEAD>
<TITLE>AIC - Layne's Bio</TITLE>
</HEAD>
<BODY BGCOLOR="FFFFFF"  TEXT = "# 000000" LINK =
"#000000" ALINK = "#E8F13A" VLINK = "#000000" >
<CENTER>
<TABLE BORDER=0 WIDTH=522 HEIGHT=200>
<TD NOWRAP WIDTH=522 HEIGHT=200 ALIGN="RIGHT">
```

1
```
<IMG SRC="biolaypg3hed2.gif"
LOWSRC="biolaypg3hed1.gif" WIDTH=520 HEIGHT=221>
```
2
```
<IMG SRC="biolaypg3hed3.gif" WIDTH=264 HEIGHT=93
ALIGN="RIGHT"><TT><FONT SIZE="3">
```
3
```
Generally considered to be <STRONG><FONT
SIZE="+3">the dark, mysterious member</FONT
SIZE="+3"> of the group,</STRONG> Layne is actually
an <FONT SIZE="+1">e<STRONG>xtroverted
chatterbox</FONT SIZE="+1"> with a thirst</STRONG>
for knowledge. Layne appeared on celebrity Jeopardy
a few years back, <STRONG><FONT SIZE="+2">crushing
oponents Tony Danza and Dr. Ruth
Westheimer,</STRONG></FONT SIZE="+2"> and kept his
rock reputation intact when he gave Alex Trebek the
finger in a dispute over the dead sea scrolls.
A lot of the <STRONG>rumors that dogged the band
in</STRONG> recent years are a result of
<I><STRONG><FONT SIZE="+2">layne's hush-hush
```
```
involvement</I></STRONG></FONT SIZE="+2"> with the
government's biosphere project.  Layne has spent the
better part
```
4
```
<IMG SRC="biolaypg3text.gif" ALIGN="CENTER">
```
5
```
<IMG SRC="biolaypg3bot.gif" WIDTH=522 HEIGHT=113
ALIGN="CENTER">
</TD>
</TABLE>
<P>
<BR>
<CENTER>
<HR NOSHADE WIDTH =500>
<P>
<BR>
<BR>
<TT>
<A HREF="biolane4.html">Next?</A>
<P>
<BR>
<BR>
¦¦ <A HREF="bio.html">Bios</A> ¦¦
</CENTER>
</BODY>
</HTML>
```

1 Here's a **LOWSRC** trick. The **LOWSRC** image loads before the **SRC** image.

The **IMG SRC** file **"biolaypg3hed2.gif"** loads second. It's the inverse of the **LOWSRC** file, causing the animation to look as though its polarity flashes.

The **LOWSRC** image **"biolaypg3hed1.gif"** loads first.

2 The next **IMG SRC** is instructed to align to the right of the text by using the **ALIGN=RIGHT** attribute. The **<TT>** tag indicates that monospaced type will follow until its closed container is specified.

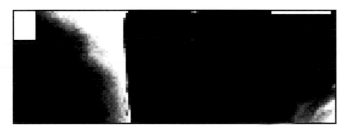

This **IMG SRC** file **"biolaypg3hed3.gif"** is instructed to align to the right of the text.

3 A lot of the **<STRONG>**rumors that dogged the band in**</STRONG>** recent years are a result of **<I>** **<STRONG>** **<FONT SIZE="+2">**layne's hush-hush involvement**</I></STRONG></FONT SIZE="+2">** with the government's biosphere project. Layne has spent the better part

A number of different tags are present here that instruct the browser to display the type differently. **<STRONG>** creates bold text on most browsers. **<FONT SIZE>** indicates that the size of the text will be higher or lower than the default depending on whether the number is positive or negative.

4 This next image aligns **CENTER** and butts up directly to the bottom of the preceding HTML text.

The **IMG SRC** file **"biolaypg3text.gif."**

5 This next image aligns **CENTER** and butts up directly to the bottom of the preceding image.

Pleasant Grove, Utah.

The **IMG SRC** file **"biolaypg3bot.gif."**

Case Study: Art Center College of Design

The Art Center College of Design site at ■ http://www
.artcent.edu) was designed by Gudrun Frommherz and
Darin Beamin. They used another technique used to
enhance HTML text to mix type sizes, fonts (Geneva
and Courier), and styles such as plain, bold, and italic.

```
throughout the pr<b>ogram. In s</b>ome classes students pursue self-directed
```

A sample line of HTML for making type bold with the <B> tag.

```
throughout the program. In some classes students pursue self-directed projects, while
```

By using the <B> tag for making text bold, Gudrun was able to
change the weights of the ASCII-based HTML typography through
mixing bold and normal text characters. These shapes created
abstract forms that are meant to please the eye and invite the
reader to study the content.

Here's the finished result on the web page.

In this example, two typefaces—Geneva and Courier—
are used, as well as setting different type sizes. This is
accomplished by using the <PRE> and <FONT> tags.

```
<PRE>
<FONT SIZE="+4"><b>A    r    t
C   e   n   t   e   r</B> </FONT>
<FONT SIZE="+2">C</font>
<FONT SIZE="+4">o    l   l   e  g   e   o  f</FONT>
<FONT SIZE="+2"><B>D</B></FONT>
<FONT SIZE="+3"><B>E      S      I
G</B></FONT>
<FONT SIZE="+2"><B>N</B></FONT>
</PRE>
```

Above is the HTML to create the words on the bottom. The
<PRE> tag forces the type to be represented in the Courier
typeface. It also instructs the browser to honor the spacing
between words and letters. The <FONT SIZE> tag *is* used
to change the size of individual letters.

A close-up view of the lettering on the bottom of the screen that
uses the <PRE> and <FONT SIZE> tags.

Digital Font Foundries

Today there are tens of thousands of PostScript and TrueType fonts available to personal computer users. It's a great benefit to be able to view and order fonts online, especially those late nights when you're designing something that's due the next day and you need a specific font you don't yet own. If you're looking for new fonts, check out these URLs:

House Industries:
■ http://www.digitmad.com/house/house.html

Letraset Online:
■ http://www.letraset.com/letraset/

Handwriting Fonts:
■ http://www.execpc.com/~adw/

Fonthead Design:
■ http://www.fonthead.com

Fonts Online:
■ http://www.dol.com/fontsOnline/

Emigre:
■ http://www.emigre.com

Agfa Type:
■ http://www.agfahome.com/products/prodfram/type.html

Internet Font Libraries:
■ http://jasper.ora.com:90/comp.fonts/Internet-Font-Archive/index.html

■ **note**

Font Legends
The following individuals are meant to spark your interest. They are just a few of the many legends in type design. You might want to check out books written by them, or about them—as well as pursue others you find of particular interest. Studying the past as well as researching 20th-century works can be a wonderful source of inspiration that effortlessly translates itself into designing meaningful web graphics.

■ Jan Tschichold
■ Laslo Moholy-Nagy
■ A.M. Cassandre
■ Kurt Schwitters
■ Matthew Carter
■ David Carson
■ El Lissitsky
■ Rudy Vanderlands
■ Bradbury Thompson
■ Lucille Tenazas
■ Neville Brody

Introduction

Getting Started in Web Design

Understanding the Web Environment

Web File Formats

Low-Bandwidth Graphics

Hexadecimal Color

Browser-Safe Color

Transparent Artwork

Background Tiles

Rules, Bullets and Buttons

Navigation-Based Graphics

Web-Based Typography

Scanning Techniques for the Web

Layout and Alignment Techniques

Animation

Sound

Interactivity

HTML for Visual Designers

Glossary

Design Resources Appendix

Index

Font 8

Varia
you c
more
The c
You c
amou
more

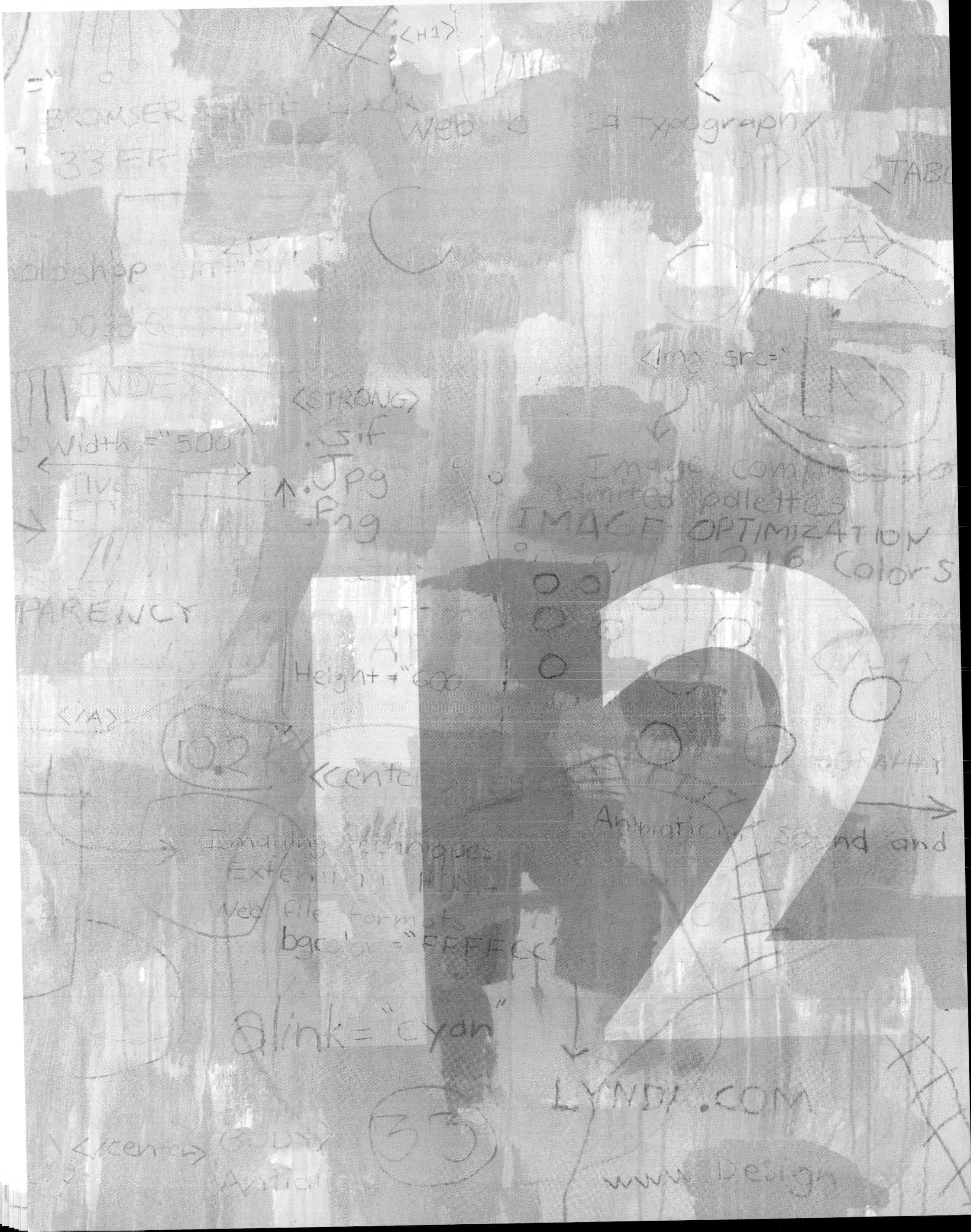

Dot Screen Patterns and Moirés

There might be times when you are asked to scan existing catalogs or product brochures to repurpose images for the web. Unfortunately, there is an inherent problem with this technique because it almost always results in unwanted dot patterns and moirés. This section covers techniques to correct this problem.

Scanned images from printed sources have specific problems when converted to RGB. The printing inks CYMK (cyan, yellow, magenta, and black) result in patterns of dots that are visible and unattractive when scanned. A close-up of a dot pattern is shown at the right to demonstrate this common scanning problem.

A simulation of CMYK printing inks that form a dot pattern.

Here's a scanned image from my book *Coloring Web Graphics*. The dot pattern problem is clearly visible.

Once this image is scaled, the dot patterns get more or less objectionable. The dot patterns change with each resize.

The best approach to this problem is to get rid of the dot pattern that appears on the image before doing any resizing. Below are some techniques for getting rid of the dots.

Other useful tools for getting rid of moirés are:

- Despeckle
- Dust and Scratch
- Unsharp mask

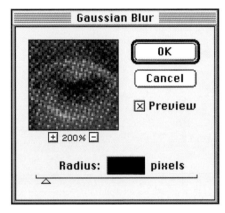

Under Filters, select Gaussian Blur. This filter causes the image to blur depending on what setting is chosen. The idea isn't to completely blur the image, but to get rid of the printing dots. The printing dots are visible within the preview window of this filter.

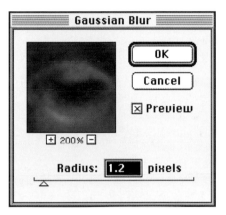

The blur setting at 1.2 pixels. No more printing dots! A higher blur setting will start to degrade the image. This will be a judgment call that you will have to make, and it will differ for every single image you work with

The resulting image does not have any dots, but it's blurry.

The trick is to resize the image smaller. This will cause the blurry appearance to become sharper and less noticable.

At this point, you can add a sharpening filter to eliminate some blur. You should have no evidence of the dot pattern! The Sharpen filter increases the contrast between light and dark areas, so use it sparingly.

Voilà! This image is perfectly acceptable for the web. You may choose to add a little extra saturation to the image using techniques described earlier.

Selections

Selecting artwork is an art unto itself. Selections enable you to apply certain image editing features to specific parts of an image without affecting others. Selections are also commonly referred to as masks or alpha channels. Every time you make a selection in Photoshop, you are creating a mask. An alpha channel is simply a permanently stored record of the selection.

This chapter describes numerous image editing techniques that can improve the quality of scanned imagery. If you understand how to select areas of an image, any of these processes can be applied to specific areas of a needy image. A good command of selection techniques is crucial to creating good-looking scanned artwork.

Photoshop Selection Tools

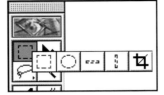

The selection tools in Photoshop include 3 main selection tools, with a couple of variations within each. They are the Marquee, the Lasso, and the Magic Wand Tool.

The Marquee

The Marquee Tool can create either a square, rectangular, elliptical, or circular selection. When an image is selected, you'll see marching ants around the area you specified. The circular marquee can be accessed by holding the mouse down on the marquee icon from the toolbar. You can also call these tool menus forward on the screen and alternate between them by pressing the "M" key on your keyboard.

Each selection tool has its set of options. To access this option window, press Return or Enter on your keyboard to bring the menu forward.

Here are the Options Palettes for the other selection tools. The two most important features within the Options Palettes are feathering and anti-aliasing. Feathering makes the edges of the selection soft by fading the edges off by the number of pixels indicated. Anti-aliased makes the edges of the selection blend seamlessly with its background.

The Magic Wand

The Magic Wand makes selections based on a tolerance in terms of value in pixels (0-255). Checking Anti-aliased enables the edges of the magic wand selections to be blended.

The Lasso

The Lasso Tool enables you to freely draw shapes around what you want to select. The other tool associated with the Lasso Tool is the Polygon Lasso Tool, which enables you to draw with straight connecting lines that connect up to the beginning. This is accessed by holding down the Option key on a Mac, or the Alt key on a PC.

Photoshop Selection Modifiers

In addition to all of these tools, modifier keys enable you to make more complex selections.

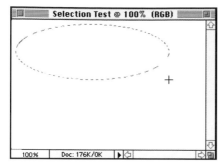

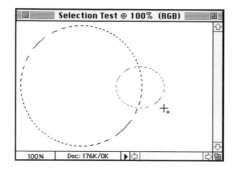

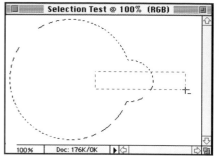

Let's begin with a simple elliptical selection. This shape can be drawn freehand, without using any modifier keys.

If you hold down the Shift key while making the selection, it will be constrained to become a perfect circle. If you were using the rectangular marquee, this modifier would create a perfect square. To add a selection to another selection, simply hold down the Shift key before you make your second selection.

To cut out a section of a selection, use the Option key on Macs or the Ctrl key on PCs.

Painting Quickmask Selections in Photoshop 4.0

Sometimes, the marquee and lasso selection tools are too limited. Painting a selection is the answer! If you want to paint or draw your mask, you can do so by using the Quickmask feature in Photoshop. The Quickmask enables you to paint a mask directly onto your image. Although it looks like it's coloring your image, it's not—it's actually making a selection.

You can toggle your selections and Quickmasks by the Quickmask button on the main toolbar. To apply your Quickmask, you simply leave the Quickmask mode by toggling back to Selection Mode on the toolbar. You can use any tool to create a Quickmask image—Paintbrush, Airbrush, Pencil, Gradient, and so on. You can also run your mask through filters for desired effects.

The Quickmask settings are located at the bottom of the Photoshop 4.0 Toolbar. The setting at the left indicates Selection Mode, and the setting at the right indicates Quickmask mode.

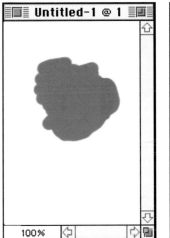

Here's an example of what the Quickmask selection looks like, before you toggle back to the Selection Mode.

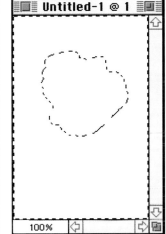

Once you toggle to Selection Mode, the marching ants appear based on the selection shape you painted.

■ **tip**

More on Photoshop

For a complete rundown of other possible selection techniques, you might consult a dedicated Photoshop book or the official manual.

Introduction

Getting Started in Web Design

Understanding the Web Environment

Web File Formats

Low-Bandwidth Graphics

Hexadecimal Color

Browser-Safe Color

Transparent Artwork

Background Tiles

Rules, Bullets and Buttons

Navigation-Based Graphics

Web-Based Typography

Scanning Techniques for the Web

Layout and Alignment Techniques

Animation

Sound

Interactivity

HTML for Visual Designers

Glossary

Design Resources Appendix

Index

13
<H1>
Web typography
<Img src="
<STRONG>
.Gif
.Jpg
Png
Width="500"
Image compression
palettes
IMAGE OPTIMIZATION
216 Colors
PARENCY
Height="600"
</A>
10.2
<center>
Animation, sound and
Extending HTML
Web file formats
bgcolor="FFFFCC"
LYNDA.COM
</center>
www Design

Alignment Hell

A web page has no fixed size. Some browsers have predefined sizes that the viewing window fits to; others let you size the screen to fill your monitor. Some of your audience will see your page through tiny portable computer screens. Others will have 21" monitors. Some of your audience will change the font size defaults, which will make everything line up differently than you planned.

Imagine if you had to fit lots of information on a piece of paper, but no one could tell you the size of the paper you had to work with. And imagine trying to fit that information onto the paper artistically, with a little more finesse than left-justifying every image, headline, and text block. Also imagine that the tools to change position and alignment were strange and unintuitive and didn't work everywhere.

Is it any wonder that few designers know how to do web page layout well? Making a web page behave the way you want it to is a challenging task. This chapter examines alignment issues from a few different angles:

- Defining the size of a web page
- Using HTML alignment tags
- Using invisible spacers for alignment
- Using tables for alignment
- Aligning foreground and background images

Once you've examined all the possibilities this chapter covers, you'll see that it's possible to beat the odds and create interesting layouts in HTML. What is possible is not easy, however, because HTML was never intended to be a page layout description language.

When I wrote the first edition of *Designing Web Graphics*, we were in the era of Browser Hell. There were so many different kinds of browsers, and no one browser had the clear market advantage of being the one for which to design.

These examples demonstrate what can happen when using some of the alignment techniques described in this chapter with browsers that don't support table tags. Fortunately, both MSIE and Netscape abound now, and these pitfalls to using alignment techniques are not as prevalent anymore.

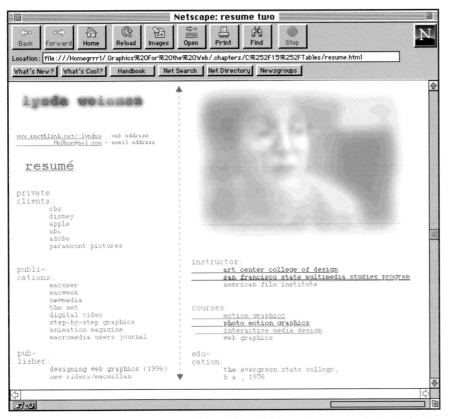

Here's an example of a three-column table and the <PRE> tag alignment methods displayed in Netscape 1.1. These methods of alignment are discussed in-depth within this chapter. During the era of Browser Hell, this was a pretty tricky alignment accomplishment.

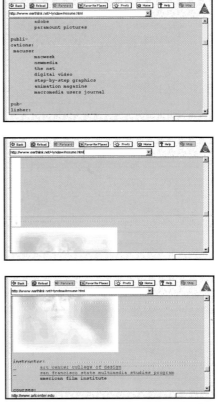

In a browser that didn't support tables, this type of alignment technique created a disaster! Here's the identical HTML file that failed and had to be displayed accross five separate screens. No one misses those days of Browser Hell!

Defining the Size of a Web Page

"Small is better" seems to be the credo of web design. Because there is no fixed size to a web page, you get to define one yourself. Taking into account that people might be looking at your work in small windows, it makes the most sense to define a small page size to work with. Yes, but how small is small?

I tend to err on the conservative side when suggesting width restrictions for graphics on a web page. 640 pixels is the average width of an average computer monitor—even on many portables— and I think there should be some breathing room around that. On the Macintosh, Netscape's opening screen defaults to 505 pixels across. I've picked 480 pixels as a good width for an opening graphic or headline. That's the approximate width of the menu bar for Netscape's home page. This rule is not cast in stone. I'm simply describing the sizes of some of the environments your page will be viewed in and arriving at a size based on how I would want my graphics to be viewed.

Lack of a defined web page size can be dealt with creatively. Carina Feldman, who recently received an M.F.A. in Graphic Design from Art Center College of Design, challenged the unlimited size of a web page by creating a long, vertical text graphic that forces viewers to scroll down many computer screens to finish reading.

Carina Feldman's long, vertical graphic that plays with lack of defined space (■ www.quicklink.com/~zigzag).

Because web pages can scroll vertically or horizontally, there are no length or width restrictions to contend with on a web document. The size of the artwork you choose to put on any given page dictates the size of the page. If you position artwork that spans horizontally or vertically, the page fits to the size of your artwork. Scroll bars appear in most browsers automatically when the artwork is oversized in either direction.

If you want your opening graphic to be visible on most computer monitors, however, you may want to think about composing your opening page graphic (splash screen or menu bar) so that it can be seen on a portable computer. Most portable computer screens today are 640x480, and some are 640x400.

Based on this information, I think opening screen graphics and headline text, or whatever you hope the viewer will see at first glance on your page, should be no taller than 350 pixels.

Some artists choose to make wider screens than my conservative estimate of 480 pixels. There are lots of clever ways to tell your audience how wide to open the browser window, as shown by the following examples.

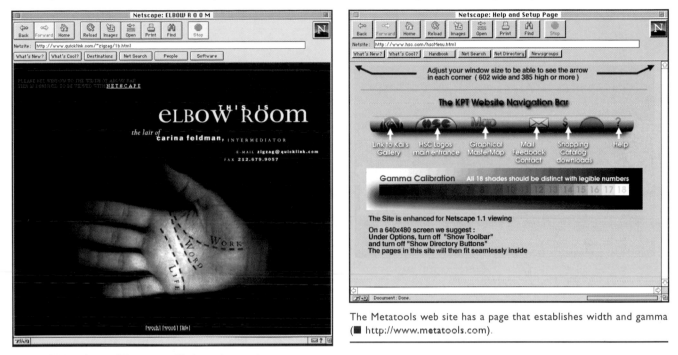

Carina Feldman's site (■ www.quicklink.com/ zigzag).

The Metatools web site has a page that establishes width and gamma (■ http://www.metatools.com).

As you can see, the size of your page is up to you. Take your average end viewer's monitor capabilities into account to make informed design decisions about sizing. Carina's pages are great for personal expression, but if you are hired to design a page for a client, it most likely would be important to make the page read at first glance under standard monitor conditions.

JavaScript for Establishing Page Size

It's a good idea to check out your pages on different size monitors. Not everyone can be so lucky to own lots of different size monitors, so Steven Younis came up with a very cool JavaScript that would simulate monitor sizes. Feel free to check your pages through his site:

■ http://www.dot.net.au/younis/window.html

Go to ■ http://www.dot.net.au/younis/window.html to check out Steven's cool JavaScript.

Here's the code, in case you want to try this yourself. Be sure to credit Steven if you use it on your own site.

```
<!-- THIS PAGE WAS CREATED WITH WORLD WIDE
WEB WEAVER 2.0 IN ORDER TO SEPARATE THIS PAGE
INTO MULTIPLE SECTIONS COMMENT TAGS HAVE BEEN
PLACED AT SPECIFIC LOCATIONS. REMOVING OR
EDITING THESE COMMENTS WILL CAUSE WEB WEAVER
TO NOT RECOGNIZE SECTIONS -->
<HTML>
<HEAD><TITLE>New Window</TITLE>
<SCRIPT LANGUAGE="JavaScript">
<!--Activate Cloaking
//***************************************** CREDITS
****************************************************
//
//   Web Page Monitor Tester
(Last updated-December 12, 1996)
//   Written by:  Steven Younis (younis@dot.net.au)
//
//   Younis Graphics-http://www.dot.net.au/younis
//
//**************************************************
**************************************************
**
//Deactivate Cloaking-->
</SCRIPT>
</HEAD><BODY><!-- BEGIN BODY HEADER SECTION -->
<!-- BEGIN MAIN BODY SECTION --><H2>
Web Page Monitor Tester</H2>
<HR NOSHADE><P>
<FORM>
Open a window 640 x 480 pixels:
<INPUT TYPE=BUTTON VALUE="640x480"
onClick="window.open ('window.html','640x480',
'toolbar-yes,status=yes,scrollbars=yes,
location=yes,menubar=yes,directories=yes,width=640,
height=480')"><P>
Open a window 800 x 600 pixels:
<INPUT TYPE=BUTTON VALUE="800x600"
onClick="window.open ('window.html','800x600',
'toolbar=yes,status=yes,scrollbars=yes,
location=yes,menubar=yes,directories=yes,width=800,
height=600')"><P>
<HR><P>
Default Netscape Browser sizes:<P>
<B>640 x 480</B><BR>
Mac = 470x300:
<INPUT TYPE=BUTTON VALUE="Mac"
onClick=" window.open('window.html','Mac',

'toolbar=yes,status=yes,scrollbars=yes,
location=yes,menubar=yes,directories=yes,width=470,
height=300')"><BR>
PC  = 580x300:
<INPUT TYPE=BUTTON VALUE="PC"
onClick="window.open
('window.html','PC','toolbar=yes,status=yes,
scrollbars=yes,location=yes,menubar=yes,
directories=yes,width=580,height=300')"><P>
<B>800 x 600</B><BR>
Mac = 470x430:
<INPUT TYPE=BUTTON VALUE="Mac"
onClick="window.open('window.html','Mac',
'toolbar=yes,status=yes,scrollbars=yes,
location=yes,menubar=yes,directories=yes,
width=470,height=430')"><BR>
PC  = 580x430:
<INPUT TYPE=BUTTON VALUE="PC"
onClick="window.open('window.html','PC',
'toolbar=yes,status=yes,scrollbars=yes,
location=yes,menubar=yes,directories=yes,width=580,
height=430')"><P>
<B>1024 x 768</B><BR>
Mac = 470x600:
<INPUT TYPE=BUTTON VALUE="Mac"
onClick="window.open
('window.html','Mac','toolbar=yes,status=yes,
scrollbars=yes,location=yes,menubar=yes,
directories=yes,width=470,height=600')"><BR>
PC  = 580x600:
<INPUT TYPE=BUTTON VALUE="PC"
onClick="window.open('window.html','PC',
'toolbar=yes,status=yes,scrollbars=yes,
location=yes,menubar=yes,directories=yes,width=580,
height=600')"><P>
<P>
<HR><P>
Close this Window:
<INPUT TYPE=BUTTON VALUE="Close"
onClick="window.close()">
</FORM>
<P><HR NOSHADE><P>
<FONT SIZE=-1>Copyright &#169; 1996,
<A HREF="MAILTO:younis@dot.net.au">
Steven Younis</A>.</FONT>
<!-- BEGIN BODY FOOTER SECTION --></BODY></HTML>
```

Using HTML for Alignment

HTML was not designed to be a QuarkXPress or PageMaker. I don't think the original authors ever dreamed of it as a tool for page layout that would satisfy the needs of graphic designers. It was originally invented to support the scientific community and to include diagrams and image tables that were associated with massive quantities of technical writings. Formatting handles such as left justifying and indenting a list of words suited the needs of that community just fine.

We're asking a lot more of HTML than it was ever designed to do, which is OK. HTML originators thought they were inventing one thing for one purpose, and it laid the ground-work for other purposes—including layout design! HTML has limited alignment capabilities, but web designers worth their weight should know how to use all of them.

On the following pages I have provided a useful list of HTML tags for aligning text and images.

Text Alignment Tags

These tags relate to text elements.

Paragraph breaks: Insert this tag where you want spaces between paragraphs:

`<P>`

Line breaks: Put this tag where you want to have the text wrap to the next line:

`<BR>`

Centering text: Use this tag before you center text and/or images, and use the closed tag when you want text below it to return to left-justified formatting.

`<CENTER>`

Preformatted text: Preformatted text typically uses a different font, such as the typewriter-style Courier, instead of the default Times Roman. The <PRE> tag lets you set the spacing and indents of your type. (For more examples of the <PRE> tag, check out Chapter 11, "Web-Based Typography," and Chapter 17, "HTML for Visual Designers.")

`<PRE></PRE>`

No break: Use this tag if you want the browser width to dictate where the text breaks. The closed tag signifies when you want the no break formatting to end.

`<NOBR></NBR>`

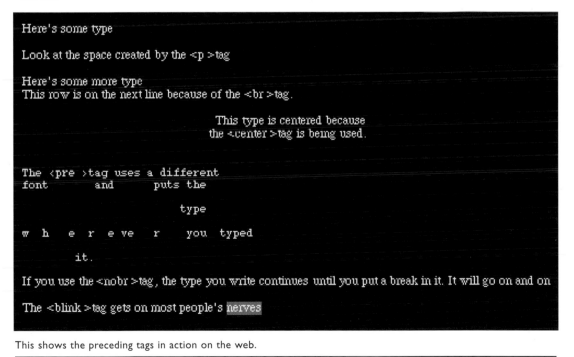

This shows the preceding tags in action on the web.

Image and Type Alignment Tags

These tags cause text to align in relationship to the images it's next to.

<ALIGN=TOP> Align text to the top of your image:

`<IMG SRC=filenamehere.gif ALIGN=TOP>`

<ALIGN=BOTTOM> Align text to the bottom of your image:

`<IMG SRC=filenamehere.gif ALIGN=BOTTOM>`

<ALIGN=MIDDLE> Align text to the middle of your image:

`<IMG SRC=filenamehere.gif ALIGN=MIDDLE>`

Image Alignment Tags

The following tags align the images to the left or right of the screen.

Image left justified:

`<IMG SRC=filenamehere.gif ALIGN=LEFT>`

Image right justified:

`<IMG SRC=filenamehere.gif ALIGN=RIGHT>`

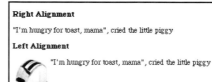

Horizontal and Vertical Space Tags

The horizontal and vertical space tags allow you to insert empty space around a graphic, creating breathing room.

HSPACE: I've used the <HSPACE=XX> tag in the following code to put 40 pixels of breathing room to the left and right of the toaster image.

```
<HTML>
<HEAD> <TITLE> Alignment Test</TITLE> </HEAD>
<BODY BGCOLOR="ffffff">
<IMG SRC="ltoast.jpg" ALIGN=LEFT HSPACE=40>"I'm hungry for toast, mama!", <BR>cried the little piggy.<BR CLEAR=all>
</BODY>
</HTMLl>
```

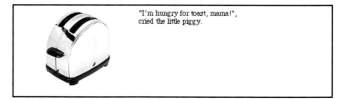

VSPACE: To demonstrate what adding <VSPACE=value> does, I experimented with the following code:

```
<HTML>
<HEAD> <TITLE> Alignment Test</TITLE> </HEAD>
<BODY BGCOLOR="ffffff">
<IMG SRC="ltoast.jpg" ALIGN=LEFT HSPACE=40
VSPACE=80>"I'm hungry for toast, mama!",
<BR>cried the little piggy.<BR CLEAR=all>
</BODY>
</HTML>
```

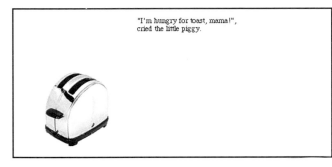

WIDTH and HEIGHT Attributes

These attributes work by allowing you to specify the width and height values (in pixels) of a graphic. This can accomplish two things: it causes the text on the page to load before the graphic while making space for the graphic to come into the proper location. Using WIDTH and HEIGHT attributes within HTML is very important for downloading speed, and many plug-in <EMBED> tags require that you include width and height information. (See chapters 14 and 16 for more information on plug-ins and embedding.)

There's a lesser-known feature of <WIDTH> and <HEIGHT> tags, however. If you put smaller or larger values in these tags, they will actually shrink or scale your image. In the following example, the actual dimension of the toaster image is 102x115 pixels. By putting a width of 53 and height of 60, I shrunk the image in half. By putting a value of 240x214, I scaled it to be twice as big.

The following sections illustrate these alignment tags.

```
<HTML>
<HEAD> <TITLE> Alignment Test</TITLE> </HEAD>
<BODY BGCOLOR="ffffff">
<IMG SRC="ltoast.jpg" WIDTH=60 HEIGHT=53
ALIGN=LEFT>"I'm hungry for toast, mama!",
<BR>cried the little piggy.<br >
<P>
<P>
<IMG SRC="ltoast.jpg" WIDTH=240 HEIGHT=214
ALIGN=LEFT>"I'm hungry for toast, mama!",
<BR>cried the little piggy.<BR>
</BODY>
</HTML>
```

This exhausts the possibilities that widely supported HTML tags offer for alignment.

Next, we move on to alignment techniques without using HTML. These involve making custom artwork that serves to align images, instead of relying on code.

Alternatives to HTML Using Artwork

Using images for alignment involves creating spacer art. This art exists on the web page for the sole purpose of making spaces between text and images. For the spacer art to be invisible, you have two options.

Make the spacer art the same color as your background. To do this, use the <BODY BACKGROUND> or <BODY BGCOLOR> tag to create a solid color or colored background pattern tile, or both. Make sure your spacer art is one color and assign that color to be transparent, saving the one-color artwork as a transparent GIF. These methods are described in more depth in Chapters 5, "Hexadecimal Color," and 7, "Transparent Artwork."

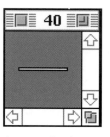

An example of spacer art.

Using Spacers for Alignment

The following is what the HTML code would produce without using any spacers or alignment techniques. The toaster photographs are from a CD-ROM collection from Classic PIO Partners (800-370-2746). I've named the artwork respectively: ltoast.jpg, ftoast.jpg, and rtoast.jpg.

```
<HTML>
<HEAD> <TITLE> Alignment Test</TITLE> </HEAD>
<BODY BGCOLOR="ffffff">
<IMG SRC="ltoast.jpg"><IMG SRC="ftoast.jpg"><IMG SRC="rtoast.jpg">
</BODY>
</HTML>
```

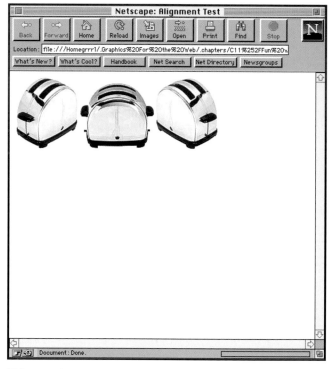

This example uses no spacers.

The following is the HTML code to use white spacer art between each image to give them a little breathing room. I made a file in Photoshop that was 40 pixels wide and 1 pixel high, and named it 40space.jpg.

```
<HTML>
<HEAD> <TITLE> Alignment Test</TITLE> </HEAD>
<BODY BGCOLOR="ffffff">
<IMG SRC="40space.jpg"><IMG SRC="ltoast.jpg"><IMG
SRC="40space.jpg"><IMG SRC="ftoast.jpg"><IMG
SRC="40space.jpg"><IMG SRC="rtoast.jpg">
</BODY>
</HTML>
```

If I used the same spacer in front of each image, I could create a consistent left indent.

```
<HTML>
<HEAD> <TITLE> Alignment Test</TITLE> </HEAD>
<BODY BGCOLOR="ffffff">
<IMG SRC="40space.jpg"><<IMG SRC ="ltoast.jpg">
<P><<IMG SRC ="40space.jpg"><<IMG SRC ="ftoast.jpg">
<P><<IMG SRC ="40space.jpg"><<IMG SRC ="rtoast.jpg">
</BODY>
</HTML>
```

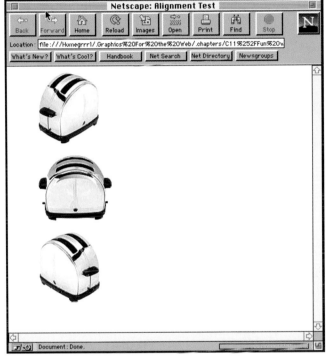

This example uses the space in front of each image.

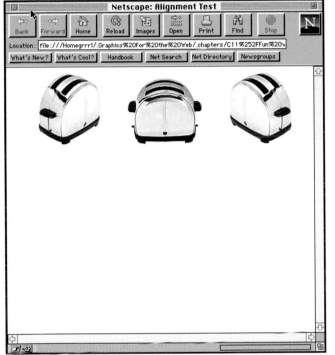

This example uses the 40-pixel wide spacer between each image.

■ tip

WIDTH and HEIGHT Attributes for Spacers

You don't have to make the spacer art the correct size. Using the WIDTH and HEIGHT attributes, you can stretch a single pixel GIF to become any size you wish. David Siegel is the master of the single pixel GIF trick. Check out his instructions at ■ http://www.dsiegel.com/tips/wonk5/single.html.

He also wrote a great book called *Creating Killer Web Sites*, published by Hayden Books (ISBN: 1-568302-894), which teaches a lot of helpful table and alignment techniques.

Aligning a Graphic to a Patterned Background

One of the frustrating things about web design is the strange offset phenomenon that exists between foreground and background images. There's no solution for it, but working with backgrounds that have small intricate patterns as opposed to large obvious patterns can trick the eye into forgiving the offset.

Here's an example of a foreground image Bruce Heavin made that has been precomposited over a complex background in Photoshop.

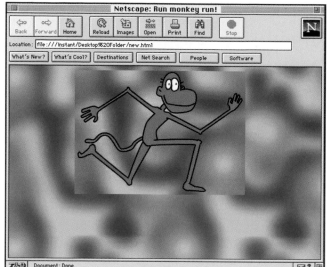

The identical complex background was used as a seamless tile in the <BODY BACKGROUND> tag of this HTML. Notice the mismatched edge? There's nothing that can be done about this offset, especially because the offset amount differs on Mac and PC versions of browsers.

Here's an example of artwork by Richard Downs (■ http://www.earthlink.net/~downsart/). It's been created against a complex background, but the background pattern is very tight and detailed.

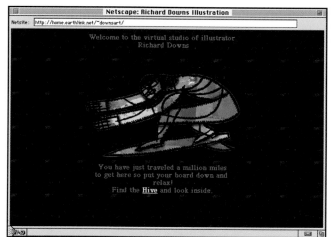

Even though the same offset mismatch exists here, it's barely noticeable because the small pattern is much more forgiving.

Tables for Alignment

Tables for the web were originally conceived to produce columns of text or numbers in individual cells, much like a spreadsheet or chart. Even though tables were invented to support text and numbers, you can put graphics inside table cells, too. All the graphic tags we've described so far work within the table tags. Because of this, I've made a distinction in this chapter between data tables and graphic tables.

You'll see a lot of attention in other books and online sources paid to data tables. The same tags that support data can also support graphics, and herein lies a great power waiting to be unleashed. The graphic designer who knows how to use tables for page layout control will be a much happier camper than the one who doesn't. Learning to program tables will offer lots of formatting options that HTML doesn't directly support.

There are great online tutorials for learning to program tables. I've seen online support only for data tables, not graphic tables. Still, data table principles are crucial to understand if you're going to use graphic tables. Some of my favorite online sources for table instruction follow.

This is a site to watch for all kinds of great online tutorials. The authors are Japanese, so the English is a little stilted, but the instruction on tables and many other HTML tags is indispensable:
- http://ncdesign.kyushuid.ac.jp/howto/text/Normal/table.html

Table instruction from the Netscape site itself:
- http://home.mcom.com/assist/net_sites/tables.html

You will learn about how to program graphics tables later in this chapter, but first you should understand the basic kind of web tables: data-based tables.

> ### ■ note
>
> #### WYSIWYG Tables
> It should be noted that almost all WYSIWYG HTML editors let you create tables without programming the code. It's so much easier to use them—instead of hand coding—that it's really worth your time to invest in one of them. It's important to understand how tables in HTML work, however, because it's still necessary, from time to time, to edit the automatic code WYSIWYG editors generate.

Data Tables

Data-based tables are quite possibly what the HTML standards committee (■ http://www.w3c.com) had in mind when they endorsed the code. These are the typical kinds of tables that you'll see on most sites. They contain text and numbers, links, and occasional graphics. They have telltale borders around the cells, which look slightly dimensional, by employing embossed lines of varying width to divide individual chart sections.

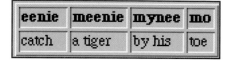

Data tables default to use embossed lines to divide the cells and sections.

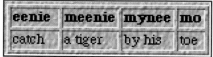

If you use a pattern background or solid color background, the embossing shows through and looks as if it's a lighting effect.

Table borders are sort of like horizontal rules on steroids—the HTML code magically manufactures vertical and horizontal lines of different widths and thicknesses with a few choice strokes of code and tags. They seem complicated by appearance, but you will probably be surprised at how easy they are to create and use.

HTML Table Tags

When creating data or graphics tables for the web, you work with the same HTML tags. The table tags allow you to put information inside individual cells. Understanding the tag structure for data tables enables you to work with the graphic tables later in this chapter.

You always begin a table with **<TABLE>** and end it with the **</TABLE>** tag. The **<TR> </TR>** tag stands for starting and ending a new row. The **<TH> </TH>** tag delineates the header and makes the text in that row bold. The **<TD> </TD>** tag stands for the content of each data cell.

Here's an example of such code, with the HTML below:

```
<TABLE>
<TR> <TH>eenie
</TH><TH>meenie</TH><TH>mynce
</TH><TH>mo</TH></TR>
<TR><TD>catch</TD><TD>a tiger</TD><TD>
by his</TD><TD>toe</TD></TR></TABLE>
```

eenie	meenie	mynee	mo
catch	a tiger	by his	toe

The **<TABLE BORDER>** tag gives the table that embossed look and feel. Here's an example of such code, with the HTML below:

```
<TABLE BORDER>
<TR> <TH>eenie
</TH><TH>meenie</TH><TH>mynee</TH>
<TH>mo</TH></TR>
<TR><TD>catch</TD><TD>a tiger</TD><TD>
by his</TD><TD>toe</TD></TR></TABLE>
```

eenie	meenie	mynee	mo
catch	a tiger	by his	toe

The **<COLSPAN>** tag allows one row to fill more than one column. Here's an example of such code, with the HTML below:

```
<TABLE BORDER>
<TR><TH COLSPAN=4> A poem,by someone</TH>
<TR> <TH>eenie
</TH><TH>meenie</TH><TH>mynee</TH>
<TH>mo</TH></TR>
<TR><TD>catch</TD><TD>a tiger</TD><TD>
by his</TD><TD>toe</TD></TR></TABLE>
```

A poem, by someone			
eenie	meenie	mynee	mo
catch	a tiger	by his	toe

The **<ROWSPAN>** tag takes up columns and rows. It is not any specified size or shape; the dimensions are dictated by the content you insert. Here's an example of such code, with the HTML below:

```
<TABLE BORDER>
<TR><TH ROWSPAN=4> A poem, by someone</TH>
<TR><TH>eenie
</TH><TH>meenie</TH><TH>mynee</TH>
<TH>mo</TH></TR>
<TR><TD>catch</TD><TD>a tiger</TD><TD>
by his</TD><TD>toe</TD></TR></TABLE>
```

A poem, by someone	eenie	meenie	mynee	mo
	catch	a tiger	by his	toe

The **<TABLE WIDTH=# of pixels>** and **<TABLE HEIGHT=# of pixels>** tags allow you to dictate the shape of the table by pixels. Here's an example of such code, with the HTML below:

```
<TABLE BORDER WIDTH=300 HEIGHT=100>
<TR> <TH>eenie
</TH><TH>meenie</TH><TH>mynee</TH>
<TH>mo</TH></TR>
<TR><TD>catch</TD><TD>a tiger</TD><TD>
by his</TD><TD>toe</TD></TR></TABLE>
```

eenie	meenie	mynee	mo
catch	a tiger	by his	toe

The **<TABLE CELLSPACING=# of pixels>** tag puts a thicker line weight around the cells. Here's an example of such code, with the HTML below:

```
<TABLE BORDER CELLSPACING=10>
<TR> <TH>eenie
</TH><TH>meenie</TH><TH>mynee</TH>
<TH>mo</TH></TR>
<TR><TD>catch</TD><TD>
a tiger</TD><TD>
by his</TD><TD>toe</TD></TR></TABLE>
```

eenie	meenie	mynee	mo
catch	a tiger	by his	toe

The **<TABLE CELLPADDING=# of pixels>** tag puts a uniform space inside the cells, governed by the number of pixels entered after the **=** (equal) sign. Here's an example of such code, with the HTML below:

```
<TABLE BORDER CELLPADDING=10>
<TR> <TH>eenie
</TH><TH>meenie</TH><TH>mynee</TH>
<TH>mo</TH></TR>
<TR><TD>catch</TD><TD>a tiger</TD><TD>
by his</TD><TD>toe</TD></TR></TABLE>
```

eenie	meenie	mynee	mo
catch	a tiger	by his	toe

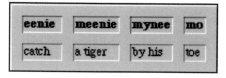

You can adjust the alignment of data inside cells by using the **<VALIGN>** tag, which allows you to specify top, middle, bottom, and baseline alignments. Here's an example of such code:

```
<TABLE BORDER HEIGHT=100>
<TR> <TH>eenie
</TH><TH>meenie</TH><TH>mynee</TH>
<TH>mo</TH></TR>
<TR><TD VALIGN=top>catch</TD><TD
VALIGN=middle>a tiger</TD><TD VALIGN=bot-
tom>by his</TD><TD
VALIGN=baseline>toe</TD></TR></TABLE>
```

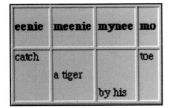

You can also specify, right, left, and middle alignment values within the <TR>, <TH>, and <TD> tags by using the word align. Here's an example of such code:

```
<TABLE BORDER WIDTH=300>
<TR> <TH ALIGN left>eenie </TH><TH ALIGN
left>meenie</TH>
<TH ALIGN left>mynee</TH>
<TH ALIGN left>mo</TH></TR>
<TR><TD ALIGN=left>catch</TD>
<TD ALIGN=left>a tiger</TD>
<TD ALIGN=left>by his</TD>
<TD ALIGN=left>toe</TD></TR></TABLE>
<TABLE BORDER WIDTH=300>
<TR> <TH ALIGN=right>eenie </TH>
<TH ALIGN=right>meenie</TH>
<TH ALIGN=right>mynee</TH>
<TH ALIGN=right>mo</TH></TR>
<TR><TD ALIGN=right>catch</TD>
<TD ALIGN=right>a tiger</TD>
<TD ALIGN=right>by his</TD>
<TD ALIGN=right>toe</TD></TR></TABLE>
```

eenie	meenie	mynee	mo
catch	a tiger	by his	toe

You can also put graphics inside tables, by using the **<IMG SRC="name.gif">** tag, instead of text or values. Here's an example of such code, with the HTML below:

```
<TABLE BORDER>
<TR> <TD>
<IMG SRC="catcha.gif"></TD></TR></TABLE>
```

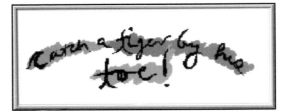

Here's an example of mixing text and graphics inside cells of a table:

```
<TABLE BORDER>
<TR> <TH>eenie </TH><TH>
<IMG SRC="meenie.gif"></TH><TH>mynee</TH>
<TH>mo</TH></TR>
<TR><TD>catch</TD><TD >a tiger
</TD><TD>by his</TD><TD >
<IMG SRC="toe.gif"></TD></TR></TABLE>
```

eenie	meenie	mynee	mo
catch	a tiger	by his	toe

This last example shows how to insert graphics into your tables by using the **<IMG SRC>** tag. The following section explains how you can work with graphics more seamlessly, by eliminating the telltale border around table cells.

Graphic Tables for Page Layout Design

Table support is the first real hook we've had to being able to control layout of page design. If you use tables to create a design grid, all the things that HTML has kept you from doing are suddenly possible. You want a vertical row of linked type in the middle of your page, or a vertical rule graphic? No problem! You want your graphics aligned left or right to a specific grid defined by pixels? No problem! You want to define the size of your page and not let the browser do that for you? No problem! Basically, if you're used to working with PageMaker or Quark, you're used to working with design grids. Tables take much more effort, but if you do some preplanning, you can use them much the same way.

This example of a page within @tlas shows how tables help them align graphics. The borders are turned on intentionally to show where the tables are.

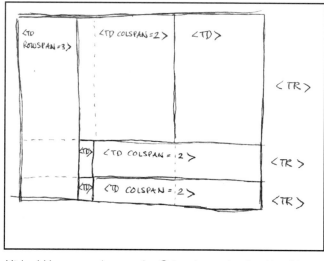

Michael Macrone, webmaster for @tlas, always sketches his tables on paper before programming the code. It helps him know how many rows and columns he needs.

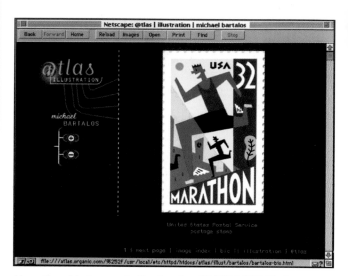

Here, the table is turned off, using the <TABLE BORDER=0> attribute. Check out @tlas at ■ http://www.atlas.organic.com.

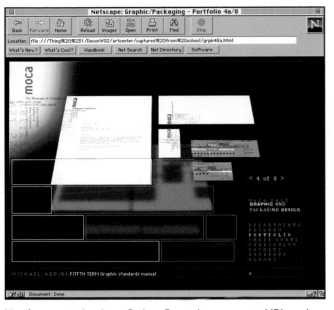

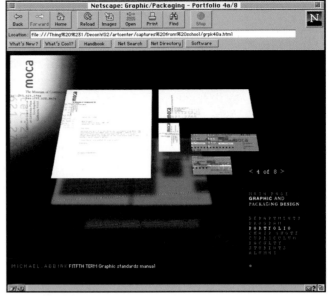

Here's an example where Gudrun Frommherz, a recent MFA graduate from Art Center College of Design, used a table to place invisible GIFs over a large JPEG background image. The invisible GIFs were programmed to link to other pages. Note: This would work reliably on a single-system intranet. Alignment inconsistencies between platforms are described on page 312.

The finished screen shows no evidence of the tables because the borders are turned off. You can, however, click on the blurry stacks of paper on the screen image and be linked to other pages. This is an incredibly cool trick, because it effectively enables you to add links to huge <BODY BACKGROUND> images. Because the image is a JPEG, it's small enough for easy web viewing.

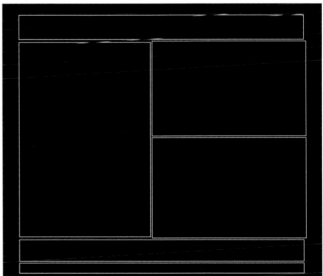

This page (■ http://www.mixingmessages.si.edu) designed by Elizabeth Roxby looks like a single image.

Actually, it's a table with a single image cut apart into many images. This enabled the designer to optimize each section as a JPEG or a GIF, depending on the best compression for each respective section.

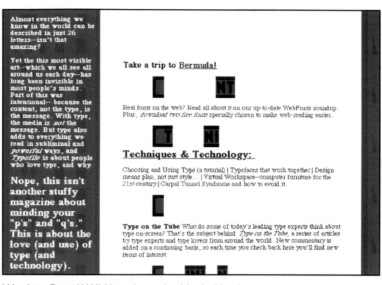

Watching Daniel Will Harris' page load looks like the entire page is animated. In reality, he's broken apart his single images into many images and positioned them with tables. It gives a Venetian blind effect when the page is loaded.

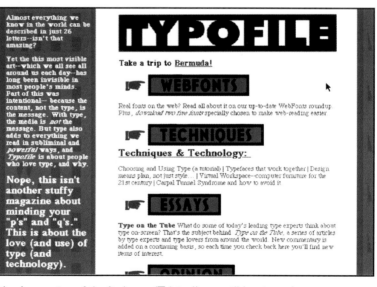

Here's a section of the final page (■ http://www.will-harris.com).

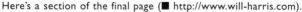

Warning: Text in Tables Can Get Messed Up Easily

As wonderful as tables are for forcing text and images into exact positions, there's one major snafu. Text tables are dependent on the size of the text. If you've created dainty text boxes and your end viewers decide to change their default sizes for text, your table is going to look terrible. For this reason, tables with graphics only are much more reliable than tables with text or a combination of the two. I'm not suggesting you don't use tables for text, but understand that you run the risk that these tables might not look as you intended on everyone's system.

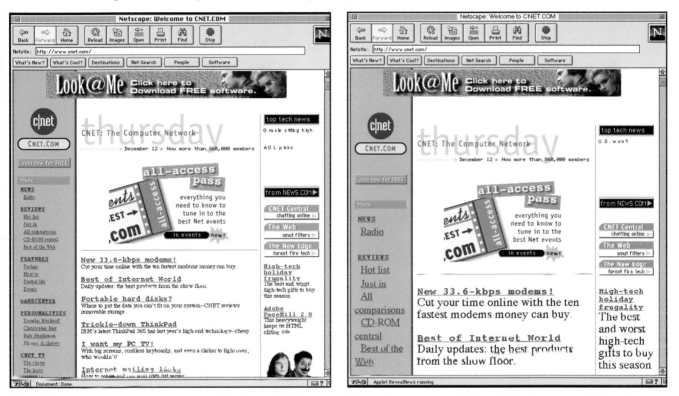

■ http://www.cnet.com makes great use of tables for a tabloid-style newspaper layout.

Here's the same page, with the default fonts changed. Though not terrible, this is probably NOT what the designers had in mind. You always run the risk of unpredictable settings when your page is reliant on tables and text.

Alignment Without Tables

The <PRE> tag, which was discussed in Chapter 11, "Web-Based Typography," can also be used for alignment purposes. Here's Crystal Waters' (author of *Web Concept & Design* and *Universal Web Design* from New Riders) home page. It uses the <PRE> tag exclusively, and looks pretty darn cool if I might say so myself!

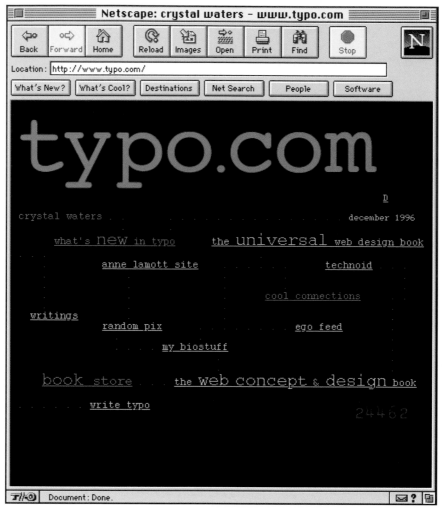

Check out ■ http://www.typo.com for very interesting layout ideas using the <PRE> and <FONT SIZE> tags.

It's interesting to study Crystal's HTML below to see how she used the <PRE> tag:

```
<HTML>
<HEAD>
<TITLE>crystal waters - www.typo.com</TITLE>
</HEAD>
<BODY bgcolor="#000000" text="#cccccc"
link="#cccccc" vlink="#999999">
<CODE><FONT SIZE=3>
<A HREF="./about.html"><IMG SRC="./t.gif"
WIDTH="419" HEIGHT="86" VSPACE="10" BORDER="0"></A>
<A HREF="./imagedes.html#typologo">D</A>
<BR clear=all>
<PRE><FONT SIZE=4 COLOR="#6699FF">crystal waters . .
. . . . . . . . . . . . . . . </FONT>
<FONT SIZE=3>december 1996
<FONT SIZE=4 color="#6699FF">          .          .
<A HREF="./new.html">what's
<FONT SIZE=6>new</FONT> in typo</A>
<A HREF="../uwd/uwd.html">the <FONT SIZE=6>
universal</FONT> web design book</A>
. . .                              .
.            <A HREF="./lamott/lamott.html">
anne lamott site</A>          . . . . . .
<A HREF="../technoid/technoid.html">technoid</A> . .
.
.          .          .          .
.
.          .          .          .
.
.          .          .
```

```
<A HREF="./cool/cool.html">cool connections</A>
. .
.              .              .
.
<A HREF="./writings/writings.html">writings</A>
.              .                      .
<A HREF="./pix/pix.html">random pix</A>        . . .
. . . . . .
<A HREF="./kudos.html">ego feed</A>        .
.              .                      .
. . . .
<A HREF="../crystal/crystal.html">my biostuff</A>
.
.                      .
.

<FONT SIZE=6>
<A HREF="./store/store.html">book</FONT>
<FONT SIZE=5>store</A></FONT> . . .
<A HREF="./wcd/wcd.html">the <FONT SIZE=6>web</FONT>
<FONT SIZE=6>concept</FONT> &
<FONT SIZE=6>design</FONT> book</A></PRE>
<CODE><FONT SIZE=4>
<!--sirius counter II-->
<IMG ALIGN=right HEIGHT="32" WIDTH="65"
SRC="/cgi bin/Count2?uname=crystal¦
num=2¦udir=1¦dtype=num¦dmax=6¦pad=N">
<FONT SIZE=4 COLOR="#6699FF">. . . . . . </FONT>
<A HREF="mailto:typo@typo.com">write typo</A>
<BR clear=all>
</BODY>
</HTML>
```

The Adobe Acrobat Solution

Another solution to alignment hell is to say to hell with HTML altogether and use PDFs (**P**ortable **D**ocument **F**ormat) instead. Adobe's Acrobat product (■ http://www.adobe.com/prodindex/acrobat/main.html), which enables you to generate and view PDF files, has survived several ill-fated attempts to be successfully marketed as an HTML alternative.

PDF originated as a document transfer solution. The idea behind PDF was that you could save a document in a high-end layout program, complete with fonts and alignment styles, and distribute the document to anybody, even if they didn't own the software the document was originally created with. PDFs performed this task very well and enjoyed little, if any, competition.

PDF in its initial incarnation knew nothing of web delivery. The files were huge by web standards and were formatted to look good in print, not on computer screens. Of course, no one can blame Adobe. The web did not exist when Acrobat and PDF were first released!

Early web-based PDF attempts were crippled by a product that had too many components, was too large to download, and had files that were too large for the web and didn't look good either. Version 3.0 of Acrobat solves a lot of the early wrinkles for the following reasons:

- It's possible to create PDF files in many applications now, and you can author PDF files without owning Acrobat.

- PDF files can stream on the web. You don't have to download an entire PDF document before seeing and viewing pages. This makes it much less frustrating for end viewers.

- The Acrobat plug-in (available for free from: http://www.adobe.com/prodindex/acrobat/readstep.html) is much smaller to download than the entire application.

- Web-based PDF files can be optimized better than was possible in earlier versions.

- PDF files can be inline elements of standard HTML web pages.

- PDF files now support anti-aliasing on-the-fly and display text properly for screen-based viewing.

- PDF supports very cool transition effects, such as wipes and venetian blind effects with multiple pages.

- PDF supports the ability to link to internal content or outside URLs.

This is not to say that PDF still doesn't suffer from its attempts to retrofit itself into a web-based delivery medium. Any time a format depends on plug-in installation by the end viewer, accessiblity is limited. PDF is unfortunately a RAM-hungry monster. Even on my machine (with 72mb of RAM!), I had PDF files stop working when viewed on the web, and had to suffer through several browser crashes.

I don't recommend PDFs as an alternative to HTML, but I do think they provide a viable means of distributing information over the web that is not well suited for HTML. Already published and designed magazine articles and books are prime candidates for PDF delivery because the material is already successfully designed and can't be easily converted to HTML and maintain accurate integrity. PDF basically mimics print, with the enhanced and important advantages of being able to include internal and external hyperlinks.

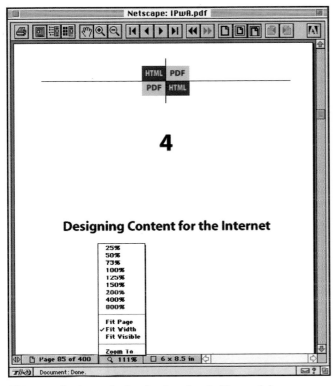

This example shows the Acrobat interface inside a web browser. One of the cool features of a PDF file is that it can be scaled all the way up to 800%.

At 400% the EPS-based artwork still looks fantastic. This would not be true if it you zoomed into standard web image formats, such as GIF, PNG, or JPEG.

■ tip

More Information on PDF Authoring

Acrobat plug-in
■ http://www.adobe.com/prodindex/acrobat/readstep.html

Internet Publishing With Acrobat
Publisher: Adobe Press
Author: Gordon Kent
Retail Price: $40 ▪ ISBN: 1-56830-300-9

Online (PDF) version of the above book
■ http://www.novagraphix.com/Internet_Publishing_with_Acrobat/

PDF Transitions
■ http://www.novagraphix.com/Internet_Publishing_with_Acrobat/
finder/transitions/index.html

David Siegel's PDF Pages
■ http://www.killersites.com/3-pdf/

Adobe Magazine (PDF form)
■ http://www.adobemag.com/

Building PDFs (Web Tutorial Information)
■ http://www.projectcool.com/developer/acrobat/

Cascading Style Sheets

Many web developers hope that **C**ascading **S**tyle **S**heets (CSS) will be the answer to alignment hell. CSS enables you to define the font, the indent, the justification, the leading, the spacing, and/or the color of your web page.

There are three different methods with which to implement CSS: one that enables you to embed this information for a single page, another that enables you to apply a style to an element of a page, and another that enables you to link to the style information, thereby potentially affecting many pages. One clear advantage to using CSS is that everything is created using tags and ASCII, meaning that CSS files are significantly smaller than pages that include invisible spacers and images for typography. Doesn't it sound great?

Like any new technology, there's a shakeout period where all the dust has to settle before you jump in. At the time this chapter was written, CSS was endorsed by the W3C (■ http://www.w3.org) and had been implemented only by Microsoft Internet Explorer (both Mac and PC versions). Netscape 4.0 had announced plans to support CSS using JavaScript, but no specs had been posted to its site.

The advantages to using CSS will be numerous, but if you plan to implement them today you're talking about maintaining two sets of pages: those that are CSS compliant, and those that use all the other alignment workarounds this chapter suggests. With only one browser's support, you're going to exclude more of your audience than not if you become an early adopter of CSS.

If you're really anxious to get a head start using CSS, I would suggest reading up on CSS, downloading a version of MSIE (■ http://www.microsoft.com), and experimenting with the new tags. My guess is WYSIWYG editors will support CSS as soon as the browsers duke it out and some standards are established.

If you'd like to read more about CSS, or check out some examples and code, here are some great URLs:

Web Review's Feature on CSS
■ http://webreview.com/96/11/08/feature/

HotWired's Web Monkey
(Check out the Threads section—read what the public's feelings are about CSS!)
■ http://www.webmonkey.com/browsers/96/33/index0a.html

Download Microsoft's TrueType Fonts
(Then move on to the CSS Gallery)
■ http://www.microsoft.com/truetype/

Microsoft's How-To CSS Tutorials
■ http://www.microsoft.com/truetype/css/gallery/entrance.htm

Microsoft's CSS Gallery

As usual, the best way to learn about something on the web is to reverse-engineer how it was constructed. Visit Microsoft's CSS gallery (■ http://www.microsoft.com/truetype/css/gallery/entrance.htm) for plenty of examples. I've selected a few samples from Microsoft's site.

This series of simple examples are at ■ http://www.microsoft.com/truetype/css/gallery/extract1.htm. The content for each page is the same, but the style information is different.

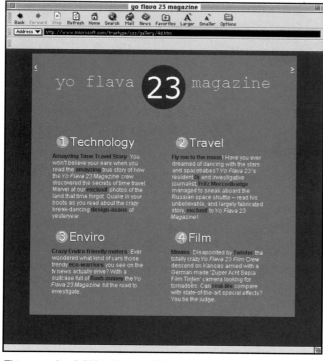

This example of CSS is found at ■ http://www.microsoft.com/true-type/css/gallery/4d.htm. Notice how you can overlay text over text, and text over shapes. These layering capabilities are not found within HTML. This entire page is less than 5k. If you were using GIF images and spacers, this page could easily be much larger.

Here's the code:

```
<HTML>
<HEAD>
<TITLE>yo flava 23 magazine</TITLE>
<STYLE>
<!--BODY {background:darkblue;color:black}
P{color:black;font-size:12px;
font-family: Arial, sans-serif}.copy
{color: white; margin-left:-4px;
margin-right:6px; margin-top:10px;
font-size:12px;
font-family: Arial, sans-serif}.plus
{color: white; margin-left:-200px;
margin-right: -200px; font-size:33px;
font-family:Courier New}.logo1
{color: darkblue; margin-top:-17px;
font-size:160px; font-weight:bold;
font-family:WingDings}.logo2
{color:azure; margin-top:-131px;
margin-right:-3px; font-size: 62px;
font-weight:bold;
font-family:Verdana}
.logo3 {color: azure;
font-size:35px; font-weight:bold;
font-family:Courier New}.ball
{color:deepskyblue; font-size:44px;
font-weight:bold;
font-family:Wingdings}.subhead
{color:darkblue; margin-left:8px;
margin-top:-39px;font-size:24px;
```

```
font-weight:bold;
font-family:Verdana}.subhead2
{color:white; margin-left:9px; margin-top:-30px;
font-size:24px; font-weight:bold;
font-family:Verdana}
B {color:darkblue} I {font-weight:bold}
A:link {font-size:18px; text-decoration:none;
font-family:Comic Sans MS
A:visited {font-size:18px; text-decoration: none;
font-family: Comic Sans MS }-->
</STYLE>
</HEAD>
<BODY>
<CENTER>
<TABLE WIDTH=560 CELLPADDING=0 CELLSPACING=0
BORDERCOLORDARK=black BORDERCOLORLIGHT=red
BORDER=0 BGCOLOR=steelblue>
<TR><TD COLSPAN=5 ALIGN=CENTER>
<TABLE WIDTH=550 CELLPADDING=0
CELLSPACING=0><TR>
<TD WIDTH=220 VALIGN=TOP><P><BR>
<A HREF="/truetype/css/gallery/4b.htm">
<SPAN STYLE="color: white">&lt;</SPAN></A>
<DIV ALIGN=RIGHT CLASS=logo3>yo flava</DIV>
</TD><TD WIDTH=110 ALIGN=CENTER>
<DIV CLASS=logo1>l</DIV>
<DIV CLASS=logo2>23</DIV></TD>
<TD WIDTH=220 VALIGN=TOP>
<P ALIGN=RIGHT><BR>
<A HREF="/truetype/css/gallery/4e.htm">
<SPAN STYLE="color: white">&gt;</SPAN></A>
<DIV ALIGN=LEFT CLASS=logo3>magazine</DIV>
</TD></TR></TABLE></TD></TR>
<TR><TD WIDTH=50 VALIGN=TOP> </TD>
<TD WIDTH=200 VALIGN=TOP>
<DIV CLASS=ball>l</DIV>
<DIV CLASS=subhead>1 Technology</DIV>
<DIV CLASS=subhead2>1 Technology</DIV>
<DIV CLASS=copy><B>Amazing Time Travel Story</B>.
You won&#146;t believe your ears when you read the
<B>amayzing</B> true story of how the <I>Yo Flava 23
Magazine</I> crew discovered the secrets of time
travel. Marvel at our <B>exclusif</B> photos of the
land that time forgot. Quake in your boots as you
read about the crazy break-dancing <B>design-
asaus</B> of yesteryear.</DIV>
</TD>
<TD ROWSPAN=3 WIDTH=50></TD>
<TD WIDTH=200 VALIGN=TOP>
<DIV CLASS=ball>l</DIV>
<DIV CLASS=subhead>2 Travel</DIV>
<DIV CLASS=subhead2>2 Travel</DIV>
<DIV CLASS=copy><B>Fly me to the moon</B>! Have you
```

```
ever dreamed of dancing with the stars and
spacebabes? <I>Yo Flava 23</I>&#146;s resident
<B>Dj</B> and investigative journalist,
<B>Fritz Mercedbadge</B> managed to sneak
aboard the Russian space shuttle &#150; read
his unbelievable, and largely fabricated story,
<B>exclusif</B> to <I>Yo Flava 23
Magazine</I>!</DIV>
</TD>
<TD WIDTH=50 VALIGN=TOP> </TD></TR>
<TR><TD VALIGN=TOP> </TD></TR>
<TR><TD WIDTH=50 VALIGN=TOP> </TD>
<TD WIDTH=200 VALIGN=TOP>
<DIV CLASS=ball>l</DIV>
<DIV CLASS=subhead>3 Enviro</DIV>
<DIV CLASS=subhead2>3 Enviro</DIV>
<DIV CLASS=copy><B>Crazy Enviro-friendly
motors</B>. Ever wondered what kind of cars
those trendy <B>eco-warriors</B> you see on the
tv news actually drive? With a suitcase full of
<B>flash-money</B> the <I>Yo Flava 23
Magazine</I> hit the road to investigate.</DIV>
</TD>
<TD WIDTH=200 VALIGN=TOP>
<DIV CLASS=ball>l</DIV>
<DIV CLASS=subhead>4 Film</DIV>
<DIV CLASS=subhead2>4 Film</DIV>
<DIV CLASS=copy><B>Movies</B>. Disapointed by
<B>Twister</B> the totally crazy <I>Yo Flava 23
Film Crew</I> descend on Kansas armed with a
German made &#145;Zuper Acht Sepia Film
Tinten&#146; camera looking for tornadoes. Can
<B>real-life</B> compare with state-of-the-art
special effects? You be the judge.
<BR> <BR> </DIV>
</TD>
<TD WIDTH=50 VALIGN=TOP> </TD>
</TR>
</TABLE>
</CENTER>
</BODY>
</HTML>
```

Introduction

Getting Started in Web Design

Understanding the Web Environment

Web File Formats

Low-Bandwidth Graphics

Hexadecimal Color

Browser-Safe Color

Transparent Artwork

Background Tiles

Rules, Bullets and Buttons

Navigation-Based Graphics

Web-Based Typography

Scanning Techniques for the Web

Layout and Alignment Techniques

Animation

Sound

Interactivity

HTML for Visual Designers

Glossary

Design Resources Appendix

Index

<BROWSER

33FF

Web 2d typography

<H1>

<TAB

<A>

otoshop

<Img src="

<STRONG>
.Gif
.Jpg
.Png

Image compressio
Limited palettes
IMAGE OPTIMIZATION
216 Colors

Width="500"

PARENCY

Height="600"

</A>

102k

<cente

GRAPHY

Extending HTML
Web file formats
bgco = "EEEECC"

sound and

link = "cyan"

LYNDA.COM

<center>

www. Design

Codecs

To make matters a little more complicated, movie formats (QuickTime, AVI, and MPEG) also use different types of compression settings and standards. These are called codecs, which stands for **co**mpressor/**de**compressor.

Appropriate Codecs for Web Movies

Movie Format	Web-Appropriate Codecs
QuickTime	Cinepak
	Indeo
AVI	Indeo
	Cinepak
MPEG	MPEG

This table lists movie file formats with appropriate codecs for web authoring. Just like there are lots of other image file formats besides those this book discusses—GIFs and JPEGs—there are many other movie codecs. They are missing from this list because I'm specifically including only those that would compress movies to reasonable sizes for modem downloading.

The codec is requested when you're saving your movie. The choices are accessed from the movie-making software you use. At this point, you choose from either web-appropriate codec: Cinepak or Indeo. The compression setting you choose is invisible to the end users. They know only whether your movie is a QuickTime, AVI, or MPEG.

The following sections look at advantages and disadvantages to the codecs appropriate for web-based movies.

Cinepak—Available for QuickTime and AVI

Cinepak offers lossy compression, which means that this compression codec causes the original movie file to lose quality. That might sound more alarming than it actually is. All web-based compression schemes are lossy. If they didn't sacrifice some quality, they couldn't produce small enough files suitable for modem transfer.

Cinepak was designed for CD-ROM authoring and does an exceptional job at playing back from a disk—be it floppy, hard disk, or CD-ROM. Cinepak has a tendency to make images look slightly blurred, and for this reason it works better on animation and graphics that have lots of solid colors rather than live action, which has lots of subtleties and changing colors. It takes a long time to render a QuickTime movie to Cinepak because of the amount of crunching Cinepak does to the file. What makes the file play back well is precisely what makes it render slowly: Cinepak takes a very large file and makes it very small—a lot of work!

Indeo—Available for QuickTime and AVI

Indeo also offers lossy compression. It has two modes: a normal and a super compressor mode. If you use the super compressor mode, Indeo will take as long as Cinepak to render, but the image quality will be much better. Indeo does an exceptional job compressing live-action-based footage. It tends to make those types of movies look sharper than Cinepak. The size in megabytes and playback speed on Indeo and Cinepak movies will be the same. Indeo is not available for Unix-based machines. They can play Indeo compressed movies, but cannot author them.

MPEG

MPEG became an early standard on the web because it was the only movie format on which Unix platform-based computers could write. The problem with MPEG movies on the web is that they typically are either video or sound files; combined video and sound movies are a rarity. This is because you need special hardware to render an MPEG movie with sound. If you are using software to compress, you must choose to either write a sound or a movie file. Now that Quick-Time is available for Unix-platforms, chances are that MPEG will become less ubiquitous.

Glossary of Animation and Digital Video Terms

FPS: FPS stands for frames per second. A movie contains a certain number of frames, and the fewer frames, the more jerky the motion and the smaller the file size.

Codec: A codec is the type of compression and decompression standard used to make the movie file smaller for web delivery.

Data rate: Data rate relates to how fast the movie data is captured.

Sprite animation: Sprite animation refers to the individual pieces of artwork required to make an animation.

How to Create Animation Content

There are lots of different animation tools and technologies, but what about the animation content itself? If you've never made animation before, you might be asking what exactly constitutes animation, per se?

Animation is actually the illusion of motion. It's really composed of a series of still images, shown in quick succession—the process of which tricks our minds into thinking that stationary artwork is truly moving. It's all fake! Making artwork for animation is an exercise in understanding how to fake motion through presenting changing artwork over time.

There are all kinds of ways to generate animation files or sequential images that change in appearance from frame to frame. Any number of animation software packages can generate sequential images in PICT, PICs, GIF, or QuickTime formats. Most of the web animation tools can import standard PICTs, GIFs, or QT formats.

You can make animation without a dedicated animation program, too. If you use an image editor, such as Photoshop, try running a filter in incremental amounts over a still image. Try drawing the same artwork three times and it will appear to jitter subtlely, or not so subtlely depending on how much each version changes. Try changing the opacity over multiple images, and you'll create artwork that appears to "fade up." Try looking at existing animation on a VCR and single-framing it, or try loading other people's animated GIFs into anima-ting GIF programs to reverse-engineer what you like. Just be sure that reverse-engineering doesn't mean stealing. The same copyright laws that apply to images apply to movies!

Introduction

Getting Started in Web Design

Understanding the Web Environment

Web File Formats

Low-Bandwidth Graphics

Hexadecimal Color

Browser-Safe Color

Transparent Artwork

Background Tiles

Rules, Bullets and Buttons

Navigation-Based Graphics

Web-Based Typography

Scanning Techniques for the Web

Layout and Alignment Techniques

Animation

Sound

Interactivity

HTML for Visual Designers

Glossary

Design Resources Appendix

Index

15
<H1>
<P>
BROWSER SAFE COLOR
Web typography
33FF
<TAB
<A>
hotoshop
<img src="
<STRONG>
.Gif
.Jpg
.Png
Width="500
Image compressio
Limited palettes
IMAGE OPTIMIZATION
216 Colors
PARENCY
Height="600
</A>
10.2 K
<center
Imaging techniques
Extending HTML
Web file formats
bgcolor="FFFFCC
Animation, Sound and
alink="cyan"
LYNDA.COM
33
</center>
www Design

Sound on the Web

Because the web has effectively created the ultimate convergence of any and all mediums, perhaps it's time to add sound to your web design bag o' tricks! Perhaps you're tired of listening only to the sound of your mouse clicking or your keyboard typing, or you're feeling brave about entering some new web authoring territory. Whatever your reason, it's now possible to program your site to provide background ambient noise, real-time audio on demand, or sound that can be downloaded and played on external sound players. This chapter examines these options and other issues related to sound.

Sound Aesthetics

Just because you can add sound to your site doesn't mean you should. Keep in mind that people have very strong musical tastes, and while you might love Balinese gamelan music as much as I do, your end viewer might prefer Martin Denny.

My suggestion is that you are careful about looping sounds—in the event that your end viewer can't stand your choice of music or sound effect, and you are effectively driving them away. Netscape has an interesting technology demo on its site that enables the end viewer to turn on or off looping sound, or change the type of music entirely.

My point is, sound can be a wonderful thing to one person and an annoyance to another. Embedding ambient sound on a web page is discussed later in this chapter, along with techniques to enable your end user to access audio controls to turn sound on and off for your site. You might think you are adding an enhancement to your site by including automatic sound, but it's my job to tell you that others might not agree.

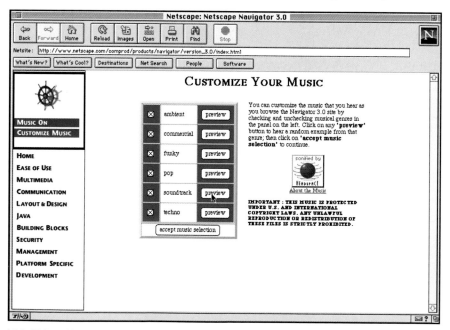

Visit ■ http://www.netscape.com/comprod/products/navigator/version_3.0/index.html to view the source of this page and other interesting sound technology demos.

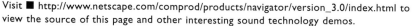

How to Get Sound Source Files into Your Computer

Just like images have to be scanned or created directly in the computer, sounds have to be scanned or digitized or created from scratch as well. This is a complex or easy undertaking, depending on whether you're attempting to achieve professional-level sound or willing to accept a few snap, crackle, and pops.

Here are some ideas for obtaining sound file sources:

■ **Capture sound from CDs**

Most sound-capture software enables you to capture sound from audio CDs. Tips for capturing from CD sources are listed later in this chapter. Be careful about copyrights and other rights—it is not legal to take sound from your favorite band and stick it on your web site or otherwise use it. For more information about copyright laws and music, check out:

The Use of Music on a Multimedia Web Site: The Legal Issues
■ http://home.earthlink.net/~ivanlove/music.html

If you're on the other end and want to create licensing agreements for sound or music you've created, you'll find some boilerplate legal contracts in this book:

Web Developer's Guide to Sound and Music
Publisher: Coriolis Group Books
Authors: Anthony Helmstetter and Ron Simpson
Retail Price: $39.95 ■ ISBN: 1-883577-95-0

■ **Purchase royalty-free sound libraries online or on CD-ROMs**

There are zillions of web sites and CD-ROMs that include royalty-free music and sound effects. Here are a couple of good starting points to check out:

Gary Lamb's Royalty-Free Music Collection
■ http://www.royaltyfree.com/

SoundScape Web Background Music for Web Pages
■ http://www.iti.qc.ca/iti/users/sean/sndscape.html

Royalty-Free Multimedia Soundtracks
■ http://www.kenmusic.com/

■ **Use the microphone that ships with your computer**

Many Macs and PCs ship with a microphone and simple sound editing software which you can use to record your voice for narration, greetings or sound effects. This is a great way to add a personal greeting to your site. I have wonderful sound bytes of my daughter singing songs and saying silly things as she was growing up that were all captured this way. Be aware, however, that professional sound designers would cringe at this recommendation! If you are planning to do professional-quality sound, use professionals! They have all kinds of equipment you won't begin to understand, which does things such as normalize, equalize, remove noise, mixing, dithering, resampling, and more...

For a little tour around some professional sound sites, try:

The MIDI Farm
■ http://www.midifarm.com/info/

Doctor Audio
■ http://www.doctoraudio.com/indextext.html

Professional Sound Corporation
■ http://www.professionalsound.com/

■ **Use sound-editing software to produce computer generated sounds**

There are dedicated sound-editing packages, just like there are dedicated image-editing software packages. Sound editing software can cut or mix together disparate clips of sound, create transitions such as fades and dissolves, and process the sound with effects like echo, reverb, and playing in reverse.

You might try reading the computer and sound trades to find hardware and software that fit your needs and budget. Or check out some suggested URLs:

Mike Sokol's Sound Advice
■ http://www.soundav.com/

Professional Sound Designer's Magazine
■ http://www.vaxxine.com/ps/

Vibe
■ http://www.vibe.com/

Digital Audio Terminology

Sample rates: Sample rates are measured in kilohertz (KHz). The sample rate affects the "range" of digitized sound, which describes its highs and lows. Sound editing software is where the initial sample rate settings are established. Standard sample rates range from 11.025 KHz, 22.050 KHz, 44.10 KHz, to 48 KHz. The higher the sample rate, the better the quality.

Bit depth or sampling resolution: Sampling resolution affects quality of sound, just like dpi resolution affects the quality of images. Standard sampling resolutions are 8-bit mono, 8-bit stereo, 16-bit mono, and 16-bit stereo.

μ-law: μ-law used to be the only file format you'd find on the web because it is generated by Unix platforms. Now that Macs and PCs are the predominant platform of the web, μ-law files are not seen as much. The sound quality is generally much lower than other sound formats, but the files are much smaller, too. μ-law files always have the file-name extension .au.

AIFC: AIFC is a new spec for the older **A**udio **I**nterchange **F**ile Format (AIFF). Both AIFF and AIFF-C files can be read by this format. AIFF and AIFC files are commonly used on SGI and Macintosh computers. Only 16-bit sound data can be recorded using this format.

MPEG: MPEG audio is well respected as a high-quality, excellent audio compression file format. MPEG audio has the advantage of a good compression scheme that doesn't sacrifice too much fidelity for the amount of bandwidth it saves. MPEG files tend to be small and sound good. On the IUMA site, there are two sizes of MPEG files: stereo and mono. MPEG audio layer 2 files always have the file-name extensions .mpg or .mp2. MPEG audio layer 3 files have an .mp3 extension.

To Stream or Not to Stream?

Streaming is the process whereby an audio or video file plays as it's being downloaded. This enables your end user to hear the sound as it's downloading, instead of waiting until the entire file is downloaded for it to play. Streaming audio is not always appropriate because your sound and music will take a quality hit in the process. At times you will prefer to set up music archives on a site for downloading, especially if you want to distribute high-quality sound that is too large in file size for smooth streaming. Because both streaming and nonstreaming audio standards exist, this chapter covers both topics.

If you are going to prepare audio files for downloading off your site, you'll need to know a few new tricks. We'll look at the HTML tags required to do this, how to make your movies and sounds small, and decide which types of helper applications you and your audience will need.

Making Small Audio Files

Audio on the web has most of the same limitations as images—many files are too large to hear as inline components of a page. In this event, your audience will be required to download audio files in order to listen to them, and it's your job to choose a file format and compression rate. You will base these decisions on the platform you're authoring sounds from and then work to reduce your file size while keeping sound quality as high as possible

Here's a look at the various audio standards and ways to reduce the size of audio files.

Rates and Bits

There are two components of an audio file that make it sound good (and take up space): the sampling rate and the bit depth, which is referred to as the sample resolution.

Sample rates are measured in kilohertz (KHz). The sample rate affects the range of a digitized sound, which defines its highs and lows. Higher sample rates result in larger file sizes. The sampling rate is set when the sound is digitized (captured) into the computer. Sound editing software is where the initial sample rate settings are established, and it should be set according to the type of sound being sampled. Some types of sounds can deal with lower sampling rates better. Narration, for example, doesn't depend on high and low ranges to sound good. Here are some sampling rates:

- 8 KHz
- 11 KHz
- 22.050 KHz
- 44.1 KHz
- 48 KHz

Sampling resolution dictates how much range the sound has in highs and lows. Higher kilohertz settings result in a bigger file size. The sampling resolution is also set when the sound is digitized (captured) into the computer. Sound editing software allows users to dictate which sample resolution the sound is captured at. Because noise is introduced at lower sample rates, it's necessary to evaluate individual sound elements to see how far down the sampling resolution can be set without introducing unacceptable noise. You can create digital sound at the following resolutions:

- 8-bit mono
- 8-bit stereo
- 16-bit mono
- 16-bit stereo

Generally when you first digitally record or "sample" a sound, you want to record it at 16-bit resolution at the 44.1 KHz sampling rate. Just like an image scan, it's always best to start with the most information and reduce down. Later, after processing the sound to your satisfaction with digital audio editing applications, you would resample the final file down to 8-bit, 22.05 KHz.

Audio File Formats

Many types of audio files are found and used on the web. Choosing which one to use is often determined by what kind of computer system and software you're authoring sounds from. Here's a breakdown of the various formats:

■ μ-law

μ-law used to be the only file format you'd find on the web because it is generated by Unix platforms. Now that Macs and PCs are the predominant platform, μ-law files are not seen as much. The sound quality is generally considered much lower than the other sound formats described here. It is used much less often now, as a result. If you are going to author μ-law files, they should be saved with an .au extension.

■ AIFF

AIFF was developed by Apple and is used on Macintoshes and SGIs. It stands for **A**udio **I**nterchange **F**ile **F**ormat. It can store digital audio at all the sample rates and resolutions possible. You'll also hear about MACE (**M**acintosh **A**udio **C**ompression/**E**xpansion), which is the built-in compression standard for AIFF files. Just like in video, what compression you use is invisible to the end listener. It does dictate the size and quality of your end result, however. If you are going to author AIFF files, they should be saved with an .aif extension.

■ WAVE

WAVE was developed by Microsoft and IBM and is the native sound file format to Windows platforms. Like AIFF, it can store digital audio at all the sample rates and resolutions possible. Basically, WAVE and AIFF files are considered equals in terms of quality and compression, and are easier to use depending on which platform you are authoring from. If you are going to author WAVE files, they should be saved with a .wav extension.

■ MPEG

MPEG audio is well respected as a high-quality, excellent audio compression file format. The only problem is that encoding MPEG requires extra hardware that is out of reach of many audio content creators. Because MPEG files aren't native to any specific platform, your audience will need to download a helper application to hear them. If you are going to author MPEG sound files, they should be saved with the .mpg extension.

■ RealAudio

RealAudio was the first example of streaming audio on the web. Streamed audio files come over the phone lines in small chunks, so the entire file doesn't have to be downloaded before it can be heard. The file can be up to one hour long because the data is coming in as you're hearing it—not first downloading fully to your hard drive. The sound quality is often compared to that of an AM radio station. Because of quality limits, it's best used for narration and not for music or other sounds. You must have the RealAudio player installed on your system to hear sounds play as soon as you click on a link that supplies real audio source material. You can author Real-Audio content by using the RealAudio encoder, which can be obtained by accessing the RealAudio site (■ http://www.realaudio.com). You won't be able to offer RealAudio files from your web site unless your provider has paid RealAudio a server licensing fee. Contact RealAudio for more information.

Tips for Making Web-Based Sound Files

Several free or shareware applications can convert from or to μ-law, AIFF, WAV, and MPEG files, so chances are your audience will be able to access your sounds regardless of which file format you choose to support. Typically, Mac authors will choose AIFF, PC authors will choose WAV or MPEG, and Unix authors will pick μ-law because those are the file formats supported natively by their systems.

To properly prepare the files, however, you might want to use a sound editing program that offers features such as peak level limiting, normalizing, downsampling, and dithering from 16-bit to 8-bit. Premiere is a great entry-level video and sound editor—although professional videographers and sound engineers will typically own higher-end dedicated editing programs. The following figure shows some of the audio filters found in Premiere.

Here are some tips for making web-based sound files:

- Digitize at the standard audio CD sample rate and resolution (44 KHz and 16-bit). Downsample the file to the preferred sample size of 22 KHz or 11 KHz. Typically, at lower sample rates the sound will be duller and have less high end. For dialogue or sounds where high end doesn't matter, lowering the sample rate creates smaller files that will be of acceptable quality.

- Halfing the sample rate will half the file size. Additionally, changing the file from stereo to mono cuts the file size in half. Use the Mix feature of audio software packages to create a mono version of a stereo file.

- If the 16-bit file is still too large, you can use dithering algorithms on audio (just like on images) to take the files down to 8-bit. Dithering will add noise, in the form of hiss (and in the worst case, electronic buzzing and chattering). Dithering will be most noticeable in files with silences between sounds.

- Because of the electronic noise, dithering should be avoided on dialogue. Dithering works great for rich, full music files such as hard rock and industrial. Another alternative is to redigitize the 16-bit audio file at 8-bit by playing back and recording a prerecorded 16-bit, 44.1 KHz sound into your digitizer. Often this creates cleaner 8-bit samples with more "punch."

- When naming audio files, as with all files being prepped for Internet distribution, they must be named with no spaces. Unlike inline images, these files are going to be downloaded by your audience. Therefore, names should be eight characters or less in length, with room for a three-letter file extension, or Windows platform users won't get to hear them!

- Make sure you've done all your sound editing (such as mixing from stereo to mono, filtering, peak level limiting, normalizing, or downsampling) before you convert to 8-bit. If you edit an 8-bit sound and then resave it, you will add electronic noise to your file. Always start with higher bit depth, and do your editing in that file before you save or dither it to 8-bit.

HTML for Downloading Sound Files

A sound file gets the <A HREF></A> tag, just like its video and image-based counterparts. But unlike video, where there might be an associated thumbnail image, sounds are usually indicated by a sound icon or hyper-text. Here are a few variations and the code you would use to produce them.

Here's the code to link your audience to a sound and let them know what file size and format it is:

```
<A HREF="snd1.aif">
<FONT SIZE=5>
Click here to download
this sound!</A>
</FONT>
<P>
Excerpt from CD:<BR>
WebaWorld<P>
Cut: Spider<P>
AIFF Sound<BR>
:30<BR>
567k
```

Or if you want to add an icon, too:

```
<A HREF="snd1.aif>
<FONT SIZE=5>
<IMG SRC="ear.gif">
Click here to download
this sound!</A>
</FONT>
<P>
Excerpt from CD:<BR>
WebaWorld<P>
Cut: Spider<P>
AIFF Sound<BR>
:30<BR>
567k
```

Audio Helper Apps and Utilities

Here's a list of useful helper applications and utilities for audio creation and playback.

For Macs

Sound Machine 2.5

(Plays AU, AIFF, and WAVE)

■ ftp://ftp.iuma.com/audio_utils/au_players/Macintosh/
sound-machine-21.hqx

SoundApp

■ ftp://mirror.apple.com/.ufs01/info-mac/gst/snd/
sound-app-151.hqx

MPEG Audio: Converts MPEG to AIFF

■ ftp://ftp.iuma.com/audio_utils/mpeg_players/Macintosh/
MPEGAudNoFPU1.0a6.hqx

MPEG CD: Plays MPEG audio

■ http://www.kauai.com/~bbal/MPEG_CD_2.0.3.sea.hqx

Brian's Sound Tool

(Converts WAVE, AU, and AIFF)

■ gopher://gopher.archive.merit.edu:7055/40/mac/sound/
soundutil/brianssoundtool1.3.sit.hqx

SoundHack

(Converts WAVE, AU, and AIFF)

■ ftp://shoko.calarts.edu/pub/SoundHack/SH0866.hqx

For PCs

Xing SoundPlayer

(Plays MPEG audio; you need a sound card)

■ ftp://ftp.iuma.com/audio_utils/mpeg_players/Windows/
mpgaudio.exe

Windows Play Any

(Plays AU, WAV, and AIFF)

■ ftp://ftp.ncsa.uiuc.edu/Web/Mosaic/Windows/viewers/
wplny12a.zip

WHAM 1.31

(Sound Converter)

■ ftp://gatekeeper.dec.com/pub/micro/msdos/win3/
sounds/wham133.zip

Automatic Music Without Downloading

As usual, the browser wars are shakin' and quakin' with new ways to add proprietary features and out-do each other. Netscape and MSIE each have their own way of adding inline sound to web pages. This section will look at both options and will then advise you how to make your site compatible with both browsers.

MSIE Audio Tags

The BGSOUND element is an MS Internet Explorer 2.0 enhancement. SRC specifies the URL of the audio file to be played. The LOOP attribute specifies how many times the sound will be played while the HTML document is displayed, and can either be a number or the string "infinite." The default for LOOP is one. As mentioned earlier in the aesthetics section of this chapter, considerable opposition to the use of this element has been expressed on the web, especially the use of LOOP=infinite because users currently have no way to disable the audio.

BGSOUND

<BGSOUND SRC="...">	The BGSOUND element will cause an audio file to play automatically as an inline sound element. You can insert either .wav or .midi files.
<BGSOUND SRC=" LOOP="...">	To make the sound loop, insert this attribute. The default ..." is 1 time, unless specified.

To view Microsoft's tutorial page on these tags and attributes, check out:
■ http://www.microsoft.com/kb/articles/q156/1/54.htm

Netscape Audio Tags

Netscape's sound tags work with its LiveAudio plug-in, which comes preinstalled in Netscape versions 3.0 and higher. This means that the tags all revolve around the <EMBED> tag, which is standard for all plug-in based HTML.

LiveAudio plays audio files in WAV, AIFF, AU, and MIDI formats. Audio controls appear according to the size specified in the WIDTH and HEIGHT parameters in the <EMBED> tag. You can create an audio console with any of the following six views:

- **Console**—Consists of a Play, Pause, Stop, and Volume Control lever.

- **SmallConsole**—Consists of a Play, Stop, and Volume Control lever (upon invoking this view of the applet class, a sound will "autostart" by default). This view will have smaller buttons than the standard Console buttons.

- **PlayButton**—A button that starts the sound playing.

- **PauseButton**—A button that pauses (without unloading) the sound while it is playing.

- **StopButton**—A button that ends the playing of sound and unloads it.

- **VolumeLever**—A lever that adjusts the volume level for playback of the sound (and adjusts the system's volume level).

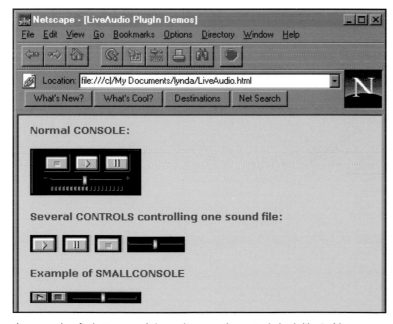

An example of what some of the audio console controls look like in Netscape.

These views may be used many times on one web page, with all the view instances controlling one sound file or many sound files, depending on how the file is called in the HTML or JavaScript.

HTML Syntax

```
<EMBED SRC= [URL]
AUTOSTART=[TRUE¦FALSE]
LOOP=[TRUE¦FALSE¦INTEGER]
STARTTIME=[MINUTES:SECONDS]
ENDTIME=[MINUTES¦SECONDS]
VOLUME=[0-100]
WIDTH=[# PIXELS]
HEIGHT=[# PIXELS]
ALIGN=[TOP¦BOTTOM¦CENTER¦BASELINE¦LEFT¦RIGHT ¦TEXTTOP¦MIDDLE¦ABSMIDDLE¦ABSBOTTOM]
CONTROLS=[CONSOLE¦SMALL CONSOLE¦PLAYBUTTON¦PAUSEBUTTON¦STOPBUTTON¦VOLUMELEVER] HIDDEN=[TRUE]
MASTERSOUND
NAME=[UNIQUE NAME TO GROUP CONTROLS SO THAT THEY CONTROL ONE SOUND]...>
```

SRC="..."	The URL of the source sound file.
AUTOSTART=[TRUE|FALSE]	Setting the value to TRUE allows the sound, music, or voice to begin playing automatically when the web page is loaded. The default is FALSE.
LOOP=[TRUE|FALSE|INTEGER]	Setting the value to TRUE allows the sound to play continuously until the stop button is clicked on the console or the user goes to another page. If an INTEGER value is used, the sound repeats the number of times indicated by the integer.
STARTTIME=[MINUTES:SECONDS]	Use STARTTIME to designate where in the sound file you would like playback to begin. If you want to begin the sound at 30 seconds, you would set the value to 00:30 (implemented only on Windows 95, NT, and Macintosh).
ENDTIME=[MINUTES:SECONDS]	Use ENDTIME to designate where in the sound file you would like playback to end. If you want to stop the sound at 1.5 minutes, you would set the value to 01:30 (implemented only on Windows 95, NT, and Macintosh).
VOLUME=[0–100]	This value must be a number between 0 and 100 to represent 0 to 100 percent. This attribute sets the volume for the sound that is playing [unless the MASTERVOLUME (see NAME attribute on the following page) is used; then this value sets the sound for the entire system]. The default volume level is the current system volume.

WIDTH=[# PIXELS]	This attribute is used to display the width of the console or console element. For the CONSOLE and SMALLCONSOLE, the default is WIDTH=144. For the VOLUMELEVER, the default is WIDTH=74. For a button, the default is WIDTH=37.
HEIGHT=[# PIXELS]	This attribute is used to display the height of the console. For the CONSOLE, the default is HEIGHT=60. For the SMALLCONSOLE, the default is HEIGHT=15. For the VOLUMELEVER, the default is HEIGHT=20. For a button, the default is HEIGHT=22.
ALIGN=[TOP|BOTTOM|CENTER| BASELINE|LEFT|RIGHT|TEXTTOP| MIDDLE|ABSMIDDLE|ABSBOTTOM]	This attribute tells Netscape Navigator how you want to align text as it flows around the consoles. It acts similarly to the <IMG> tag.
CONTROLS=[CONSOLE| SMALLCONSOLE|PLAYBUTTON| PAUSEBUTTON|STOPBUTTON| VOLUMELEVER]	This attribute defines which control a content creator wishes to use. The default for this field is CONSOLE.
HIDDEN=[TRUE]	The value for this attribute should be TRUE, or it should not be included in the <EMBED> tag. If it is specified as TRUE, no controls will load and the sound will act as a background sound.
MASTERSOUND	This value must be used when grouping sounds together in a NAME group. This attribute takes no value (it must merely be present in the EMBED tag), but tells LiveAudio which file is a genuine sound file and allows it to ignore any stub files. Stub files have a minimum length necessary to activate LiveAudio.
NAME=[UNIQUE NAME TO GROUP CONTROLS TOGETHER THAT THEY CONTROL ONE SOUND]	This attribute sets a unique ID for a group of CONTROLS elements so that they all act on the same sound as it plays. For example, if a SOUND content creator wishes to have one sound controlled by two embedded objects (a PLAYBUTTON and a STOPBUTTON), he must use this attribute to group the CONTROLS together. In this case, the <MASTERSOUND> tag is necessary to flag LiveAudio and let it know which of the two <EMBED> tags actually has the sound file you wish to control. LiveAudio ignores any EMBED with no <MASTERSOUND> tag. If you want one VOLUMELEVER to control multiple NAMEs (or system volume), create an EMBED by using the VOLUMELEVER CONTROL. Set NAME to MASTERVOLUME.

JavaScript Functions for LiveAudio

LiveAudio includes the capability to defer loading a sound file until the Play button is pushed. This enables a web page designer to comfortably embed several sounds on one page, without worrying about page load time.

To implement this feature, the web designer must create a file like the following:

```
<SCRIPT LANGUAGE=SoundScript>
OnPlay(http://YourURL/YourSound.aif);
</SCRIPT>
```

This file should be saved and named as a sound file (such as script1.aif). When the Play button is pushed, the URL you defined for the OnPlay function is loaded.

LiveAudio

To play a sound as a background sound for a web page:

```
<EMBED SRC="mysound.aif" HIDDEN=TRUE>
```

To have several CONTROLS controlling one sound file:

```
<EMBED SRC="mysound.aif" HEIGHT=22 WIDTH=37
CONTROLS=PLAYBUTTON NAME="MyConsole" MASTERSOUND>
<EMBED SRC="stub1.aif" HEIGHT=22 WIDTH=37
CONTROLS=PAUSEBUTTON NAME="MyConsole">
<EMBED SRC="stub2.aif" HEIGHT=22 WIDTH=37
CONTROLS=STOPBUTTON NAME="MyConsole">
<EMBED SRC="stub3.aif" HEIGHT=20 WIDTH=74
CONTROLS=VOLUMELEVER NAME="MyConsole">
```

To use a SMALLCONSOLE:

```
<EMBED SRC="mysound.aif" HEIGHT=15 WIDTH=144
MASTERSOUND CONTROLS=SMALLCONSOLE>
```

LiveConnect

LiveAudio is LiveConnect enabled. The following functions will work in JavaScript to control a loaded LiveAudio plug-in:

```
Controlling functions (all Boolean):
play('TRUE/FALSE or int','URL of sound')
stop()
pause()
start_time(int seconds)
end_time(int seconds)
setvol(int percent)
fade_to(int to_percent)
fade_from_to(int from_percent,int to_percent)
start_at_beginning() = Override a start_time()
stop_at_end() = Override an end_time()
State indicators (all Boolean, except *, which is
an int):
IsReady() = Returns TRUE if the plug-in instance
has completed loading
IsPlaying() = Returns TRUE if the sound is
currently playing
IsPaused() = Returns TRUE if the sound is
currently paused
GetVolume() = Returns the current volume
as a percentage * from:
```

Netscape's Documentation on These Tags

■ http://www.netscape.com/comprod/products/navigator/version_3.0/index.html

---

■ **note**

Cross-Browser Compatibility

Ok, you've reviewed the tags for each of the browsers; suppose you want to make a site that works for either or both?

Try this:

```
<EMBED SRC="sound.wav" AUTOSTART=TRUE
HIDDEN=TRUE>
<NOEMBED><BGSOUND="sound.wav"></NOEMBED>
```

Other Sound Options

Sound is a huge subject, worthy of entire books! There are many other sound options available to you for web delivery. Here is a brief synopsis of a few noteworthy ones.

QuickTime: QuickTime movies can be hidden from view or include control consoles. This makes their MIDI-compatible file format ideal for streaming audio. Many of the tags listed in Chapter 14, "Animation," work with sound files, too. Visit the QuickTime site for more details:

■ http://www.quicktime.apple.com

Macromedia Director/Streaming Audio: Director is one of the oldest authoring tools around for multimedia. Shockwave, a plug-in for web browsers, enables Director content to be viewed on web pages. Streaming audio is now a feature supported by the Shockwave plug-in. To develop streaming audio content, you need to learn to use Director and program interactivity with a proprietary language called Lingo. For more about Director, Shockwave, and Lingo, look to Chapters 14, 16, and 18.

Sound Tips:

■ http://www.macromedia.com/shockwave/director5/tips.html#sound

Shockwave Audio FAQ:

■ http://www.macromedia.com/support/technotes/shockwave/developer/shocktechnotes/audio/swafaq.html

Streaming Audio Tips:

■ http://www.macromedia.com/support/technotes/shockwave/developer/shocktechnotes/audio/longswa.html

RealAudio: RealAudio is the oldest streaming and most well-known audio technology on the web. It has three components:

> ■ The RealAudio Player plays files encoded in the RealAudio format.
> ■ The RealAudio Encoder encodes files into the RealAudio format.
> ■ The RealAudio Server delivers RealAudio over the Internet or your company network.

In order to hear RealAudio files, you must have the plug-in. In order to author RealAudio files, you need to convert your sound files so that they work in the RealAudio format. To download the encoder:

> ■ http://www.realaudio.com/products/encoder.html

The RealAudio Server is the only piece of the puzzle that costs money. It enables you to distribute RealAudio content from your site.

Introduction

Getting Started in Web Design

Understanding the Web Environment

Web File Formats

Low-Bandwidth Graphics

Hexadecimal Color

Browser-Safe Color

Transparent Artwork

Background Tiles

Rules, Bullets and Buttons

Navigation-Based Graphics

Web-Based Typography

Scanning Techniques for the Web

Layout and Alignment Techniques

Animation

Sound

Interactivity

HTML for Visual Designers

Glossary

Design Resources Appendix

Index

BROWSER SAFE COLOR

33 FF

Web 16   334 typography

Photoshop

0033

INDEX

Width = "500"

PARENCY

<STRONG>
.Gif
.Jpg
.Png

Height = "600"

</A>

10.2

<center>

Imaging techniques
Extending HTML
Web file formats
bgcolor "FFFFCC"

alink = "cyan"

<center> BODY
Antialias

33

<Img src="

Image com...
Limited palettes
IMAGE OPTIMIZATION
216 colors

Animation Sound and

LYNDA.COM

www.Design

16

Interactivity

Interactivity is a huge subject that overlaps with other chapters of this book and can't be isolated on its own as one practice or technique. The web is interactive by nature. At the very core of hypertext and hyperimages is the fact that the end user gets to make decisions about what information he or she wants to see displayed. It's up to us as web designers to make sure that we service this end user to the best of our abilities. Interactivity, when used correctly, can be a great enhancement to any site.

Here is a brief list of some of the features that qualify as interactive elements to add to a site:

- Counters
- Forms
- Guestbooks
- Chat/avatars
- Ad banners
- Button rollovers

Interactivity is something a printed page cannot do that the web excels at. As publishers of information, thinking in terms of interactivity is an entirely new kind of mind-set. You'll hear the buzzword "building community" if you hang around web designers long enough. By interacting with your end user, you are indeed building a community. If you do it well you can create goodwill, or it can backfire on you as an invitation to criticism or harassment.

This chapter will review some of the interactive technologies and techniques available today. There are many opportunities to add interactivity to sites, but these features are often difficult for "mere mortals" to program or implement. Being a nonprogrammer myself, I shy away from adding certain features on my site, even though I'd love to implement them. So in this chapter I'll direct my readers (you!) to helpful URLs so that you can learn more about adding interactivity to your sites.

Interactivity Role Models

Before getting to specific tools and techniques, you should check out a couple of inspirational sites that use interactivity very well. One of my personal favorites is ■ http://www.amazon.com, an online bookstore that has an "interactive" mind-set.

Besides the things you would expect in a bookstore—the ability to search and order books—Amazon has implemented a few neat twists of their own:

- ■ They have a form that invites authors and publishers to review their own books
- ■ They have a form that interviews authors
- ■ They invite readers with different forms to review and rate books
- ■ They allow customers to enter search information so that they can notify customers when other books of interest become available
- ■ They invite you to create a bookstore on your site and teach you how

They have indeed created a sense of community and involvement that a traditional bookstore could not easily match.

Another favorite site with an interactive mind-set is ■ www.iuma.com. Their site invites musicians to submit audio and video clips, and creates a worldwide distribution avenue that bypasses the traditional music publishing model. They help underground bands get an audience (and the possibility for record deals, too).

IUMA has a database of thousands of music and video clips, enabling end users to easily locate music styles that they like and order products from independent musicians. They have created a service that a traditional music store could not offer and a traditional music publisher could not afford. IUMA is an example of a web-centric publishing model that offers something which has never before been possible.

Interactivity Versus Difficulty

Many of the interactive enhancements this chapter discusses are created with programming instead of standard HTML. If HTML makes your eyes glaze over to begin with, then the notion of learning programming might cause a total meltdown. Programming is not for everyone, nor should it be. This chapter is meant to provide an overview of options and technologies, not a tutorial for learning programming.

The most common types of interactive programming involve CGI, technically known as **C**ommon **G**ateway **I**nterface. CGI is a type of scripting that extends the capabilities of HTML. CGI is the communication protocol that the web server (the computer that sends web pages out to the world to see) uses to interact with your end user's browser and external scripts. CGI scripts can be written in any number of computer languages—Perl, sh, C, C++, or AppleScript to name a few.

CGI scripts are hidden from view on a server. It is not possible to view the source within HTML or deconstruct how these types of scripts are written. Conversely, with HTML and JavaScript it is possible to view, copy, and paste the source code. This is always helpful and welcomed by nonprogrammers. CGI scripting is not something anyone can learn overnight. This chapter does not attempt to teach CGI; it instead describes the function, shows some scripts and how they work, and offers resources to help you learn more.

■ **note**

What Kind of Server?

To make CGI matters a tad more complicated, you must know the type of server you're using before uploading a CGI script and getting it to work on your site. Different servers on different platforms require different types of scripts. If you don't maintain your own server, check with your web administrator to ensure that you are using the correct types of CGI. Your web administrator might also keep a public or private CGI directory (often called /cgi.bin/) that you will need to locate.

Like many subjects on the web, there's a huge amount of information regarding CGI and scripts. You'll find many web sites with free scripts, tutorials, and links pages. Here are a few favorites:

Matt's Scripts and Archives
■ http://worldwidemart.com/scripts/index.shtml

Selena Sol's CGI-Script Archives
■ http://www2.eff.org/~erict/Scripts/

Perl/HTML Archives
■ http://www.seas.upenn.edu/~mengwong/perlhtml.html

Felipe's AppleScript Samples
(for use w/Mac HTTP)
■ http://edb518ea.edb.utexas.edu/scripts/cgix/cgix.html

WebSTAR Examples
■ http://www.starnine.com/development/extending.html

Fun and Wacky Scripts + Great CGI Introduction
■ http://netamorphix.com/cgi.html

The CGI Book
(examples and book support, mailing list, etc.)
■ http://www.cgibook.com

Robert Stockton's Guide to Perl CGI Programming
■ http://www-cgi.cs.cmu.edu/cgi-bin/perl-man

Meng Weng Wong's mailto.cgi Tutorial
■ http://icg.stwing.upenn.edu/mailto.html

Links to All Kinds of Scripts
■ http://www.cbil.vcu.edu:8080/cgis/cgis.html

Freeware Scripts!
■ http://www.webcom.se/projects/freeware/

Excellent Mac-Based CGI Links, FAQs, and Tutorials
■ http://www.comvista.com/net/www/cgilesson.html

Counters

Adding a counter to your page is a form of interactivity. It tells your visitors about your site's traffic and helps you keep track of those numbers, too. Aesthetically, counters can range from straight HTML-style text to custom-made graphics. An amusing site for counter design inspiration is:

Museum of Counter Art
■ http://www.merlinmedia.com/counter/index.html

If you are going to create your own custom counter number art, you must make sure that each character is the exact same height and width as the next. You can ensure this by setting up an image file in any imaging software at the set size you want for each numeric character. Copy the image and create your numbers inside the same file over and over (10 times—0 through 9) and resave the artwork in a numbered sequence. Most counter scripts will require .gif files.

Adding a counter requires CGI. There are about a zillion counter CGIs for public distribution on the web. If you follow the links on this page, you'll be kept busy checking out link after link. Setting up your own counter requires that you deal with uploading a CGI script. If you don't want to hassle with setting up a CGI for your counter, you can pay money to ■ http://www.dig-its.com to keep track of your counts for you. You can use their database and CGI scripts, and need only to copy and paste a simple HTML tag onto the pages you want to use a counter. A pricing guide is located on their site.

For Windows Servers
■ http://www.digitmania.holowww.com/software.html

For Macintosh Servers
■ http://www.io.com/~combs/htmls/counter.html

For Unix Servers
■ http://www.fccc.edu/users/muquit/Count.html

Forms

Forms can be used for anything on your site—from e-mail to questionnaires to humor. There are two parts to adding forms: the HTML and the forms processing, which involves CGI and database functionality. The HTML for forms can be inserted into frames or tables for further alignment refinement (see Chapter 13, "Layout and Alignment Techniques," or Chapter 10, "Navigation-Based Graphics").

Forms processing is what happens to the data once your end user enters it into your form. The CGI for forms processing takes the data and does whatever it's told to do with it. It might be that you're keeping track of e-mail addresses through your form. Or calculating an order. Or taking a poll. Whatever function your form is supposed to fill, the CGI must be programmed to intercept the data and either store it or send it onward to a database.

Here are some good reference URLs to help with forms processing:

The NCSA Site

■ http://www.ncsa.uiuc.edu/SDG/Software/Mosaic/Docs/fill-out-forms/overview.html

Forms Processing Tutorial

■ http://www.ithaca.edu/computing/quick_guides/forms/overview.html

---

■ **tip**

HTML for Buttons within Forms

The HTML required for forms is fairly easy, and is possible to program without any programming knowledge, other than HTML. Here's a breakdown of HTML required to generate buttons within forms.

checkboxes

```
input type=checkbox
```

radio buttons

```
input type=radio
input type radio name=checked
```

buttons

| Submit Query | Reset |

```
input type=submit
input type=reset
```

custom type within the button

| Billing Information | Gum? What's that? |

```
input type=submit value="Billing information"
```

pull-down menus

```
1-2
3-4
5-6
Gum? What's that?
```

```
<select><option selected>Gum? What's that?
</select>To create scrolling menus:<select>
<option>1-2 <option>3-4 <option>5-6
<option selected>Gum? What's that?
</select>
```

Guestbooks

Guestbooks help cultivate that sense-of-community thing I talked about earlier. Most people welcome the opportunity to share their thoughts, especially if they can remain anonymous. This can create goodwill, but it also can backfire. Sometimes the entries in my guestbook read like a lovefest, and other times they read like Ripley's Believe it or Not. Guestbooks require CGI too, and parameters can be established to allow or disallow duplicates, external HTML, profanity, anonymity, and anything else definable.

Here's an example of the source code for the guestbook on my site. It was written by my brother, William Weinman, who gives it away for free on his site:
■ http://www.cgibook.com/guestbook/source.html

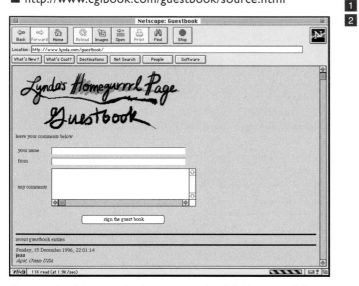

An example of this guestbook in action at Lynda's Homegurrrl Site:
■ http://www.lynda.com/guestbook/.

A guestbook is a common CGI program that is usually built in two parts: one for creating the listings and one for reading them back. Commonly, the part that creates the listings is built around an HTML forms interface, and the part that reads the listings is implemented as a server-side include.

There is one main HTML page for both entering the guestbook information and viewing the most recent entries.

```
<HTML>
<HEAD>
<TITLE>Guestbook</title>
</HEAD>
<BODY BGCOLOR="#ffffff">
<IMG SRC=guestbook.gif ALT="Guestbook"
WIDTH=333 HEIGHT=60 ALIGN=right>
<BR CLEAR=all>
<P>leave your comments below
```
1 `<FORM ACTION="guest.cgi" METHOD=post>`
2 `<TABLE>`
```
<TR>
<TD>
your name
<TD>
<INPUT NAME="name" SIZE=50>
<TR>
<TD>
from
<TD>
<INPUT NAME="from" SIZE=50>
<TR>
<TD>
any comments
<TD>
<TEXTAREA NAME="comments"
ROWS=5 COLS=50></TEXTAREA>
<TR>
<TD> <!-- empty for spacing -->
<TD ALIGN=center>
<BR>
<INPUT TYPE=submit
```

```
VALUE="
sign the guestbook">
</TABLE>
</FORM>
```
3 `<HR NOSHADE SIZE=3>`
```
recent guestbook entries
```
4 `<!-- #exec CMD="readbook.pl" -->`
```
</BODY>
</HTML>
```

1 The **<FORM>** tag is used to specify the name of the CGI program and the method used to pass the values from the form.

2 A **<TABLE>** tag is being used to align the form.

3 This is creating a black horizontal rule between guestbook entries.

4 This is the server-side include for reading the guestbook. The program **readbook.pl** will run and its output will be included in the HTML in place of this line.

The guestbook is implemented as two different Perl programs. The program readbook.pl is run with a server-side include from the HTML, and guest.cgi is run from the <FORM> tag to get the data for a new entry in the guestbook. Let's start by looking at guest.cgi.

5
```perl
#!/usr/bin/perl
$lockfile="/tmp/guestbook.lock";
$mydata="/home/billw/var/guestbook/guestbook.$$";
$datafile="/home/billw/var/guestbook/guestbook.dat";
```
6
```perl
print "content-type: text/html\n\n";
# make sure we have POST data
$ct = $ENV{"CONTENT_TYPE"};
$cl = $ENV{"CONTENT_LENGTH"};
# check the content-type for validity
if($ct ne "application/x-www-form-urlencoded")
```

```perl
{printf "I don't understand content-type: %s\n",
$ct;
exit 1
;}
# get each of the query strings from the input
stream
read(STDIN, $qs, $cl);
@qs = split(/&/,$qs);
foreach $i (0 .. $#qs) {
$qs[$i] =~ s/\+/ /g;
$qs[$i] =~ s/%(..)/pack("c",hex($1))/ge;
($name, $value) = split(/=/,$qs[$i],2);
$qs{$name} = $value;
}
```
7
```perl
# convert any HTML to entities
foreach $q (keys %qs) {
$qs{$q} =~ s/</&lt\;/g;
$qs{$q} =~ s/>/&gt\;/g;
$qs{$q} =~ s/"/&quot\;/g;
}
$name = $qs{"name"};
$from = $qs{"from"};
$comments = $qs{"comments"};
$today = &getdate;
```
8
```perl
# create the record
open(MYDATA, ">$mydata");
print MYDATA <<RECORD;
<record>
Date: $today
Name: $name
From: $from
Comments: $comments
</record>
RECORD
# only one of us can write to
# the main data file at a time
&lock;
```
9
```perl
# put the new record at the top of the data file
# by reading the rest of the datafile into the
# end of the new datafile . . .
open(DATA, "<$datafile");
while(<DATA>) { print MYDATA; }
```

```
close(DATA);
close(MYDATA);
# then put the new datafile in the place of the
# old one.
rename($mydata, $datafile);
# done with the main datafile
&unlock;
print <<CONF;
<HTML>
<HEAD>
<TITLE>
Guestbook
</TITLE>
</HEAD>
<BODY BGCOLOR=#ffffff>
<IMG SRC=guestbook.gif ALT="Guestbook"
WIDTH=330 HEIGHT=60 ALIGN=right>
<BR CLEAR=all>
<BR><CODE>
<P>you may need to press the RELOAD button <BR>
after you go <A HREF=index.html>back</A> <BR>
if you want to see your entry <BR>
</CODE>
</BODY>
</HTML>
CONF
# lock and unlock
#
# file locking routines to make sure only one
# person writes to a data file at a time
#
sub lock
{
local ($oumask);
# create the lock file world-writable
$oumask = umask(0);
for($i = 0; !open(LOCK, ">$lockfile"); $i++) {
# wait a sec and try again
sleep 1;
# after 30 seconds, just unlock it
```

```
&unlock if ($i > 30);
}
close(LOCK);
umask($oumask);
}
sub unlock
{
# just delete the lockfile (unlink is unix-ese for
delete)
unlink($lockfile);
}
# getdate
#
# make a printable version of today's date and time
#
sub getdate
{
my($month, $day, $time);
my($sec, $min, $hour, $mday, $mon, $year, $wday,
$yday, $isdst) =
localtime(time);
$month = ("January", "February", "March", "April",
"May", "June",
"July", "August", "September", "October",
"November", "December")[$mon];
$day = ("Sunday", "Monday", "Tuesday", "Wednesday",
"Thursday",
"Friday", "Saturday")[$wday];
$year = ($year > 95) ? $year + 1900 : $year + 2000;
$time = sprintf("%02d:%02d:%02d", $hour, $min,
$sec);
# $today is the printable date
return ($today = "$day, $mday $month $year, $time");
}
```

5 This line at the top of the program identifies the Perl interpreter as the program used to execute this file. It is a common way to run Perl scripts under Unix.

6 This prints out a MIME **"Content-Type"** header to tell the web browser that it will be receiving HTML. All CGI programs must start output with a MIME header.

7 This section converts any HTML in the form data to entities that can be printed. This effectively prevents users from putting any HTML (for example, <IMG SRC=http:// www.hell.org/devil.jpg>) into their entries.

8 Here we create the actual record in the guestbook database. The database is actually a text file, with each record delimited by **<RECORD>** and **</RECORD>** in the file. This makes it easy for the reading program to find the beginning and ending of each record.

9 For the purpose of a guestbook, we want to make sure each new record goes at the beginning of the file, rather than the end. This is the code that accomplishes that.

After writing the record to the MYDATA file, it opens the DATA file and reads it into MYDATA after the new record. Then it closes both files and renames MYDATA to overwrite the DATA file. This results in a new copy of DATA that contains the new record at the head instead of the tail.

```perl
#!/usr/bin/perl
$datafile="/home/billw/var/guestbook/guestbook.dat";
$| = 1; # flush stdout on each write
open(DATA, "<$datafile");
while(<DATA> && $i++ < 100) {loop if $_ ne
"<record>";
($date) = <DATA> =~ /Date: (.*)/;
($name) = <DATA> =~ /Name: (.*)/;
```
10 (line: `$| = 1; # flush stdout on each write`)
11 (line: `while(<DATA> && $i++ < 100) {loop if $_ ne`)

```perl
($from) = <DATA> =~ /From: (.*)/;
($comments) = <DATA> =~ /Comments: (.*)/;
$comments .= "\n";
while(chomp($c = <DATA>) && ($c ne "</record>")) {
$comments .= "$c\n";
}
print "<HR NOSHADE SIZE=3>\n";
print "$date\n";
print "<BR><STRONG>$name</STRONG>\n";
print "<BR><EM>$from</EM>\n";
print "<BLOCKQUOTE><PRE>$comments</PRE></BLOCK-
QUOTE>\n";
}
```
12 (line: `print "<HR NOSHADE SIZE=3>\n";`)

10 The **$|** variable is a special variable in Perl that controls the behavior of the output buffer. If the variable is zero (the default condition), all output is buffered (that is, it can be held on to) by the operating system until the operating system gets around to dealing with it. If it is nonzero, the output buffer is flushed (that is, the output is written immediately) as soon as the write action is finished.

It is important to set this to nonzero to make sure that the HTML that is sent to the output actually gets there in the order that you send it. Not setting this can lead to some very confusing results.

11 This is the code that deciphers the data file. It looks for lines that start with **"Date:", "Name:"**, and so on, and stores their contents in variables. It also looks for **"<RECORD>"** and **"</RECORD>"** that marks the beginning and ending of each record.

12 Notice that what we send here is HTML. It will be included right in the stream of HTML that is sent to the browser.

Ad Banners

Ugh. This is a tough subject for me, because I have a love/hate attitude toward ad banners. I preferred the noncommercial web before ad banners existed and littered the design integrity of so many sites. I reluctantly include information about ad banners here because, despite my ambivalence, they are firmly a part of the web landscape now.

Having made my own tastes known, I realize that many of you want to know about ad banner creation. For one thing, television commercials, although annoying, are also a medium in which enormous creativity and design excellence is found. As an animation teacher for many years, I saw that most of the opportunities for cool stuff were under the guise of "advertising." Not only that, but a lot of sites can't run for free, and advertising sponsorship is a needed and necessary evil. Furthermore, I also know of many professional design firms that are making more money designing advertising banners than web sites!

Most ad banners are accepted in GIF or JPEG format. Animated GIFs (see Chapter 14, "Animation") are a great file format for ad banners. Just beware that site audiences can be easily annoyed by these critters—especially looping ones. However, a successfully designed animated ad banner will hold your attention without annoyance.

There are no standard specs for ad banners. You might be asked to design a variety of sizes for a client. If you want to create banners for yourself and not a paying client, there are some interesting services on the web that trade banners for free:

■ http://www.linkexchange.com/

In the true spirit of web interactivity, Link Exchange has also set up the following newsgroup:

Newsgroup: le.discuss
■ news://news2.linkexchange.com/le.discuss

This newsgroup covers general Link Exchange Comments/Questions/Problems/Promotional Issues, Banner Design, Click-Thru Ratios, Advertising Issues, International Advertising, Web Design in regard to building a better site, Questions about Search Engines /Directories/Yellow Pages, and so on.

Sample frames from an ad banner I created for my book *Deconstructing Web Graphics*. Ad banners can be single frames, or contain many frames such as this example. This animation contains 15 separate images and conveys much more information about my book than a single frame could possibly communicate. It was created in Photoshop and GIFBuilder (■ http://iawww.epfl.ch/Staff/Yves.Piguet/clip2gif-home/ GifBuilder.html).

Chat Environments and Avatars

In future editions of this book, I predict this section will grow bigger as visual chat areas and avatars become a viable digital design medium for illustrators and designers. Unlike e-mail, chat is real-time, where participants send electronic messages in large group forums. There are currently more options for nonvisual chat software applications, but the future will bring a different sort of chat experience that will involve full multimedia, such as sound, movies, animated characters, and even voice.

For now, there are a few early adopter-based technologies that include avatars (icons for chat participants) and worlds (environmental backdrops). Here's a brief URL list to check out some of the software options for visual and nonvisual chat software:

WebCrawler's List of Chat Software Options
- http://webcrawler.com/select/chat.tools.html

The Palace
- http://www.thepalace.com/

IRC FAQ
- http://www2.undernet.org:8080/~cs93jtl/irc_faq.txt

ICHAT
- http://www.ichat.com/

A custom environment for a Palace-based chat environment that Bruce Heavin created for *The Net* magazine.

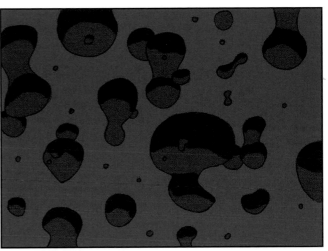

Bruce created custom views of the environment—the inside of the lava lamp on the table. Visitors can even chat inside the lava lamp!

The visual environment in a virtual chat space can attract a specific clientele, or inspire subjects of conversation, just like the real world.

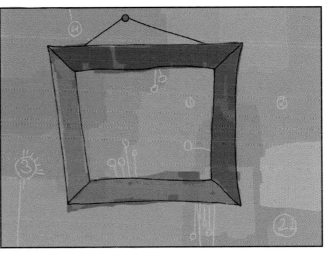

The Palace is scriptable, so it can be programmed to do extra things, like enable end users to draw on the wall. Bruce made areas, such as inside this frame, where visitors can add their own pictures.

Mouse Rollovers

Mouse rollovers are very popular in CD-ROM-based multimedia, and will be on the web as soon as people learn how to make them. On the web we have a few visual cues for hyperlinks, such as the hand symbol, the bounding box around linked graphics, and underlines below text. These are fairly limited visual signals. Rollovers offer much greater design flexibility.

A rollover can make type appear to glow, change the color of an icon, or make a sound. The possibilities for rollover effects are limited by your imagination only. This section will evaluate two technologies for rollovers: JavaScript and Macromedia Director/Shockwave.

JavaScript MouseOvers

JavaScript is a programming language developed by Netscape. Unlike Java, C, Perl, or sh, however, you can view the JavaScript code within HTML documents. This makes it very easy to learn and "borrow" from others' sites. Proper netiquette recommends that you always leave references to the originator within the code if you do copy the scripts. These credits are usually left in comment tags, which look like this:

```
//So-and So's Amazing Rollover Script//
or like this
<!...So-and So's Amazing Rollover Script...!>
```

You'll see these types of credits in the following examples.

Joe Maller's JavaScript Rollover

Joe Maller, a digital designer in NYC and computer imaging instructor at Parsons Institute, uses his site as an experimental playing field for all types of new web technologies. Check his stuff out at ■ http://www.joemaller.com. The following tutorial was written by Joe and is also on his site.

Declaring Images in the Script

In the <SCRIPT> section of the <HEAD> of the document, you need to first declare the images you will later use for your rollover. The JavaScript to set up those images looks like this:

```
Image1= new Image(100,150)
Image1.src = "your_image.gif"
Image2 = new Image(100,150)
Image2.src = "your_other_image.gif"
```

Each image must have two lines: the first sets its size, and the second sets its source and the location and name of the image. The numbers within the parentheses refer to width and height, in that order. Note that JavaScript is case sensitive; TheDog is not the same as thedog.

Naming Image Objects

JavaScript 1.1, as implemented in Netscape Navigator 3.0, defines images as objects. That means the JavaScript now recognizes images as more than just HTML.

To replace an image, you must give JavaScript some way of identifying where you will replace the images. Do this by either inserting NAME="Rupert" into the <IMG...> tag, or by learning to refer to images in JavaScript's Array syntax: document.images[2]

The above refers to the third image tag in the HTML document (you're programming now—zero counts first). I prefer to simply name my images, and that's what I've done in this example.

For JavaScript to recognize a rollover, the object rolled over must be a link; regular text is ignored. Here is the HTML code for the image that will be replaced during a rollover:

```
<A HREF="link.html"
onMouseOver="SwapOut()"
onMouseOut="SwapBack()">
<IMG NAME="Rupert"
SRC="your_image.gif"
WIDTH=100
HEIGHT=150>
</A>
```

Notice the name attribute's appearance in the <IMG...> tag.

What's "onMouseOver"?

onMouseOver and onMouseOut are event handlers that tell JavaScript what to do when an event occurs. The command given is the function within the quotes. onMouseOver="blorg()" tells JavaScript to execute the function blorg().

Functions

Functions are predefined sets of commands that JavaScript will execute when only the name of the function is called. Functions are usually stored in the <SCRIPT> section of the <HEAD> of the document, the same place we declared the images earlier. The standard format for defining a function is:

```
function SwapOut() {
document.Rupert.src = Image2.src; return true;
}
```

joe_blink.jpg   joe open.jpg

Joe's mouseover effect causes his eyes to blink. It's fun—and worth trying at at home!

■ **note**

Notes and Problems

LOWSRC—If you use the low source tag on an image, you might experience unwanted reloads of that image before every image swap.

Image Size—The size of the image is set by the image you will be replacing. Replacement images will be stretched to fit.

Putting It All Together

The following is the complete code for a simple document that will change images. Don't believe me? Try it. Here's the code:

```
<HTML>
<HEAD>
<TITLE>
Doubter's page
</TITLE>
<SCRIPT LANGUAGE="JavaScript">
<!-- hide from none JavaScript Browsers
Image1= new Image(121,153)
Image1.src = "joe_open.jpg"
Image2 = new Image(121,153)
Image2.src = "joe_blink.jpg"
function SwapOut() {
document.Rupert.src = Image2.src; return true;
}
function SwapBack() {
document.Rupert.src = Image1.src; return true;
}
// - stop hiding -->
</SCRIPT>
</HEAD>
<BODY BGCOLOR="#FFFFFF">
<CENTER>
<P>
<A HREF="http://www.joemaller.com/"
onmouseover="SwapOut()"
onmouseout="SwapBack()">
<IMG NAME="Rupert"
SRC="joe_open.jpg"
WIDTH=121
HEIGHT=153
BORDER=0>
</A>
</P>
If you use this, please give me credit.
</CENTER>
</BODY>
</HTML>
```

Bill Weinman's JavaScript Rollover

This example demonstrates that rollovers, like many things, can be done more way than one. This is Bill's script:

```
// bill's suave mouseover javascript
// (c) 1996 wew   http://www.weinman.com/wew/
//
// If you want to use this, go ahead;
but please leave
// this notice here so that other people
know where it
// came from.   —wew.
//
// how many items in the array
numitems = 6
// the offset to the first GIF that's
going to change.  This is
// the number of GIFs on the page before
the first one that
// will swap, minus 1.
offset = 7
// creates the array for the GIFs.
don't touch this.
Atitles = new Array(numitems)
// this initializes the array.
for(i = 0; i < numitems; i++)
{
Atitles[i] = new Image()
}
// blankgif is the default GIF.
this one's white 1 pixel x 1 pixel.
// WARNING: transparent GIFs create problems on
MacIntoshim!
blankgif = "white.gif"
// These are the GIFs that will overlay
the white ones when the
// mouse is over them.
Atitles[0].src = "tbio.gif"
Atitles[1].src = "tproj.gif"
Atitles[2].src = "tbook.gif"
Atitles[3].src = "tbear.gif"Atitles[4].src =
"tlinks.gif"
Atitles[5].src = "tmail.gif"
// this function swaps out the GIFs,
and updates the status line.
function description(m,i) {
status = m
imgtmp = document.images[offset + i].src
document.images[offset + i].src = Atitles[i].src
return true;
}
// this function restores the blankgif and
the status line.
function clearstat(i) {
status=""
document.images[offset + i].src = blankgif
return true;
}
</script>
```

Bill's images and file names follow:

Bear	Bio	Links	Email	Projects
bbear.gif	bbio.gif	blinks.gif	bmail.gif	bproj.gif

Director/Shockwave/Lingo-Based Interactive Web Pages

Shockwave is the name of a plug-in that enables Director-based multimedia projects to be played on the web. Multimedia can be described as anything that combines sound, animation, images, text, and interactivity.

Unlike JavaScript, Macromedia Director is an authoring program for creating interactive multimedia for kiosks and CD-ROMs, and it has been around many years longer than the web itself. The Shockwave file format boasts an impressive compression ratio of three to one, making the Director files one third of their usual size.

Afterburner is the free post-processing tool that offers authors who create Director multimedia projects the ability to convert them so that they can be distributed over the web. Once Afterburner has converted a Director project, that project becomes a Shockwave file. You can download Afterburner from Macromedia's site at ■ http://www.macromedia.com/shockwave/devtools. html#director.

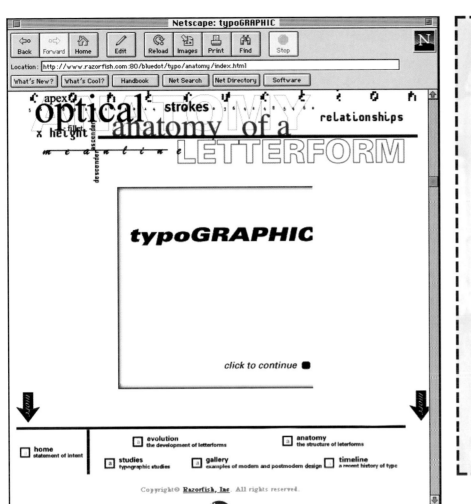

The centered window with the "click here to continue" button is the embedded Shockwave document. This example is taken from ■ http://www.razorfish.com/bluedot/typo/anatomy/.

■ note

Shockwave Versus JavaScript
Director projects (which later get converted to Shockwave) can be much more robust than what is possible through Java-Script. With the added power (a paint and animation interface, and a proprietary programming language called Lingo) comes a steeper learning curve. You can't see the source code for a Director project like you can a JavaScript, making it impossible to reverse engineer what others have done. Learning Shockwave and Director requires buying the program, reading the manual and/or third-party books, and/or joining users groups or discussion groups. The power is definitely greater, but the learning curve may not be worth it to you. For more information, visit ■ http://www.macromedia.com.

Leroy's Click and Drag

Bruce Heavin includes a simple Shockwave piece on his site.

Leroy's Click and Drag is at ■ http://www.stink.com/leroy/leroy.html. Every graphic on this page is click and dragable.

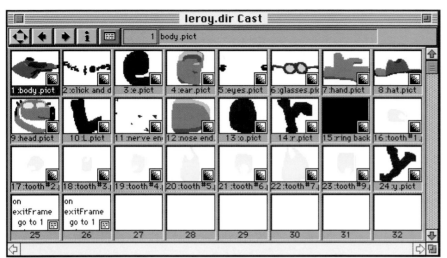

The leroy.dir Cast window shows each element of artwork used in the Director project.

By clicking the Movable check box, Bruce created an interactive experience making each piece of artwork movable.

Designing the Interface for the Anatomy Shockwave Project

Stephen Turbek spent several weeks teaching himself Macromedia Director so he could program some of his own experiments with interface design. The Anatomy section in the typoGRAPHIC site (■ http://www.razorfish.com/bluedot/typo/) gave him an opportunity to produce his first published Director project, where he was able to test some of his theories about human interface design. Stephen's interface design succeeded by creating custom navigation controls that blended seamlessly with the overall aesthetic of the site.

A main concern to Stephen was understanding how to make a person learn a new interface. The "red dot" became a unifying design theme in his project. After the user learned that the dot changed to red and could be clicked to go to the next screen, the navigation for the piece was established.

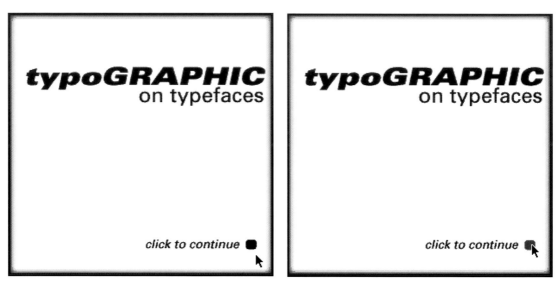

When the end user's cursor passes over the black rectangle, it turns red. This rollover effect signifies that the rectangle is a button that triggers interactive events.

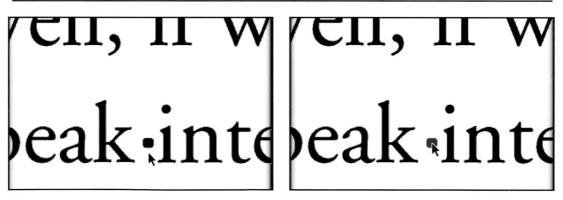

The red cursor metaphor is reinforced as a navigational cue in subsequent screens without the need to repeat the instructions "click to continue." The end user is being trained how to use the interface without further explanation.

A current trend in advanced multimedia and game design is to break away from obvious buttons with words on them. By using a simple red dot instead of a bulky button or conventional arrow icons, Steven was able to keep the design of his Shockwave piece much more elegant and consistent with the established aesthetic of the typoGRAPHIC site. It's important to designers that interfaces integrate with the overall look and feel of an interactive experience.

Stephen also strove to create an inviting interface that enabled users to explore and learn without cumbersome navigation graphics. He carried the rollover effect of objects changing from black to red throughout the piece. The next section of the project offered definitions for the anatomy of type, inviting the user to interact with red circles.

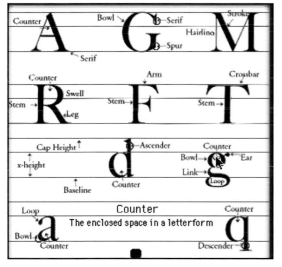

When a cursor travels over a red circle, the definition of the term is displayed at the bottom of the frame. The familiar black dot at the bottom of the image signifies that it can be clicked to advance to the next screen.

Another important component of Stephen's piece was to create maximum interactivity for the audience. Rather than a simple slide show, he chose to let the user move type around onscreen themselves, to view the differences between serifs and typeface weights. This created a much more compelling example than simply showing visual examples of the differences.

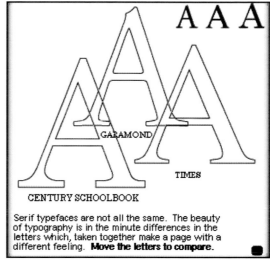

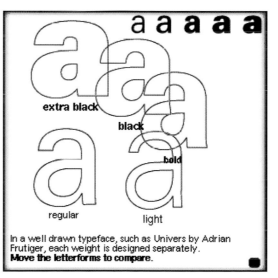

Stephen designed two screens that enable the user to move the letterforms into position. This level of interactivity is new to the web and justifies using extra tools such as Director and Shockwave.

Deconstructing the Lingo for Shockwave

Adding interactivity to Director projects is accomplished through using a proprietary programming language called Lingo. Lingo is touted as an easy programming language—although non-programmers might not necessarily agree with that analysis. Learning Lingo is possible by studying the manuals that are shipped with Macromedia Director or through third-party books and Usenet groups. This is the view of the artwork from within Director's Paint window.

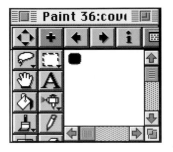

In order to color the black dot, it had to be a separate sprite (piece of artwork) within the Director project .

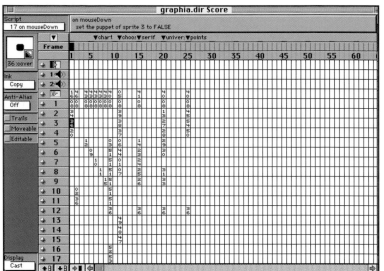

Inside the Director Score window, the black dot is in the channel #3 position. Note in the Lingo script that follows how this artwork is referred to as "sprite 3," even though the artwork is named cover.pict, and is in the number 36 position in the Cast window.

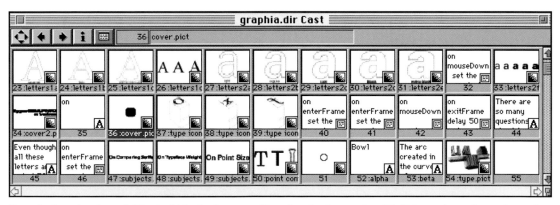

If you look at the channel #3 cel within the Score, you'll notice the tiny number 36. This number reflects the position of the sprite that's been assigned in the Cast Member window.

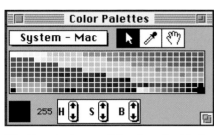

The Lingo is also specifying the color black turn to red with the cursor rollover. Black is #255 within the Mac System palette.

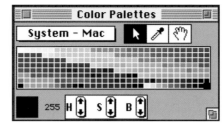

Red is #217 within the Mac System palette.

The cursor turns red by instructing the color of the black (255) sprite to turn red (217). It's possible to set a custom palette within Director, but the Mac System palette is in use in this project. The Lingo for the red cursor rollover effect follows:

```
on enterFrame
set the puppet of sprite 3 to TRUE
if rollOver(3) = TRUE then
set the forecolor of sprite 3 to 217
else set the forecolor of sprite 3 to 255
end if
end
On exitFrame
go to the frame
end
```

To create the early slide-show effect, Stephen inserted delay times, which cause each frame of artwork to pause for a specified amount of time. Delays within Lingo are measured in ticks. One second is 60 ticks, so each delay in this piece is a little less than a second. Here's the Lingo:

```
on exitFrame
delay 50
end
```

These three screens appear in succession, like a slide show. The slide-show effect was accomplished by assigning each frame to have a delay within the Lingo programming.

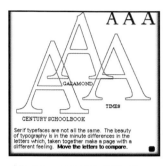

Allowing users the ability to move images around on-screen, such as the three letterforms here, is accomplished by assigning the object to be movable.

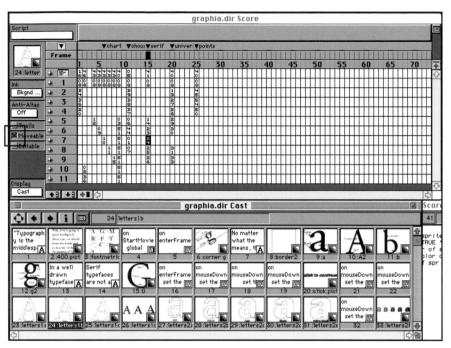

Note how the number 24 is highlighted in the Director Score. To its far left is a check box called Movable. By clicking this, the sprite is able to be moved by the end user. This piece of artwork is sprite number 24 in the Cast window. It also has been set to use Bkgnd ink, which instructs the program to mask the background color of the graphic. In this case, the graphic's background color was white, so under the Bkgnd ink setting the white was assigned to be transparent.

Besides checking the Movable check box, another way to assign movability to an object is through Lingo. The advantage to using Lingo for this purpose is that the movable attribute can be turned off or be dependent on other actions. Clicking on the Movable check box is less flexible because it's a global setting that lasts the entire duration of the Director project.

This is the Lingo to add movable functionality to a sprite:

```
set the movable of sprite x=true
```

> ■ **note**
>
> **Director 5 Supports Shockwave**
>
> Director 5 has been released since Stephen made the Shockwave example on typoGRAPHIC. Some of the upgrade's improvements are support for anti-aliased text and the capability to save directly in the Shockwave format without the use of Afterburner.

Shocking Director

The final step to preparing the Director document is to turn it into a web-based Shockwave document. This is done with a free utility called After-burner, which can be downloaded from:

- http://www.macromedia.com/shockwave/devtools.html#director

Afterburner is a post-processor that compresses and prepares Director movies for uploading to an HTTP server that will make them available to Internet users. This can now be done in Director 5.0 directly, without using Afterburner. Uncompressed movies should be in .dir or .dxr format. After compression with Afterburner, they will be in .dcr format. HTTP servers should set the MIME-Type for .dcr files to "application/x-director."

To include the Shockwave piece within the typoGRAPHIC site, the following HTML was used:

```
<EMBED SRC="images/graphia.dcr" WIDTH=304 HEIGHT=300>
```

It's extremely important to include the dimensions of Shockwave documents in HTML code. The file will not function without it.

Although Stephen did not choose to do this on the typoGRAPHIC site, it is possible to code the HTML so an alternative image displays on browsers that do not support plug-ins by using the following tag:

```
<NO EMBED>
```

After the <NO EMBED> tag, an alternative graphic could be inserted that would be visible only to browsers that do not have the Shockwave plug-in installed or don't support the plug-in.

Font

Introduction

Getting Started in Web Design

Understanding the Web Environment

Web File Formats

Low-Bandwidth Graphics

Hexadecimal Color

Browser-Safe Color

Transparent Artwork

Background Tiles

Rules, Bullets and Buttons

Navigation-Based Graphics

Web-Based Typography

Scanning Techniques for the Web

Layout and Alignment Techniques

Animation

Sound

Interactivity

HTML for Visual Designers

Glossary

Design Resources Appendix

Index

<H1>

BROWSER SAFE COLORS

33FF

Web 0   ed typography

oloshop

0033

INDEX

Width="500"

PARENCY

<STRONG>

.Gif
.Jpg
.Png

<Img src="

Image compressio
limited palettes
IMAGE OPTIMIZATION
216 Colors

</A>

Height="600

10.2

<center>

Imaging techniques
Extending HTML
Web file formats
bgcolor="FFFFCC"

Animation sound and

OGRAPHY

link="cyan"

<center> BODY
Antialias

LYNDA.COM

www Design

17

<IMG SRC="#" ALT="#">	Contains an image and a text description for viewers who don't have graphical web browsers.
<IMG SRC="#" HEIGHT=# WIDTH=#>	Allows for specifying image dimensions and causes HTML text to load before large graphics.
<A HREF="#"><IMG SRC="#"></A>	Contains a linked image and automatically generates a border around the image in whatever link color has been specified.
<A HREF="#"><IMG SRC="#" BORDER=0></A>	Ensures that there's no border on browsers that support this feature.
<A HREF="#"><IMG SRC="#" BORDER=#></A>	Depending on the value, puts a heavier or lighter border around the linked image.

List Tags and Attributes

<UL>	Unorganized list: Generates an indented list with bullets.
<OL>	Organized list: Generates numbers in front of list.
<LI>	Puts a bullet in front of each item, indents the text, and creates a line break at the end of each item.
<DL>	Definition list: Produces an indented list with no bullets.
<DD>	Produces items in a definition list.

Table Tags

<TABLE></TABLE>	Put at the beginning and end of tables.
<TH></TH>	Makes bold text or numbers and accepts table attributes.
<TD></TD>	Includes text, numbers, or images and accepts table attributes.

Table Tags and Attributes

ALIGN="left, right, or center"	Aligns text or images in table.

VALIGN="top middle, bottom, or baseline"	Vertically aligns text or images in table.
ROWSPAN=#	Denotes the number of rows in a table.
COLSPAN=#	Denotes the number of columns in a table.
WIDTH=#	Specifies the width of the table by pixels.
CELLPADDING=#	Sets the space between the border and content of table.
CELLSPACING=#	Adjusts the thickness of the borders.

Linking Tags and Attributes

<EMBED></EMBED>	For use with plug-ins.
<NOEMBED></NOEMBED>	For non-plug-in-based content.

Frames Tag and Attributes

<FRAMESET></FRAMESET>	Initiates frames.
COLS	Specifies the numbers of columns and widths in a <FRAMESET>.
ROWS	Specifies the rows and their height in a <FRAMESET>.
SCROLLING	Turn on or off scrolling when content is larger than the frame.
TARGET	Lets you set _blank, _self, _parent, or_top attributes (see Chapter 10, "Navigation-Based Graphics").
FRAMEBORDER	Enables you to turn borders on or off.

Linking Tags and Attributes

<A></A>	Anchors text.
<A HREF="URL"></A>	Links the image or text to an URL.

Comments Tag

<! ... >	Sets comments that appear as notes for the HTML document but won't show up on the actual web page.

Introduction

Getting Started in Web Design

Understanding the Web Environment

Web File Formats

Low-Bandwidth Graphics

Hexadecimal Color

Browser-Safe Color

Transparent Artwork

Background Tiles

Rules, Bullets and Buttons

Navigation-Based Graphics

Web-Based Typography

Scanning Techniques for the Web

Layout and Alignment Techniques

Animation

Sound

Interactivity

HTML for Visual Designers

Glossary

Design Resources Appendix

Index

<H1>
Web
typography
<img src="
<STRONG>
.gif
.jpg
png
Limited palettes
IMAGE OPTIMIZATION
216 Colors
PARENCY
Height="600
</A>
10.2
<<center
Imaging techniques
Extending HTML
Web file formats
bgcolor="FFFFCC"
sound and
alink="cyan
LYNDA.COM
</center>
www. Design
g

Glossary

8-bit graphics: A color or grayscale graphic or movie that has 256 colors or less.

8-bit sound: 8-bit sound has a dynamic range of 48 dB. Dynamic range is the measure of steps between the volume or amplitude of a sound.

16-bit graphics: A color image or movie that has 65,500 colors.

16-bit sound: Standard CD-quality sound resolution. 16-bit sounds have a dynamic range of 96 dB.

24-bit graphics: A color image or movie that has 16.7 million colors.

32-bit graphics: A color image or movie that has 16.7 million colors plus an 8-bit masking channel.

active navigation: Point-and-click navigation, where the end user guides the information flow.

adaptive dithering: A form of dithering in which the program looks to the image to determine the best set of colors when creating an 8-bit or smaller palette. See dithering.

additive color: The term for RGB color space that uses projected light to mix color.

AIFC: A sound file format. AIFC is a new spec for the older Audio Interchange File Format (AIFF). Both AIFF and AIFF-C files can be read by this format.

aliasing: In bitmapped graphics, the jagged boundary along the edges of different-colored shapes within an image. See anti-aliasing.

animated GIF: Part of the GIF89a spec that supports multiple images, and streams and displays them sequentially.

anti-aliasing: A technique for reducing the jagged appearance of aliased bitmapped images, usually by inserting pixels that blend at the boundaries between adjacent colors.

artifacts: Image imperfections caused by compression.

attributes: Defined appearances or behaviors of 3D objects. For example, a lighting attribute would affect the color and light of an object. A texture attribute would affect the surface texture of an object.

authoring tools: Creation tools for interactive media.

avatar: A visual icon chosen or designed by an end user that is used as a persona within chat environments.

AVI: Audio-Video Interleaved. Microsoft's file format for desktop video movies.

bit depth: The number of bits used to represent the color of each pixel in a given movie or still image. Specifically: bit depth of 1=black-and-white pixel; bit depth of 2=4 colors or grays; bit depth of 4=16 colors or grays; bit depth of 8=256 colors or grays; bit depth of 16=65,536 colors; bit depth of 24=(approximately) 16 million colors.

bitmapped graphics: Graphics that are pixel based, as opposed to object oriented. Bitmapped graphics are what the computer can display because it's a pixel-based medium, whereas object-oriented graphics can be viewed in high resolution once they are sent to a printer. Graphics on the web are bitmapped because they are viewed from a computer-screen-based delivery system.

brightness: Adds white or tints an image, whereas lack of brightness adds black or tones an image.

browser: An application that enables you to access World Wide Web pages. Most browsers provide the capability to view web pages, copy and print material from web pages, download files from the web, and navigate throughout the web.

browser-safe colors: The 216 colors that do not shift between platforms, operating systems, or most web browsers.

cache: A storage area that keeps frequently accessed data or program instructions readily available so that you do not have to retrieve them repeatedly.

CGI: Common Gateway Interface. A web standard for extending the functionality of HTML. CGI always involves the combination of a live web server and external programming scripts.

chat: A real-time multiple user e-mail environment.

Cinepak: Cinepak is very high form of movie compression. The compression type is called "lossy" because it causes a visible loss in quality.

client: A computer that requests information from a network's server. See server.

client pull: Client pull creates a slide show effect with HTML text or inline images. It is programmed within the <META> tag.

client side: Client side means that the web element or effect can run locally off a computer and does not require the presence of a server.

client-side imagemap: A client-side imagemap is programmed in HTML, and does not require a separate map definition file or to be stored on a live web server.

CLUT: Color LookUp Table. An 8-bit or lower image file uses a CLUT to define its palette.

color mapping: A color map refers to the color palette of an image. Color mapping means assigning colors to an image.

color names: Some browsers support using the name of a color instead of the color's hexadecimal value.

complementary colors: Created from opposing color hues on the color wheel.

compression: Reduction of the amount of data required to re-create an original file, graphic, or movie. Compression is used to reduce the transmission time of media and application files across the web.

contrast: The degrees of separation between values.

counter: Counts and displays the numbers of hits on a web page.

data rate: Data rate relates to how fast movie data was captured.

data streaming: The capability to deliver time-based data as it's requested, much like a VCR, rather than having to download all the information before it can be played.

dithering: The positioning of different-colored pixels within an image that uses a 256-color palette to simulate a color that does not exist in the palette. A dithered image often looks noisy, or composed of scattered pixels. See adaptive dithering.

dpi: Dot Per Inch. A term used mostly by print graphics-based programs and professionals, and is a common measurement related to the resolution of an image. See screen resolution.

extension: Abbreviated code at the end of a file that tells the browser what kind of file it's looking at. For example, a JPEG file would have the extension .jpg.

fixed palette: An established palette that is fixed. When a fixed palette web browser views images, it will convert images to its colors and not use the colors from the original.

forms processing: Forms that enable users to enter information on web pages are created by using HTML and CGI, and their function is typically referred to as forms processing.

fps: Frames Per Second. A movie contains a certain number of frames, and the fewer frames, the more jerky the motion and the smaller the file size.

frames: Frames offer the ability to divide a web page into multiple regions, with each region acting as a nested web page.

ftp: File Transfer Protocol. An Internet protocol that enables users to remotely access files on other computers. An ftp site houses files that can be downloaded to your computer.

gamma: Gamma measures the contrast that affects the midtones of an image. Adjusting the gamma lets you change the brightness values of the middle range of gray tones without dramatically altering the shadows and highlights.

gamut: A viewable or printable color range.

GIF: A bitmapped color graphics file format. GIF is commonly used on the web because it employs an efficient compression method. See JPEG.

GIF89a: A type of GIF file that supports transparency and multi-blocks. Multi-blocks create the illusion of animation. GIF89a files are sometimes referred to as "transparent GIFs" or "animated GIFs."

group: A VRML term. Grouping objects enables collections of objects to be treated as single objects. The group is a container for all the objects so that nodes can be applied to multiple objects. If an object has two colors, chances are it has two groups.

guestbook: A type of form that enables end users to enter comments on a web page.

hexadecimal: A base 16 mathematics calculation, often used in scripts and code. Hexadecimal code is required by HTML to describe RGB values of color for the web.

HTML: HyperText Markup Language. The common language for interchange of hypertext between the World Wide Web client and server. Web pages must be written using HTML. See hypertext.

HTTP: HyperText Transfer Protocol is the protocol that the browser and the web server use to communicate with each other.

hue: Defines a linear spectrum of the color wheel.

hybrid-safe colors: Pre-mixed, interlaced browser-safe colors that give the illusion of colors outside the 216 safe spectrum but are still browser safe.

hypertext: Text formatted with lines that enable the reader to jump among related topics. See HTML.

imagemaps: Portions of images that are hypertext links. Using a mouse-based web client such as Netscape or Mosaic, the user clicks on different parts of a mapped image to activate different hypertext links. See hypertext.

inline graphic: A graphic that sits inside an HTML document instead of the alternative, which would require that the image be downloaded and then viewed by using an outside system.

inlining: The process of embedding one VRML file into another.

interlaced GIFs: The GIF file format allows for "interlacing," which causes the GIF to load quickly at low or chunky resolution and then come into full or crisp resolution.

ISP: Acronym for Internet Service Provider.

Java: A programming language developed by Sun Microsystems that is cross-platform compatible and supported by some web browsers.

JavaScript: A scripting language that enables you to extend the capabilities of HTML. Developed by Netscape.

JPEG: Acronym for Joint Photographic Experts Group, but commonly used to refer to a lossy compression technique that can reduce the size of a graphics file by as much as 96 percent. See GIF.

lighting: 3D artwork responds to lighting in a realistic manner, so lighting will affect overall appearance and color.

links: Emphasized words in a hypertext document that act as pointers to more information on that specific subject. Links are generally underlined and may appear in a different color. When you click on a link, you can be transported to a different web site that contains information about the work or phrase used as the link. See hypertext.

lossless compression: A data compression technique that reduces the size of a file without sacrificing any of the original data. In lossless compression, the expanded or restored file is an exact replica of the original file before it was compressed. See compression.

lossy compression: A data compression technique in which some data is deliberately discarded in order to achieve massive reductions in the size of the compressed file.

mask: The process of blocking out areas in a computer graphic.

MIME: Multipurpose Internet Mail Extensions. An Internet standard for transferring nontext-based data such as sounds, movies, and images.

moiré: A pattern that results when dots overlap. This problem often occurs when scanning printed materials.

MPEG: MPEG audio is a high-quality audio compression file format.

µ-law: µ-law is a sound file format rendered by Unix platforms. The sound quality is generally much lower than other sound formats, but the files are much smaller, too.

object-oriented graphics: A graphic image composed of objects such as lines, circles, ellipses, and boxes that can be moved independently. This type of graphic is used for print-based design because it can be printed at a higher resolution than a computer screen. See bitmapped graphics.

object resolution: Relates to how many polygons form a shape. High object resolution includes many polygons, looks the best, and takes the longest to render. Low-resolution objects have fewer polygons and render faster.

passive navigation: Animation, slide shows, streaming movies, and audio. Basically anything that plays without the end user initiating the content.

plug-in: Plug-ins are supported by some browsers, and extend the capability of standard HTML. They need to be installed in the end user's plug-in folder, found inside the browser software folder.

PNG: An acronym for Portable Network Graphics. PNG is a lossless file format that supports interlacing, 8-bit transparency, and gamma information.

PostScript: A sophisticated page description language used for printing high-quality text and graphics on laser printers and other high-resolution printing devices.

primary colors: The theory behind primary colors is that these colors are the starting point from which any other colors can be mixed. On the computer, the primary colors are red, green, and blue because color mixing is additive (created with light). With pigment the primary colors are red, blue, and yellow because color mixing is subtractive.

progressive JPEG: A type of JPEG that produces an interlaced effect as it loads and can be 30 percent smaller than standard JPEGs. It is not currently supported by many web browsers.

provider: Provides Internet access. See ISP.

quick mask: A Photoshop technique for making masks. See mask.

QuickTime: System software developed by Apple Computer for presentation of desktop video.

render: The computer process of calculating 3D data and displaying the results on the computer screen.

rollover: A type of navigation button that changes when the end user's mouse rolls over it.

sample rates: Sample rates are measured in kilohertz (KHz). Sound-editing software is where the initial sample rate settings are established. Standard sample rates range from 11.025 KHz, 22.050 KHz, 44.10 KHz, to 48 KHz. The higher the sample rate, the better the quality. The sample describes its highs and lows.

sampling resolution: Sampling resolution affects quality, just like dpi resolution affects the quality of images. Standard sampling resolutions are 8-bit mono, 8-bit stereo, 16-bit mono, and 16-bit stereo.

saturation: Defines the intensity of color.

screen resolution: Screen resolution generally refers to the resolution of common computer monitors. 72 dpi is an agreed upon average, although you will also hear of 96 dpi being the resolution of larger displays.

search engine: A type of application, commonly found on the web, that enables you to search by keywords for information or URLs.

server: A computer that provides services for users of its network. The server receives requests for services and manages the requests so that they are answered in an orderly manner. See client.

server push: Server push is the method of requesting images or data from the server and automating their playback. It involves CGI and the presence of a live web server.

server side: Server side means any type of web page element that depends on being loaded to a server. It also implies the use of a CGI script.

server-side imagemap: A server-side imagemap requires that the information about the imagemap be saved within a "map definition file" that needs to be stored on a server and accessed by a CGI script.

splash screen: A main menu screen or opening graphic to a web page.

sprite: An individual component of an animation, such as a character or graphic that moves independently.

tables: Tables create rows and columns, as in a spreadsheet, and can be used to align data and images.

tag: ASCII text indicators with which you surround text and images to designate certain formats or styles.

texture map: 2D artwork that is applied to the surface of a 3D shape.

transparent GIFs: A superset of the original GIF file format that adds header information to the GIF file, which signifies that a defined color will be masked out.

true color: The quality of color provided by 24-bit color depth. 24-bit color depth results in 16.7 million colors, which is usually more than adequate for the human eye.

URL: Uniform Resource Locator. The address for a web site.

value: The range from light to dark in an image.

Video for Windows: A multimedia architecture and application suite that provides an outbound architecture that lets applications developers access audio, video, and animation from many different sources through one interface. As an application, Video for Windows primarily handles video capture and compression, and video and audio editing. See AVI.

WYSIWYG: Pronounced wizzy-wig. A design philosophy in which formatting commands directly affect the text displayed on-screen so that the screen shows the appearance of printed text.

Introduction

Getting Started in Web Design

Understanding the Web Environment

Web File Formats

Low-Bandwidth Graphics

Hexadecimal Color

Browser-Safe Color

Transparent Artwork

Background Tiles

Rules, Bullets and Buttons

Navigation-Based Graphics

Web-Based Typography

Scanning Techniques for the Web

Layout and Alignment Techniques

Animation

Sound

Interactivity

HTML for Visual Designers

Glossary

Design Resources Appendix

Index

Design Resources

Design Conferences

American Center for Design
■ http://www.ac4d.org

Web Design and Development
■ http://www.web97.com/

International Design Conference
■ http://www.idca.org

TED
■ http://www.ted.com/

MacWorld Expo
■ http://www.mha.com

Seybold
■ http://www.sbexpos.com/

SIGGRAPH
■ http://www.siggraph.org

Web Design Classes

Naugatuck Valley Community Technical College
■ http://www.leonline.com/nvctc/

Project Cool
■ http://www.projectcool.com

Duquesne University
■ http://the-duke.duq-duke.duq.edu/commhome.htm

EEI Communications
■ http://www.eei-alex.com/training/

San Francisco State Multimedia Studies Program
■ http://msp.sfsu.edu

Parsons School of Design
■ http://www.parsons.edu/

School of Visual Arts
■ http://www.sva.edu/

Art Center College of Design
■ http://www.artcenter.edu

Rhode Island School of Design
■ http://www.risd.edu/

American Institute of Graphic Arts
- http://www.dol.com/AIGA/

DGEF
(Dynamic Graphics Educational Foundation)
- http://199.224.94.160/DGEF/

Interactive Telecommunications Program
- http://www.itp.tsoa.nyu.edu/

Graphics Artists Guild
- http://www.gag.com

Magazines

Adobe Magazine
- http://www.adobemag.com

Communication Arts
- http://www.commarts.com

Digital Video Magazine Online
- http://www.zdent.com/~ziffnet/cis/

Dynamic Graphics Magazine
- http://199.224.94.160/DGEF/Dynamic/

Web Review
- http://www.webreview.com/

Web Week
- www.webweek.com

DT&G Magazine
- http://www.Graphic-Design.com

Review
- http://www.itp.tsoa.nyu.edu/~review/

I.D.® Magazine
- IDMAG@aol.com

Step-By-Step Magazine
- CompuServe 74431,2241

Miscellaneous

Suzanne Stephen's Web Design Source List
- http://www.opendoor.com/StephensDesign/URLs/index.htm

Lynda's Homegurrrl Web Design List
- http://www.webmonster.net/lists/

Web Reference
- http://www.webreference.com

Introduction

Getting Started in Web Design

Understanding the Web Environment

Web File Formats

Low-Bandwidth Graphics

Hexadecimal Color

Browser-Safe Color

Transparent Artwork

Background Tiles

Rules, Bullets and Buttons

Navigation-Based Graphics

Web-Based Typography

Scanning Techniques for the Web

Layout and Alignment Techniques

Animation

Sound

Interactivity

HTML for Visual Designers

Glossary

Design Resources Appendix

Index

BROWSER

33FF

otoshop

INDEX

Width ="500"

PARENCY

</A>

10.2

<H1>

Web

<STRONG>
.Gif
.Jpg
Png

Height = "600"

<center>

Imaging techniques
Extending HTML
Web file formats
bgcolor = "FFFFCC"

link = "cyan"

<center>

3d typography

<IM

<TABL

<A>

<img src="

Image compressio
Limited palettes
IMAGE OPTIMIZATION
216 Colors

OGRAPHY

Animation sound and

LYNDA.COM

www Design

Index

Symbols and Numbers

μ-law format, 366
<!...> tag, 415
1-bit transparency, 53
3D buttons, 249
3D objects, 284
3D Web Workshop, 348
6x6x6 palette (cube), 141
8-bit transparency, 53
16-bit browser-safe colors, 153
24-bit JPEG versus 24-bit PNG, 109
40space.jpg file, 311
216clut.cpl file, 149, 154
@tlas site, 318

A

<A HREF>...</A> tag, 47, 129, 215, 218, 221, 228,
   230, 235, 240, 269, 338, 368, 414-415
<A>...</A> tag, 415
absolute path names, 410
aco file extension, 147
active link and color, 125
active navigation, 418
ad banners, 388-389
adaptive dithering, 80, 418
adaptive palettes, 50-51, 80, 86, 111, 152
additional expenses, 5
additive color, 135, 418
Adobe Acrobat and alignment, 324-326
Adobe Illustrator, 155
    exporting type to Photoshop, 268
    filters, 210
    GIFs, 155
    horizontal rules, 210-211
    problems with web graphics, 155
Adobe Magazine site, 326
Adobe PageMill, 157
Adobe site, 154, 324, 326
    GIF89a export plug-in, 178-179
Afterburner, 396, 405
Agfa Type site, 275
aif file extension, 366
AIFC (Audio Interchange File Format), 363, 418

AIFF (Audio Interchange File Format), 366
aliased graphics, 78-79, 172, 418
Alice in Chains site, 270
Alien Skin site, 249
<ALIGN=BOTTOM> tag, 308
<ALIGN=MIDDLE> tag, 308
<ALIGN=TOP> tag, 220, 308
alignment, 300
    Adobe Acrobat, 324-326
    CSS, 327-329
    graphics and patterned background, 312
    horizontal and vertical space tags, 308-309
    HTML, 306-321
    problems, 301
    tables, 313-321
    without tables, 322-323
<ALINK=> tag, 412
alpha channel-based transparency, 53
alpha channels, 61, 186
<ALT> tag, 243
Altavista site, 6-7
Amazon site, 379
AMUG site, 123
animated GIFs, 48, 54-55, 334, 418
    authoring tools, 54
    download speeds, 350
    frame delays, 350
    interlacing, 351
    looping, 350
    Mosaic, 54
    MSIE, 54
    Netscape, 54
    optimization, 350
    palettes, 351
    transparency and disposal methods, 350-351
animated wipe effect, 203
animation
    aesthetics, 333
    animated GIFs, 334, 350-351
    AVI movies, 344
    Cinepak, 355
    codecs for movies, 354
    content creation, 357
    guidelines, 333
    Indeo, 355
    Java, 336
    JavaScript, 337
    movie creation tips, 352
    MPEG, 356
    plug-ins, 335

QuickTime movies, 338-343
    server push, 345
    small-sized movies, 353
    streaming, 54
    technologies, 334-349
    terms, 356
    tools, 346-349
anti-aliasing graphics, 77, 172, 418
Anton, Peter, 270
AOL (America Online) browsers, 30
Apple Color Picker, 157
<APPLET> tag, 336
<AREA SHAPE> tag, 241
Art Center College of Design site, 274
artifacts, 418
Ascii Paint, 261
ASCII text, 260-261
attributes, 418
au file extension, 366
audio files, 365-367, 369
authoring, 27, 33, 418
avi file extension, 344
AVI movies, 344, 418

B

<B>...</B> tag, 258, 274, 413
<B><FONTSIZE>...</FONT></B> tag, 195
background color, 17, 124-125
    cross-platform gray differences, 212
    format to save as, 169
    hexadecimal values, 168
    hybrid colors, 159-161, 163
    setting exact color, 167-169
    solid patterns, 169
background images, 130
background tiles, 16, 171, 190-203
banding, 80-81
Bandwidth Conservation Society, 113
banners, 388-389
Barnett, Don, 158, 163
<BASE> tag, 247
baseline shift, 255
batch processing, 114, 117, 182
BBEdit, 157
bclut2.aco file, 146-147, 152-153
Beach, David, 284
Beamin, Darin, 274
<BGCOLOR TEXT LINK VLINK ALINK> tag, 17
<BGSOUND> tag, 370

bidding for jobs, 5
bit depth, 40-42, 418
    audio files, 365
    GIF file format, 49, 77
    monitors, 42-43
    Photo-Paint, 111
    Photoshop, 84
    PNG format, 60
    sound, 363
bitmap graphics, 154, 418
Black Box filters, 249
<BLINK>...</BLINK> tag, 258
blinking text, 258
blorg() function, 393
body elements, 16
<BODY LINK> tag, 229
body tags, 412
body text, 254-256
<BODY>...</BODY> tag, 16-17, 124-125, 127, 129-130,
    159, 168-169, 190-191, 194, 246, 310, 312, 319, 412
Boersma, Jay, 213
boilerplate contracts, 5
bold text, 258
borders, 129, 131, 240, 314-315
Boutell site, 60, 239, 243
Boutell, Thomas, 60, 177, 239
Box Top Soft site, 113

 tag, 218, 307, 413
Brian's Sound Tool, 369
brightness, 418
Brody, Neville, 275
Browser Watch site, 30-31
browser-safe colors, 78, 121, 136, 419
    16-bit, 153
    adaptive palette, 152
    color charts, 142-145
    converting images to, 146
    ensuring artwork stays, 151
    FreeHand, 156
    GIFs (Graphic Interchange Format), 151
    illustration-based artwork, 138-139
    importance of, 141
    JPEG, 151
    mixing photos and illustrations, 152
    photograph-based artwork, 140
    reasons to use, 137
    removing unwanted, 153
    thousands of colors, 153
    web artwork delivery and, 147

browser-safe palettes, 50-51, 87, 141, 147
    applying and reducing depth, 153
    Fractal Design Painter, 150
    hexadecimal values within, 141
    Paint Shop Pro, 148
    Photo-Paint, 149
    Photoshop, 147
    RGB values within, 141
browsers
    AOL (America Online), 30
    default font, 253
    definition, 419
    differences in, 29
    giving information about graphic, 243
    HTML and different, 30-31
    Java support, 336
    Mosaic, 30
    MSIE, 30
    Netscape, 30
    palettes, 136
    plug-ins, 332
    plug-ins and animation, 335
    role in displaying images, 136
    text-based, 243
Building PDFs site, 326
bullets
    changing shape of, 216-217
    custom-made, 218-219
    HTML, 214-218
    image-based, 214
    shiny, 3D bubble, 219
    solid circle, 215
buttons, 220-221, 249

C

Cache, 419
Calculator II, 123
Caltech Logo Tutorial site, 181
Carson, David, 275
Carter, Matthew, 275
Cassandre, A.M., 275
CD-ROM drives, 11
<CENTER>...</CENTER> tag, 17, 131, 259, 307, 413
centering
    items, 17
    tables, 131
    text, 131, 259, 307
CERN server, 235, 237
CGI (Common Gateway Interface), 236, 345, 380-382, 419

CGI Book site, 381, 384
CGI-Script Archives site, 381
CGSD site, 61
chat environments, 390-391, 419
chrome-style effect, 266
Cicinelli, Joseph, 123
Cinepak, 355, 419
Claris Homepage, 157
Classic PIO Partners, 310
client, 419
client pull, 419
client-side imagemaps, 234, 241-242, 248, 419
clip art, 213, 221
Clip Art Server site, 213
CLUT (Color LookUp Table), 146, 419
clut file, 150
clut.bcs file, 156
CMYK color space, 135, 157
CNX Software site, 243
<CODE>...</CODE> tag, 253, 413
codec, 356
color, 17
    active link, 125
    additive, 135
    assigning to images, 146
    background, 17, 124-125, 130
    browser-safe, 121, 136-141
    changing headlines, 265
    CMYK vs. RGB color space, 135
    cross-platform calibration issues, 34-35
    hexadecimal values, 120-123, 137
    hybrid, 158-161, 163
    individual lines of text, 128
    limited palette, 137
    links, 125, 129
    non-browser safe and color shifting, 137
    number capable of displaying, 40-42
    predithered patterns, 158
    screen-based, 134-135
    setting exact background, 167-169
    subtractive, 135
    tables, 131
    text, 124-125
    visited links, 125
    web as publishing medium, 134
color charts, 142-145
color mapping, 50-51, 419
color names, 126-127, 419
color picker-based applications, 157
color-related tags, 124-131

ColorWeb, 157
comment tags, 415
comparing pricing standards, 5
compression, 46, 419
   general rules for, 113
   graphics, 46
   guide to, 88-108
   JPEG file format, 57
   lossless, 48, 60
   lossy, 46, 48, 57
   LZW, 48, 76
   photographs, 46
   run-length, 76
   tools and resources, 113
compression charts, 88-108
contrast, 419
copyrights and embedding information, 63
Corel site, 154
CorelDraw, 154
counters, 382, 419
Cris site, 158
cross-platform authoring
   authoring for, 33
   brightness and contrast of graphics, 37
   color calibration issues, 34-35
   gamma differences, 35
   graphics, 32-37
   monitor bit depth, 42
   pages looking different on different systems, 37
cross-platform differences, 8-9
CSS (cascading style sheets), 327-329
custom palette, 86, 111
custom-made bullets, 218-219
c|net site, 21, 321

D

D Siegel site, 311
data rate, 356, 419
data streaming, 419
data tables, 313-314
DCR file extension, 405
<DD> tag, 216, 414
DeBabelizer
   batch processing, 182
   HVS color plug-in, 113
   transparent GIFs (TGIFs), 182-183
Dec site, 184
decompression and JPEG file format, 57
default font or leading, 253

defining your role, 5
definition lists, 216
design firm experience, 5
designing web pages
   additional expenses, 5
   bidding for jobs, 5
   boilerplate contracts, 5
   comparing pricing standards, 5
   control and HTML, 18
   cross-platform differences, 8-9
   defining your role, 5
   educational experiences, 4
   learning HTML, 15-17
   maintaining pages, 5
   pricing, 5
   search engines, 6
   system requirements, 10-12, 14
   tools, 8
   working for design firm, 5
Dig Frontiers site, 113
Digimarc site, 63
digital audio terminology, 363
digital video terms, 356
digital watermarks, 63
Digits site, 382
dir file extension, 405
Disney Online site, 259
displaying images, 17
dithering, 80-83, 419
   GIF file format, 77, 82
   illustration-based artwork, 138-139
   Photoshop, 84
   smaller file size and, 82
<DL>...</DL> tag, 216, 414
Doan, Hung, 344
Doctor Audio site, 362
documents
   basic structure, 411
   body text, 254
     embedding digital watermarks, 63
     headline text, 254
dot screen patterns, 292-294
download time and file size, 194
dpi (dots per inch), 280-281, 419
drop caps, 254, 259
drop shadows, 176-177, 265
DSport site, 21
<DT> tag, 216
dxr file extension, 405

E–F

Earth Link site, 361
Echonyc site, 123
educational experiences, 4
<EM>...</EM> tag, 258, 413
<EMBED>...</EMBED> tag, 309, 335, 338-343, 371-374, 415
embedding, 47, 339-341
embossed effect, 211
Emigre site, 275
exact palette, 86
Excite site, 6-7
extension, 419

FAQ on Transparency site, 177
Fefe's Transparency Apparatus site, 181
Feldman, Carina, 302-303
Felipe's AppleScript Samples site, 381
file extensions, 409
file formats
    digital watermarks, 63
    GIF, 46, 48-55, 72, 76-77
    graphics, 46
    JPEG, 46, 56-59, 72
    PNG, 60-62
    tiled background patterns, 194
    WebTV, 64-69
files
    compression, 46
    names, 409
    sizes and download time, 194
    what size really is, 74
fixed palette, 420
flat-style graphics, 88
    GIF dithered, 91
    GIF nondithered, 92
    JPEG, 93
    PNG dithered, 89
    PNG nondithered, 90
Fleishman, Glenn, 243
floating frames, 248
<FONT COLOR=>...</FONT> tag, 413
<FONT FACE> tag, 253, 262-263
<FONT SIZE=>...</FONT> tag, 254, 258-259, 273-274, 322, 413
<FONT>...</FONT> tag, 128
Fonthaus site, 270
Fonthead Design site, 275
fonts
    baseline shift, 255
    basic for Macintoshs or PCs, 262

default, 253
designers, 275
drop caps, 254
HTML choices, 262-263
kerning, 255
leading, 253-254
leading adjustments, 255
looser leading adjustments, 255
monospace, 253
resizing, 258
sans serif, 253
serif, 253
sites to obtain, 275
size differences between Macs and PCs, 263
small caps, 254
tracking, 255
word spacing, 255
Fonts Online site, 275
foreground matching with background tiles, 194
<FORM>...</FORM> tag, 385
forms, 383, 420
Forms Processing Tutorial site, 383
Foxworld site, 346
fps (frames per second), 356, 420
Fractal Design Painter, 12
    loading browser-safe swatch palette into, 150
    seamless tiled background patterns, 200-201
    transparent GIFs (TGIFs), 180
Fractal Design site, 201
<FRAME> tag, 245-246
framed.html file, 245
frames
    floating, 248
    HTML, 245-247
    links, 248
    problems with, 244
    tags, 415
<FRAMESET>...</FRAMESET> tag, 245-246, 415
FreeHand, 156
freeware, 14
Freeware Scripts! site, 381
fringes, 176
Frommherz, Gudrun, 274, 319
ftoast.jpg file, 310-311
full-screen body backgrounds, 202
Fullerton, Ann E., 230
Fun and Wacky Scripts site, 381
functions, 393
FutureSplash Animator, 346

G

Galadriel site, 243
gamma, 35, 61, 420
gamut, 420
Garaffa, Dave, 30
GIF (Graphic Interchange Format) file format, 388, 420
    Adobe Illustrator, 155
    animated, 48, 54-55, 334
    bit depth, 49, 77
    color mapping, 50-51
    converting to ASCII, 261
    dithering methods, 77, 82
    GIF87a, 48
    GIF89a, 48, 420
    graphics, 48
    image visual complexity, 76
    indexed color file format, 48
    interlaced, 52
    limited color palettes, 110
    lossless compression, 48
    LZW compression, 48, 76
    matching with JPEG, 151
    Mosaic, 48
    MSIE, 48
    naming conventions, 47
    Netscape, 48
    number of colors in, 48
    photographs, 49
    precise color control, 152
    reducing colors, 110-112
    single pixel, 311
    small files, 76-77, 82-83
    tiled background patterns, 194
    transparent (TGIFs), 17, 48, 53, 170-185
GIF Construction Set/bookware, 54, 184
GIF dithered graphics
    flat-style, 91
    gradiated background and cartoony illustration, 101
    spectrum graphics, 96
    standard photograph, 106
gif file extension, 47, 194
GIF nondithered graphics
    flat-style, 92
    gradiated background and cartoony illustration, 102
    spectrum graphics, 97
    standard photograph, 107
GIF transparency tutorial site, 177
GIF Transparentifier site, 181
GIF Wizard, 113

GIF/JPEG Smart Saver, 113
GIF87a, 48
GIF89a, 48, 170, 178-179
    animated GIFs, 54, 334
GIFBuilder, 54, 349
Gifs R Us site, 213
GIFscii, 261
Giles, Aaron, 182
glows and transparent GIFs (TGIFs), 176-177
gradiated background and cartoony illustration, 88
    GIF dithered, 101
    GIF nondithered, 102
    JPEG, 103
    PNG dithered, 99
    PNG nondithered, 100
graphic file formats, 62
graphic tables, 313, 317-320
graphics. See also images
    24-bit JPEG vs. 24-bit PNG, 109
    adaptive dithering, 80
    adaptive palette, 80
    aliased, 78-79, 172
    alignment tags, 308-309
    alternative text, 243
    anti-aliasing, 77, 172
    applying browser-safe palette and
       reducing depth, 153
    banding, 80-81
    bit depth, 40-42
    bitmap, 154
    brightness and contrast, 37
    browser differences, 29
    browser-safe colors, 78
    color calibration issues, 34-35
    compression, 46
    compression charts, 88-108
    converting to browser-safe colors, 146
    cross-platform, 32-37
    designing for computer screen, 28
    difficulty in creation, 27
    dithering, 80-83
    embedding, 47
    ensuring browser-safe colors, 151
    file formats, 46
    file size, 72-73
    gamma differences, 35
    GIF file format, 48
    giving browser information about, 243
    good range from black to white, 36
    high-resolution, 38

imagemap-based, 226
linked, 129, 226, 228-229
low-bandwidth, 72-73
mixing with photos and browser-safe colors, 152
patterned background alignment and, 312
pixel measurements, 38
printed page, 28
reducing colors in GIF files, 110-112
resolution, 38-39
saving with icon in Photoshop, 75
screen dithering, 80-81
selections, 294-297
small, 72-73
space in between, 310-311
values, 36-37
vector-based, 154-156
viewing in grayscale mode, 36
what file size really is, 74
width and height, 309
graphics-based typography
Adobe Illustrator, 268
HTML for placing on web pages, 269
mixing with HTML-based typography, 270-274
Photoshop, 265-268
guestbooks, 384-387, 420
GUI (graphical user interface), 9
Guide to Perl CGI Programming site, 381

H

<H#>...</H#> tag, 258, 412
halos, 176
Handwriting Fonts site, 275
hard disks, 10, 74
Harris, Daniel Will, 320
head tags, 412
<HEAD>...</HEAD> tag, 16, 258, 392-393, 412
header information, 16
header.html file, 245-246
headings, 258
headline text, 254
changing color, 265
chrome-style effect, 266
drop shadows, 265
HTML vs. graphical, 256
lighting effects, 267
special effects for, 265-267
Heavin, Bruce, 79, 114, 153, 158, 198-199, 249, 284, 286, 391, 398-399
<HEIGHT> tag, 131, 243, 309, 311, 335

Herrick, Michael, 221
hex calculators, 123
hexadecimal code, 120-123
hexadecimal values, 137
Hidaho site, 123
high-resolution graphics, 38
Hollywood Records site, 260-261
Homegurrrl site, 55, 68, 384
horizontal rules
aligning, 209
black, 209
embossed effect, 211
fancier, 208-209
graphics as, 210- 211
HTML, 207-210
space between rule and text, 207
tags, 413
thickness, 209
user-created, 210-211
uses for, 206
width, 209
horizontal space tags, 308-309
hot images
borders, 227
color of border, 229
identifying, 227
imagemap-based graphics, 226
linked graphics and text, 226, 228-229
thicker border, 229
turning off border, 228
Hotbot site, 6-7
HotHotHot site, 79, 174
hotlist, 233
Hotwired site, 244
small caps, 254
Web Monkey page, 327
House Industries site, 275
<HR> tag, 207, 209, 413
<HREF> tag, 241
HS Design site, 281
<HSPACE> tag, 308
htm file extension, 411
HTML (HyperText Markup Language)
alignment, 306-323
attributes, 124
basic document structure, 411
browser interpretation differences, 29
bullets, 214-218
buttons on forms, 383
color-related tags, 124-131

common tags, 412-415
definition, 420
different browsers, 30-31
downloading audio files, 368
embedding images, 47
font choices, 262-263
frames, 245-247
guestbooks, 384-387
hexadecimal values and color, 120-123
horizontal rules, 207-210
hybrid-safe colors, 159
inserting graphics, 47
key aspects, 16-17
learning, 15, 19-20
online tutorials, 20
placing graphics-based typography, 269
server-side imagemap support, 240
software, 18
studying source code, 20
table tags, 315-317
tags that constantly change, 22
text-based editors, 21
tiled background patterns, 194-195
transparent GIFS (TGIFs), 170
visual designers, 408-415
WebTV unsupported tags, 66
WYSIWYG editors, 22-23
html file extension, 411
HTML for Angels site, 244
HTML-based typography
    aliased vs. anti-aliased, 264
    ASCII text, 260-261
    blinking text, 258
    bold text, 258
    centering text, 259
    drop caps, 259
    font choices, 262-263
    headings, 258
    italic text, 258
    mixed type sizes, 272-274
    mixing with graphics-based typography, 270-274
    preformatted text, 258
    resizing fonts, 258
    small caps, 259
<HTML>...</HTML> tag, 16, 411
HTTP, 420
hue, 420
HVS color plug-in, 113

hybrid colors, 158, 420
    background, 159-161, 163
    checkerboards, 160
    colors close in value, 160
    horizontal lines, 160
    HTML, 159
hypertext, 420

I

I World site, 30, 32
<I>...</I> tag, 258, 413
ICHAT site, 390
Ihip site, 243
Ikon site, 69
illustration-based artwork
    browser-safe color, 138-139
    dithering, 138-139
transparent GIFs (TGIFs), 173
Image Compression Charts
    flat-style illustration, 88
    GIF dithered, 91, 96, 101, 106
    GIF nondithered, 92, 97, 102, 107
    gradiated background and cartoony illustration, 88
    JPEG, 93, 98, 103, 108
    PNG dithered, 89, 94, 99, 104
    PNG nondithered, 90, 95, 100, 105
    spectrum illustration, 88
    standard photograph, 88
image-based bullets, 214
imagemap definition file, 235
imagemap-based graphics, 226
imagemaps, 233, 420
    CERN servers, 235
    client-side, 234, 241-242
    NCSA servers, 235
    necessity of, 235
    server-side, 234-240, 242
    software tools, 243
    tutorial URLs, 243
images. See also graphics
    assigning color, 146
    borders, 129
    common tags, 413-414
    deleting border of linked, 47
    displaying, 17
    exceeding 256 colors, 152
    hot, 226-229
    inserting, 47
    irregularly shaped, 166

linking, 47
low resolution, 10
static, 226
imaging programs, 12
<IMG DYNSRC> tag, 344
<IMG SRC> tag, 17, 47, 129, 170, 195, 210, 218, 221, 228
  235, 240-241, 246, 269, 273, 308, 317, 334, 342, 345,
  393-394, 413-414
In-Touch site, 59
Indeo, 355
Info Hiway site, 113
info.html file, 245, 247
Infomarket site, 7
Infoseek site, 7
inline graphic, 420
interactive buttons, 220
interactivity
  ad banners, 388-389
  avatars, 390-391
  CGI, 380-381
  changing images, 394
  chat environments, 390-391
  counters, 382
  Director/Shockwave/Lingo-based, 396, 398-405
  forms, 383
  guestbooks, 384-387
  JavaScript MouseOvers, 392
  mouse rollovers, 392-393, 395
  role models, 379
interlaced GIFs, 52, 421
Internet comparing to WebTV, 68-69
Internet Font Libraries site, 275
Internet Movie Tool, 342
IRC FAQ site, 390
irregularly shaped images, 166, 168-169
<ISMAP> tag, 236, 240
ISP, 421
italic text, 258
IUMA site, 284, 363, 379

J

Java, 336, 421
JavaScript, 337
  blorg() function, 393
  case sensitivity, 392
  establishing page size, 304-305
  functions, 393
  functions for LiveAudio plug-in, 374
  LiveConnect, 374

MouseOvers, 392
  naming image objects, 393
  onMouseOut event handler, 393
  onMouseOver event handler, 393
  resources, 337
  Shockwave vs., 397
JavaScript Tips of the Week site, 337
Jaz drives, 10
JB site, 280
JPEG (Joint Photographic Experts Group)
  file format, 46, 58-59, 72, 388
    24-bit vs. 24-bit PNG, 109
    artifacts, 57
    compression and decompression, 57
    definition, 421
    imprecise color information, 151
    lossy compression, 48, 57, 109
    matching with GIFs, 151
    naming conventions, 47
    number of colors in, 48
    photographs, 56-57
    photograph-based artwork, 140
    progressive vs. standard, 59
    standard photograph, 108
    subtle gradations, 56
    tiled background patterns, 194
    variety of compression levels, 58
JPEG graphics
  flat-style, 93
  gradiated background and cartoony illustration, 103
  spectrum graphics, 98
jpg file extension, 47, 194

K–L

Kai's Power Tools, 219
kerning, 255
Killer Sites site, 326
Kodak site, 285
KPT Glass Lens plug-in, 219

Lamb, Gary, 361
leading, 253-255
Letraset site, 275
LettError site, 256
<LI> tag, 215-217, 414
lighting, 421
line breaks, 307
lines of text color, 128
Lingo and interactivity, 396-405
Link Exchange site, 388

<LINK=> tag, 412
linked graphics, 226, 228-229
links
    aesthetic cues, 249
    client-side imagemaps, 248
    color, 125, 129
    definition, 421
    frames, 248
    graphics, 129
    images, 47
    items in lists, 215
    tags, 415
    text, 129
Links to Scripts site, 381
Liquid Typography site, 256
Lissitsky, El, 275
lists
    definition, 216
    indented without bullets, 216
    linking items in, 215
    nested, 215
    ordered, 216-217
    solid circle bullets, 215
    tags and attributes, 414
    within text, 215
LiveAudio plug-in, 371-374
LiveConnect, 374
lossless compression, 48, 60, 109, 421
lossy compression, 46, 48, 57, 109, 421
Loureiro, Leonardo Haddad, 184
low-bandwidth graphics, 72-73
low-resolution images, 10
lpi (lines per inch), 280
ltoast.jpg file, 310-311
Luna site, 112, 146
LView, 184
Lycos site, 7
LZW (Lempel-Ziv & Welch) compression, 48, 76

M

Mac-Based CGI Links, FAQs, and Tutorials site, 381
MACE (Macintosh Audio Compression/Expansion), 366
Macintosh
    advantages, 9
    audio helper files and utilities, 369
    basic fonts for web pages, 262
    changing monitor bit depth, 43
    font size differences from PCs, 263
    GUI, 9
    hex calculators, 123
    Netscape default screen width, 302
    PCs vs., 9
    system palette, 50-51, 87
    transparent GIFs (TGIFs), 182-183
    Web tools, 8
    what file size really is, 74
Macintosh servers and counters, 382
Macromedia Director, 162, 375, 396, 398-405
Macromedia site, 154, 162, 347, 375, 396
Macrone, Michael, 318
MacWorld site, 280
mailto.cgi Tutorial site, 381
Maller, Joe, 392
<MAP> tag, 241
<MAP NAME> tag, 241
MapEdit, 239, 241, 243
MapThis!, 243
masks, 166, 421
mathematical palette, 87
Matt's Scripts and Archives site, 381
matte lines, 176
Matter Form site, 221
Maurer, Mary, 270
McKinley site, 7
memory and tiled background patterns, 192
menu.html file, 245, 247
menu.ici file, 232
<MENU>...</MENU> tag, 247
Merlin Media site, 382
<META HTTPEQUIV=> tag, 412
MetaTools site, 249, 303
MGEG format, 363, 421
mgp file extension, 327, 366
    AVI HTML codes, 344
    changing fonts, 262
    CSS gallery, 328-329
    floating frames, 248
    learning HTML, 20
    MSIE audio tags, 370
MIDI Farm site, 362
MIT site, 241
Mixing Messages site, 319
modems, 11
Moholy-Nagy, Laslo, 275
moirés, 280, 292-294
monitors, 11
    bit depth, 42-43
    gamma differences, 35
    how many colors can be displayed, 11

not calibrated to one another, 34-35
resolution, 73
width in pixels, 302-303
monospace font, 253
Morris, Rick, 225
Mosaic, 30, 48, 54
mouse rollovers, 392-393, 395
movies, 352-354
mp2 file extension, 363
mp3 file extension, 363
MPEG Audio, 369
MPEG CD, 369
MPEG format, 356, 366
mpg file extension, 363
MSIE (Microsoft Internet Explorer), 30
   animated GIFs, 54
   audio tags, 370
   CSS (cascading style sheets), 327
   floating frames, 248
   GIF file format, 48
   PNG format, 60
   progressive JPEGs, 59
MSN site, 346
Mueller, Thomas, 256
Museum of Counter Art site, 382
music
   automatic without downloading, 370-374
   CDs and web sites with royalty-free, 361
   legal issues, 361
Muybridge site, 225

N

Native Spirits site, 230
navigation
   aesthetic cues, 249
   frames, 244-248
   hot images, 226-229
   imagemaps, 233-242
   navigation bars, 230-231
   putting links in single file that multiple
     pages can request, 232
   server include directive, 232
   storyboarding, 225
   text-based browsers, 243
navigation bars, 230-231
NC Design site, 20, 313
NCSA server, 235, 237
NCSA site, 383
Netscape, 30

alignment, 301
animated GIFs, 54
audio tags, 371-374
client-side imagemaps, 234
color names, 126-127
CSS, 327
documentation for audio tags, 374
GIF file format, 48
learning HTML, 20
LiveAudio plug-in, 371-374
PNG format, 60
progressive JPEGs, 59
proprietary alignment tags, 310
server-side imagemaps, 234
style sheet for <FONT SIZE> tag usage, 259
table tutorial, 313
netscape.pal file, 148
NLN site, 7
<NOBR>...</NOBR> tag, 307
<NOEMBED>...</NOEMBED> tag, 335, 405, 415
<NOFRAMES>...</NOFRAMES> tag, 246
non-browser safe colors, 137
North site, 184
Novagraphix site, 326

O–P

object-oriented graphics, 421
Obit site, 225
Obsolete site, 347
<OL>...</OL> tag, 216, 414
Olander, Ben, 333
online HTML tutorials, 20
Online Transparent GIF creation site, 177
onMouseOut event handler, 393
onMouseOver event handler, 393
Opentext site, 7
Optimized palette, 111
ordered lists, 216-217
Organic Online site, 333

<P> tag, 17, 207, 254, 307, 413
Paint Shop Pro, 12
   boosting colors, 112
   color depth, 112
   error diffusion, 112
   loading browser-safe swatch palette into, 148
   Nearest Color palette, 50
   nearest color reduction method, 112
   reducing color bleeding, 112

reducing colors in GIF files, 112
sorting browser-safe swatch palette, 148
transparent GIFs (TGIFs), 185
Window's colors, 112
The Palace site, 390-391
palette from last conversion, 86
Palette.cst file, 162
PALETTES file, 162
Pantone site, 157
paragraph breaks, 307
paragraphs, 17
Park, Yuryeong, 79
passive navigation, 421
path names, relative vs. absolute, 410
patterned backgrounds, 171
Paul Baker Typographic, Inc. site, 256
PC Magazine site, 21
PCs
    advantages, 9
    audio helper files and utilities, 369
    basic fonts for web pages, 262
    font size differences from Macintosh, 263
    hex calculator, 123
    Macintosh vs., 9
    Web tools, 8
PDFs (Portable Document Format), 324-326
Perl/NTML Archives site, 381
Photo CDs, 285
Photo-Paint, 12, 111, 149, 154
PhotoDisc, 349
PhotoGIF plug-in, 113
photograph-based artwork, 140
photographs
    compression, 46
    GIF file format, 49
    JPEG file format, 56-57
    mixing with graphics and browser-safe colors, 152
    transparent GIFs (TGIFs), 175
Photoshop, 12-13
    8-bit transparency and, 53
    Actions Palette, 114-117
    adaptive palette, 50, 86
    Adobe Illustrator type, 268
    aliased graphic tools, 173
    alpha channel creation step-by-step, 186
    batch processing, 114, 117
    Bicubic resampling, 282
    Bilinear resampling, 282
    bit depth, 84
    Black Box filters, 249

browser-safe palette, 87
browser-safe swatch set usage, 147
CLUT, 146
color balance, 290
Color Table changes, 85
Color Table dialog box, 146
coloring hybrid tiles, 161
converting scanned image to aliased image, 174
correcting color with Adjustment Layers, 286-287
custom palette, 86
Custom Palette setting, 152
Despeckle filter, 293
dither settings, 83
dithering, 84
dot screen patterns, 292-293
duplicate of image, 114
Dust and Scratch filter, 293
exact palette, 86
filling selection shortcut, 161
filtering and PNG format, 62
Gaussian Blur filter, 293
GIF file extension, 116
GIF89a export plug-in, 178-179
graphics-based typography, 265-268
horizontal rules, 210-211
Hue/Saturation balance, 290
HVS color plug-in, 113
hybrid color background tiles, 160
image resolution, 39
Image Size dialog box, 282
Indexed Color dialog box, 84-87, 146
Indexed Color mode, 283
interlacing and PNG format, 62
JPEG compression, 58
KPT Glass Lens plug-in, 219
levels, 288-289
loading browser-safe swatch palette into, 147
Macintosh system palette, 87
macros, 114-116
mathematical palette, 87
moirés, 292-293
Nearest Neighbor resampling, 282
Offset filter, 198-199
opening Illustrator files, 210
palette changes, 86-87
palette from last conversion, 86
patterns filling selection shortcut, 161
PhotoGIF plug-in, 113
PictureMarc plug-in, 63
PNG format, 62

popularity of, 12
post processing scans, 286-296
previsualizing tiles, 163
progressive JPEG settings, 59
ProJPEG plug-in, 113
Quickmask selections, 297
Rasterize dialog box, 210
reducing colors in GIF files, 110
resizing images, 282-283
saving image with Exact Palette, 152
saving images with icon, 75
saving RGB image as GIF, 110
seamless tiled background patterns, 198-199
selections, 294-297
special headline effects, 265-267
thumbnails of images, 114-116
tips for aliased images, 173-175
Unsharp Mask filter, 293
variations, 291
web color table, 153
what file size really is, 74
Windows palette, 87
PICT format, 53
pixels, 135
plug-ins, 332, 335, 422
PNG (Portable Network Graphics), 60-62, 422
24-bit vs. 24-bit JPEG, 109
8-bit transparency, 53, 109
8-bit transparent, 186-187
advantages, 109
alpha channels, 61, 186
bit depths, 60
cropping images and file size, 187
file sizes, 187
lossless compression, 109
plug-in sites, 61
PNG dithered graphics
flat-style, 89
gradiated background and cartoony illustration, 99
spectrum graphics, 94
standard photograph, 104
PNG nondithered graphics
flat-style, 90
gradiated background and cartoony illustration, 100
spectrum graphics, 95
standard photograph, 105
Popco site, 243
portable computers screen width in pixels, 302
<PRE>...</PRE> tag, 253, 258, 260, 274, 301,
    307, 322-323, 413

PostScript, 422
predithered patterns, 158
preformatted text, 258, 307
prescanned illustrations and transparent GIFS (TGIFs), 174
pricing Web design, 5
primary colors, 422
printing web pages, 257
processor speed, 10
professional designers, 4
Professional Sound Corporation site, 362
Professional Sound Designer's Magazine, 362
professional sound sites, 362
programs
    Adobe Illustrator, 155
    Adobe PageMill, 157
    Afterburner, 396, 405
    ASCII Paint, 261
    BBEdit, 157
    Brian's Sound Tool, 369
    Cinepak, 355
    Claris Homepage, 157
    color picker-based, 157
    Color Web, 157
    CorelDraw, 154
    DeBabelizer, 182-183
    Fractal Design Painter, 12
    FreeHand, 156
    FutureSplash Animator, 346
    GIF Construction Set, 184
    GIFBuilder, 349
    GIFscii, 261
    imaging, 12
    Indeo, 355
    Internet Movie Tool, 342
    Kai's Power Tools, 219
    LView, 184
    MapEdit, 239, 241, 243
    MapThis!, 243
    MPEG Audio, 369
    MPEG CD, 369
    Paint Shop Pro, 12, 185
    Photo-Paint, 12
    PhotoDisc Animation Series, 349
    Photoshop, 12-13
    QuickTime: Web Motion, 349
    Server-Side to Client-Side Online Converter, 243
    Shockwave, 162, 347
    Sound Machine, 369
    SoundApp, 369
    SoundHack, 369

Transparency, 182
transparent GIFs (TGIFs), 178-180
Web Fonts, 262
WebMap, 238, 241, 243
webPainter, 348
WHAM, 369
Windows Play Any, 369
Xing Sound Player, 369
progressive JPEGs, 59, 422
ProJPEG plug-in, 113

Q–R

Qaswa site, 347
QBullets, 221
QTVR (QuickTime Virtual Reality), 342-343
QuickLink site, 303
QuickTime movies, 338
    embedding tags, 339-341
    fast-start movies, 338
    flattening, 338
    QTVR, 342-343
    sound, 375
QuickTime site, 338-339, 342, 375
QuickTime: Web Motion, 349
quick mask, 422

RAM (random-access memory), 10
Raspberry Hill site, 113
Razorfish site, 347
readbook.pl file, 385
Ready, Kevin, 30
RealAudio, 375
RealAudio format, 366
RealAudio site, 366, 375
<RECORD>...</RECORD> tag, 387
relative path names, 410
render, 422
resizing fonts, 258
resolution
    graphics, 38-39
    monitors, 38, 73
    scanning, 280-281
    television, 64
resources
    Adobe Photoshop for Macintosh Classroom, 13
    Adobe Photoshop: A Visual Guide for the Mac, 13
    Calculator II, 123
    CGI (Common Gateway Interface), 381
    The CGI Book, 232
    Coloring Web Graphics, 160

converting RGB to hexadecimal, 123
    Creating Killer Web Sites, 311
    Designer Photoshop, 13
    Fractal Design Painter Creative Techniques, 201
    GIF Animation Studio, 351
    Graphic Artists Guild Handbook: Pricing & Ethical Guidelines, 5
    graphic file formats, 62
    hex calculators, 123
    HTML for the World Wide Web: Visual QuickStart Guide, 15
    HTML Quick Reference, 15
    Hybrid HTML Design: A Multi-Browser HTML Reference, 30
    imagemap tutorial URLs, 243
    Imaging Essentials, 13
    Internet Publishing With Acrobat, 326
    JavaScript, 337
    The Official Photo CD Handbook, 285
    Painter Wow! Book, 201
    PDFs (Portable Document Format), 326
    The Photo CD Book, 285
    Photo CD: Quality Photos at Your Fingertips, 285
    Photo CDs, 285
    The Photoshop WOW! Book, 13
    RGB-HEX Converter, 123
    rollovers, 422
    Start with a Scan, 285
    Teach Yourself Web Publishing with HTML 3.2 in a Week, 15
    transparent GIFs (TGIFs), 181-185
    Web Concept & Design, 225
    Web Developer's Guide to Sound and Music, 361
    Web hex converters, 123
RGB (red, green, blue), 121-123, 135, 157
RGB-HEX Converter, 123
rollovers, 422
rollover-style buttons, 249
Rosenthal, Amy, 150, 156
<ROWSPAN> tag, 316
Roxby, Elizabeth, 319
Royal Frazier's site, 54, 334
Royalty-Free Multimedia Sound Tracks, 361
Royalty-Free Music Collection site, 361
rtoast.jpg file, 310-311
rules
    clip art, 213
    horizontal, 206-212
    vertical, 213
run-length compression, 76

S

sampling rates, 363, 365, 422
sampling resolution, 363, 365, 422
sans serif, 253
saturation, 422
Scanner Comparison Table site, 280
scanners, 11, 279-280
scanning
    3D objects, 284
    dot screen patterns, 292-294
    moiré pattern, 280, 292-294
    post processing with Photoshop, 286-297
    resizing images, 282-283
    resolution, 280-281
    terms, 280
Schnoggo site, 123
Schwitters, Kurt, 275
screen
    dithering, 80-81
    resolution, 38, 422
screen-based color, 134-135
<SCRIPT>...</SCRIPT> tag, 392-393
<SCROLLING=NO> tag, 248
SCSI scanners, 280
search engines, 6-7, 422
Selck, Brandee, 284
serif, 253
server, 422
server include directive, 232
server push, 345, 422
server-side imagemaps
    borders, 240
    defining region of, 237
    HTML support, 240
    JPEG or GIF graphic, 237
    map definition file, 236
    map-processing CGI script, 236
    stages, 236
    used with client-side imagemaps, 242
shareware, 14
Shareware site, 7, 14, 21
shiny, 3D bubble bullet, 219
shmancy.gif file, 163
Shockwave, 162, 347
    custom palettes, 162
    interactivity, 396-405
    JavaScript vs., 397
Siegel, David, 311, 326
single pixel GIFs, 311

sites
    hierarchy, 26
    listing with search engines, 7
    lists, 214-219
    testing on multiple platforms, 9
small caps, 254, 259
small graphics, 72-73
Smith, Rowland, 238
soft-edges and transparent GIFs (TGIFs), 176-177
software, 12, 14
    HTML, 18
    imaging programs, 12
    shareware and freeware, 14
Sokol, Michael, 362
Sol, Selena, 381
solid circle bullets, 215
solid patterns and background color, 169
sound
    aesthetics, 360
    audio file formats, 366
    audio file tips, 367
    audio helper files and utilities, 369
    automatic music without downloading, 370-374
    bit depth, 363
    CDs and web sites with royalty-free music, 361
    cross-browser compatibility, 374
    digital audio terminology, 363
    HTML for downloading files, 368
    MPEG format, 363
    music legal issues, 361
    obtaining source files, 361-362
    options, 375
    professional sites, 362
    QuickTime movies, 375
    small audio files, 365
    streaming, 364
Sound Advice site, 362
sound cards, 11
Sound Machine, 369
SoundApp, 369
SoundHack, 369
SoundScape Web Background Music for Web Pages, 361
spectrum graphics, 88
    GIF dithered, 96
    GIF nondithered, 97
    JPEG, 98
    PNG dithered, 94
    PNG nondithered, 95
Specular site, 348
splash screen, 423

sprite animation, 356, 423
Spyglass site, 243
standard JPEGs, 59
standard photographs, 88
    GIF dithered, 106
    GIF nondithered, 107
    JPEG, 108
    PNG dithered, 104
    PNG nondithered, 105
static images, 226
Stephens, Chris, 213
Stink site, 347, 398
Stockton, Robert, 381
storyboarding, 225
streaming animation, 54
streaming sound, 364
<STRONG>...</STRONG> tag, 258, 273, 412
Submit-It site, 7
subtractive color, 135
Sullivan, Michael, 281
Sun site, 336
Synenergy site, 346
system requirements, 10-12, 14

T

table header, 131
<TABLE>...</TABLE> tag, 131, 315-316, 318, 385, 414-415
tables
    alignment, 313-321
    borders, 131, 314-315
    cell color, 131
    cell content, 315, 317
    cell dimensions, 131
    centering, 131
    centering text within cells, 131
    color, 131
    columns, 316
    data, 313-314
    definition, 423
    graphics, 313, 317-320
    headers, 131, 315, 317
    height, 316
    HTML tags, 315-317, 414-415
    mixing text and graphics, 317
    online tutorials, 313
    rows, 131, 315-317
    text, 317, 321
    thicker line weight between cells, 316
    uniform space inside cells, 316

    width, 316
    WYSIWYG HTML editors, 313
tags
    attributes, 124
    color names within, 126-128
    color-related, 124-131
    common, 412-415
    definition, 423
Takahas, Yoshinobo, 259
<TARGET> tag, 248
<TD>...</TD> tag, 131, 315, 317, 414
television, 64
Tenazas, Lucille, 275
Terran Interactive site, 349
text
    alignment and attributes tags, 413
    alignment tags, 307
    ASCII, 260-261
    blinking, 258
    body, 254
    bold, 258
    bulleted list within, 215
    centering, 259, 307
    chrome-style effect, 266
    color, 124-125
    drop caps, 259
    headline, 254
    individual line colors, 128
    italic, 258
    lighting effects, 267
    line breaks, 307
    linked, 129, 226, 228-229
    no breaks in, 307
    paragraph breaks, 307
    preformatted, 258, 307
    readability on tiled background patterns, 197
    small caps, 259
    space in between graphics and, 310
    tables, 317, 321
    tags, 412-413
text-based browsers, 243
text-based HTML editors, 21
texture map, 423
<TEXT=> tag, 412
TGA format, 53
<TH>...</TH> tag, 131, 315, 317, 414
Thompson, Bradbury, 275
tiled background patterns
    aesthetics, 197
    bandwidth limitations, 191

contrast and value, 197
determining sizes, 192-193
file formats, 194
full-screen body backgrounds, 202
how text will read on, 197
HTML (HyperText Markup Language), 194-195
images laying over, 195
layering, 191
memory, 192
obvious borders, 196
seamless, 198-201
seams, 196
skinny tiles, 203
text and images laying over, 195
title, 16
<TITLE>...</TITLE> tag, 16, 246-247, 412
tools, 8
Totally Hip Software site, 348
<TR>...</TR> tag, 131, 315, 317
tracking, 255
transparency, 166, 182
transparent 8-bit PNG, 186-187
transparent GIFs (TGIFs), 17, 48, 53, 423
clean artwork, 172
directly making on web, 181
fringes, 172, 176
glows, soft-edges, and drop shadows, 176-177
halos, 176
HTML, 170
illustration-based art, 173
Macintosh, 182-183
matte lines, 176
photographs, 175
prescanned illustrations, 174
resources, 181-185
software, 178-180
when to use, 171
Windows, 184-185
TransWeb site, 181
TrueType fonts, 327
true color, 423
Tschichold, Jan, 275
<TT>...</TT> tag, 253, 273, 413
Turbek, Stephen, 225, 400-401, 403, 405
type alignment tags, 308
Typo site, 322
Typofile site, 256
typoGRAPHIC site, 225, 256, 400-401, 405

typography
aesthetic considerations, 257
baseline shift, 255
body text, 254
drop caps, 254
graphics-based, 264-271
headline text, 254
HTML-based, 258-274
interesting URLs, 256
kerning, 255
leading, 253-255
monospace, 253
sans serif, 253
serif, 253
small caps, 254
terms, 253-255
tracking, 255
web-based, 252-257
word spacing, 255

U

U Lead site, 113
UIUC site, 259
<UL>...</UL> tag, 215, 414
Uniform palette, 111
University of Michigan site, 261
University of Texas site, 338
Unix servers, 382
uploading web pages, 411
URL, 423
<USEMAP> tag, 241

V

V Works site, 344
<VALIGN> tag, 317
van Blokland, Erik, 256
van Rossum, Just, 256
Vanderlands, Rudy, 275
vector-based graphics, 154-156
vertical rules, 213
vertical space tags, 308-309
Vibe site, 362
video cards, 11
Video for Windows file format, 344, 423
visited links, 125
visual designers
common file extensions, 409
file names, 409
HTML, 408-415

relative vs. absolute path names, 410
troubleshooting web pages, 411
uploading web pages, 411
<VLINK=> tag, 412
<VSPACE> tag, 309

W

W3C site, 314, 327
Walter, Chip, 177
watermarks, 63
Waters, Crystal, 322-323
wav file extension, 366
WAVE file format, 366
web animation, 332-357
web as publishing medium, 134
Web Conn site, 337
Web Fonts, 262
Web graphics, 26-42
Web hex converters, 123
Web pages
    active link color, 125
    alignment, 300-329
    background color, 124-125
    background images, 130
    beginning and ending, 16
    body elements, 16
    centering items, 17
    color, 17
    defining size, 302-305
    designing, 4-5
    displaying images, 17
    dividing into regions, 244-248
    header information, 16
    headings, 258
    length and width restrictions, 302
    link color, 125
    maintaining, 5
    navigation, 224-249
    paragraphs, 17
    printing, 257
    small blocks of text on, 257
    table color, 131
    testing, 410
    text color, 124-125
    title, 16
    troubleshooting, 411
    uploading, 411
    visited link color, 125

Web Reference site, 6
Web Review site, 327
Web site hierarchy, 26
Web tools, 8
Web Workstudio site, 6
web-based typography, 252-257
Webcrawler site, 7, 390
WebMap, 238, 241, 243
webPainter, 348
WebSTAR Examples site, 381
WebTV, 64-65
    comparing to Internet, 68-69
    design tips, 67
    supported and not supported features, 66
    unsupported HTML tags, 66
Weinman, William, 384, 395
WHAM, 369
<WIDTH> tag, 131, 243, 309, 311, 335
Will Harris site, 320
Windows
    native palette, 112
    servers, 382
    transparent GIFs (TGIFs), 184-185
Windows 3.1, changing monitor bit depth, 43
Windows 95, 43, 74
Windows palette, 87
Windows Play Any, 369
Winternet site, 185
Wong, Meng Weng, 381
word spacing, 255
World Wide Consortium site, 60
World Wide Web
    authoring environment, 27
    cross-platform authoring, 32-33
    difficulty in graphics creation, 27
WYSIWYG HTML editors, 22-23, 124, 241, 313, 423

X–Y–Z

Xing Sound Player, 369

Yahoo site, 6-7, 21, 213
Younis site, 304
Younis, Steven, 304-305
Yves Piquet site, 334

Ziff Davis site, 280
Zip drives, 10

\<deconstructing web graphics\>
Web Design Case Studies and Tutorials

Deconstructing Web Graphics profiles top web designers and programmers in order to demystify and analyze how they make decisions, solve complex issues, and create exceptional web sites. Adding her own voice and digital design teaching experience to the book, best-selling author Lynda Weinman selects from her list of favorite designed web sites. She walks you through how to read and understand the source code for each page, breaks down all of the technical elements, and describes the inside details straight from the designers and programmers who created the pages.

This conversational and information-rich guide offers insight into web design that is not found through any other means. Profiles of successful web designers, programmers, photographers, and illustrators allows them to share their tips, techniques, and recommendations. You'll bring your own web design skills to a higher level through studying their experiences and the step-by-step tutorials and examples found in *Deconstructing Web Graphics*.

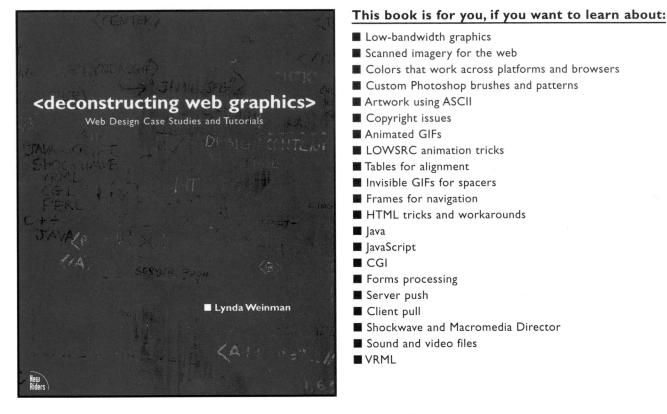

This book is for you, if you want to learn about:

- Low-bandwidth graphics
- Scanned imagery for the web
- Colors that work across platforms and browsers
- Custom Photoshop brushes and patterns
- Artwork using ASCII
- Copyright issues
- Animated GIFs
- LOWSRC animation tricks
- Tables for alignment
- Invisible GIFs for spacers
- Frames for navigation
- HTML tricks and workarounds
- Java
- JavaScript
- CGI
- Forms processing
- Server push
- Client pull
- Shockwave and Macromedia Director
- Sound and video files
- VRML

Product and Sales Information

Deconstructing Web Graphics By Lynda Weinman
ISBN:1-56205-641-7 ▪ $44.99/USA ▪ 235 pages
Available at your local bookstore or online
Macmillan Publishing ▪ 1-800-428-5331
- http://www.mcp.com/newriders

▪ http://www.lynda.com

Stop by and visit the author's up-to-date web site—read sample chapters, browse her list of web design resources, or join her mailing list-based discussion group that focuses on web design issues.

Author Biography

Lynda Weinman has authored a series of best-selling, full-color books about web graphics and design for New Riders Publishing. She has taught digital imaging, animation, multimedia and web design at Art Center College of Design, American Film Institute, and UCLA. Weinman is a featured columnist on digital graphics, animation, and the web for *New Media*, *Digital Video*, *Mac User*, *Mac Week*, *The Net*, *Step-by-Step Graphics*, *Macromedia User's Journal*, and *Full-Motion Video* magazines.

\<coloring web graphics\>
Master Color and Image File Formats for the Web

Written by Lynda Weinman and Bruce Heavin, this book features practical, accessible, and down-to-earth advice that will help you greatly expand your color web graphic design skills. The purpose of this book is to help artists, programmers, and hobbyists understand how to work with color and image file formats for web delivery. Artwork that looks good in print or on screen can easily end up looking terrible in a web browser. Web browsers and different operating systems handle color in specific ways that many web designers aren't aware of. *Coloring Web Graphics* offers in-depth answers about color, from both an aesthetic and technical perspective, and details what design constraints exist on the web and how to work around them.

A color palette of 216 browser-safe colors is identified and organized to help web designers confidently select successful cross-platform color choices and combinations. The book includes sections on color theory and understanding web color file formats as well as step-by-step tutorials that explain how to work with browser-safe colors in Photoshop, Paint Shop Pro, Photo-Paint, Painter, FreeHand, and Illustrator. The cross-platform CD-ROM includes hundreds of suggested color combinations for web page design, as well as hundreds of palettes and browser-safe clip art files.

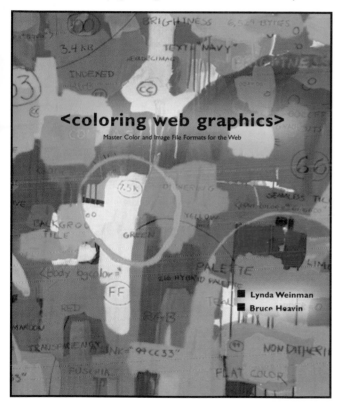

In this book, you'll learn to:

- Create colors in your artwork that won't shift or dither across multiple platforms
- Choose web-appropriate color schemes for your page designs
- Create thousands of browser-safe hybrid variations
- Use Photoshop, Paint Shop Pro, Photo-Paint, FreeHand, Illustrator, and Director to manage web-specific color

The cross-platform CD-ROM includes:

- Browser-safe color palettes
- Browser-safe color swatches for Photoshop and other imaging programs
- Browser-safe colors organized by hue, value, and saturation
- Browser-safe color clip art for web use
- Electronic versions of color swatches grouped as they are in the book
- Sample HTML pages with recommended color groupings
- Sample patterns, backgrounds, buttons, and rules

Product and Sales Information

Coloring Web Graphics By Lynda Weinman and Bruce Heavin
ISBN:1-56205-669 7 ▪ $50.00/USA ▪ 258 pages (+CD-ROM)
Available at your local bookstore or online
Macmillan Publishing ▪ 1-800-428-5331
▪ http://www.mcp.com/newriders

Stop by and visit the author's up-to-date web site—read sample chapters, browse her list of Web design resources, or join her mailing list-based discussion group that focuses on web design issues. ▪ http://www.lynda.com

Authors' Biographies

Lynda Weinman has authored a series of best-selling, full-color books about web graphics and design for New Riders Publishing. Lynda has taught and written about web design, interactive multimedia, motion graphics, and digital imaging for numerous universities and publications.
Bruce Heavin is an acclaimed painter and illustrator whose mastery of color theory is evident in all of his work. He has created artwork for clients that include Adobe, E! Entertainment Television, and has also painted the distinctive covers of all of Lynda's web design books.